Great Company

Great Company

Smart Growth, Happy Employees, Minimal Risk

Matthew Beckner

BEP

BUSINESS EXPERT PRESS

Leader in applied, concise business books

Great Company:
Smart Growth, Happy Employees, Minimal Risk

Cover design by Salman Sarwar

Interior design by S4Carlisle Publishing Services, Chennai, India

First published in 2025 by
Business Expert Press, LLC
222 East 46th Street, New York, NY 10017
www.businessexpertpress.com

ISBN-13: 978-1-63742-864-1 (paperback)
ISBN-13: 978-1-63742-865-8 (e-book)

Entrepreneurship and Small Business Management Collection

First edition: 2025

10 9 8 7 6 5 4 3 2 1

EU SAFETY REPRESENTATIVE
Mare Nostrum Group B.V.
Mauritskade 21D
1091 GC Amsterdam
The Netherlands
gpsr@mare-nostrum.co.uk

Dedicated to the spouses and families of all the Blue Canyon Technologies employees. Your love, support, and faith made it all possible. Thank you for believing in us and letting your mom, dad, wife, or husband be part of our family.

Description

This book is your guide to building a business that you're proud of, that remains true to your passions, and that lets you maintain control and avoid going bankrupt. Starting a new business is exciting, but it's also one of the most stressful things you can do. Research shows that the biggest stressors are financial uncertainty, navigating the unpredictable risks of a startup, and hiring the right team.

The secret to success lies in building a smart, low-risk strategy that includes assembling the right team and finding innovative ways to raise capital. When done right, this approach not only keeps your business on track, but also ensures that you, your employees, and your customers genuinely enjoy the journey. In *Great Company*, we bring together the best practices for today's business world, offering proven strategies to help you create a lasting, profitable business that stands out in both the marketplace and the hearts of your customers.

Whether you're an entrepreneur, a seasoned executive, or a business student eager to learn from industry experts, *Great Company* provides actionable wisdom and strategies. With real-world examples from both successful and failed startups, we highlight the challenges—and opportunities—that every new business will face. You'll walk away with the tools you need to navigate the ups and downs of entrepreneurship and build a company that thrives.

Preface

I had been wanting to write this book for about 4 years, ever since I realized that our company really was going to be acquired and that I would have to let go and leave it all behind. It was an incredible 13-year journey that is difficult to describe, but I wanted to do my best for several reasons. First, I am eternally grateful to the dozens of people who helped us along the way, sometimes with a simple piece of wisdom or advice, or an introduction to our next customer, or sharing a cautionary tale from their own company. Second, as we grew the company, we often didn't know what to do. We had a dream but lacked the knowledge to build it. It felt like trying to join an exclusive club that only admitted those who had already succeeded. Without knowing the secrets, we couldn't access the club where everyone shared the secrets. We discovered along the way that there are many paths to building a business, each of them with pros and cons. Our preference was to select methods which kept our customers and employees as happy as possible while avoiding going bankrupt or losing control of the company along the way. Small companies are special, whether you are an employee or a founder.

We didn't have a book to help us build our company, so there was a lot of trial and error which everyone had to endure. We made some mistakes and had to figure out what to do differently to avoid them in the future. I'd like to help other entrepreneurs avoid those kinds of problems in the first place. In tribute to all the people who endured those problems and helped to make our company a success, I want to pay forward the lessons learned and wisdom so that the next generation of entrepreneurs can benefit.

The title of this book intentionally has multiple implications. Yes, I want you to build a Great Company, where you and your employees thrive, enjoy what you do and know that it is meaningful for all of you and your customers. But I also want you to consider that starting and building a business is, indeed, a journey, and that the best way to enjoy the voyage is to endeavor side by side with people who inspire you, that you like, and that you can trust. In other words, travel with great company on your journey.

Contents

List of Figures and Tables

Figures

Tables

Introduction

June 23, 2008, approximately 7:00 a.m.

The three of us sat at a cramped café table, notebooks in front of us, exchanging nervous glances as if silently asking, *What have we gotten ourselves into?* George, Steve, and I were strangers—at least, we were back then. Sure, George and I worked together at a nearby satellite manufacturer, but that was the extent of our connection. Steve and George knew each other from grad school at the University of Colorado, but Steve and I? We'd never met before. Yet here we were, a mismatched trio, united by a single, audacious idea: to start a business.

A technology startup, to be precise. The catch? We didn't have a clear idea of what kind of technology or business we were going to pursue, or even what to name the company. George had been around the startup block enough to know the sting of failure. I had my own startup failures under my belt, too. But, somehow, we all agreed to meet for an hour over coffee to toss around ideas, before heading back to our "regular" jobs that paid the bills, put gas in our cars, and kept the lights on at home.

We had no roadmap. No clear plan. But one thing was certain: We were beyond excited. Excited to be "on our own," excited to take control of our own fate, and perhaps most of all, excited by the sheer possibility of what could happen next. Little did we know we were on the verge of a wild, rewarding, and at times, terrifying ride. But at that moment, we were ready to dive in.

Over the next 15 years, we would share an adventure of a lifetime, as we succeeded and failed, learned, made new friends, made a few enemies, and grew our little business from the three of us around a café table into a 350-person technology business with a four-building campus and products on orbit in space and headed to other planets. Throughout that adventure, we found that there are many right ways and several wrong ways to do almost anything. In this book, I will share with you what worked in which situations, and most importantly, how to enjoy (almost) every single day of your roller-coaster adventure.

This book has been laid out in chapter form to address various aspects of business formation, including funding, team building, culture development, product creation, marketing, processes and accounting, and other topics. The reality is that every business grows how it will and not in any predefined order. You will find that some of the topics in these chapters occur out of sequence or simultaneously. How your business grows and evolves is part of your unique adventure.

This is not a manual or a step-by-step guide for how to start and run a business. It is a collection of hard-learned lessons, guidance, and suggestions for people who want to do three things with their business.

The first goal is: Do not go broke in the process of creating your dream business. Nine out of 10 startup businesses fail over the long term. Many of those failures wipe out the founder's life savings. Statistically, there are consistent, standard reasons that startups fail, as reported by CB Insights in 2021, shown in Figure I.1.[1]

The founder of a company must adopt the mindset: *I am in charge.* You are the decision maker (along with your founding team) and should never consider yourself a victim. If you are used to being an employee, this change in mentality may take some time to set in. Employees operate in accordance with rules and executive orders, such that they don't really

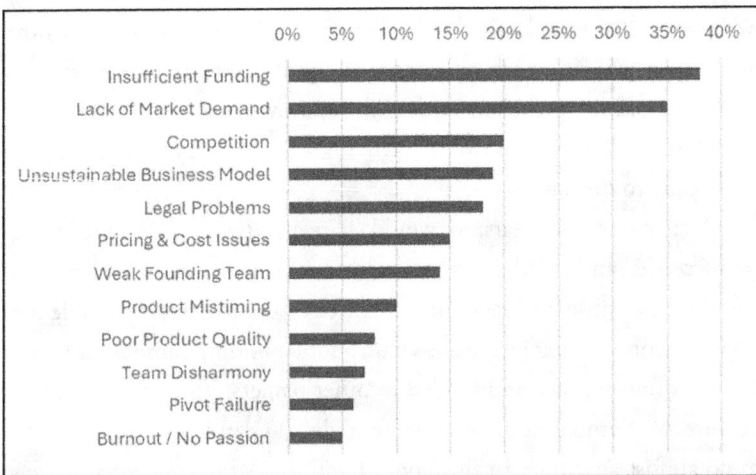

Figure I.1 Cited reasons for startup businesses' failure (CB Insights). More than one may apply

have control. "I am not in control" thinking is reflected in some of the reasons (excuses) that are given in Figure I.1. For example, "Lack of Market Demand" sounds like the market was just not very agreeable to our very fine product which we developed. How unfortunate. Take charge! The actual reason for that failure type is, "We didn't develop a product that the market wanted." Turn it around and learn the path to success: "We developed the right product, at the right time, offered at an affordable price point, and we did it so well that there was no competition!" (There—we just knocked out four of the reasons for startup business failures). If only it were that easy, but seriously, the key to success in your startup business is to take control, be proactive, make a plan, be ready to change that plan, and have a great time. Systematically, we will address all of those issues cited in the CB Reports data, but rather than focus on the reasons for failure, we will construct a plan for success, incorporating a combination of factors that align strategy, execution, and market demand. One of the biggest guiding principles is to not spend money until doing so is the next step to growing the company. Rather than spend frivolously, the idea is to be frugal until the time is right to spend, then spend smartly.

We have all seen startups secure millions of dollars of venture capital money, then spend it all building nothing, creating a lot of glamorous publicity, headlines, heat and smoke, but never creating any revenue, profit, or anything of lasting value to mankind. We will review tactics to strategically spend the money you do get, so you can maximize the amount of time for your company to become successful. If you look again at the top reasons businesses fail, they mostly boil down to *not getting the product or execution right before running out of money*. The strategy I endorse is to spend slowly until you are sure your product and team are correct. Give yourself as much runway as possible to get your company up to speed, then take flight!

The second goal of this book is to help people create companies that employees and customers love. This book is for serious entrepreneurs who envision employing dozens or hundreds of employees and want to make the business a place that you and your employees look forward to arriving each morning. A place where employees feel safe and important; where they feel like they can connect their daily actions to the success of the company.

Finally, this book is for people who want their business to make a difference in the world. Meaningful businesses change lives for the better. It is one thing to start and run a business that makes money in exchange for a product or service—that is the fundamental reason for businesses to exist. The true reward is when your creation makes a difference in people's lives, whether it is making them healthier, safer, happier, more knowledgeable, or able to achieve their own goals—that is the real payoff. If those three themes resonate with you, then you will enjoy this book.

It has been said that the secret of business success boils down to a single, four-letter word: *more*. More customers, more products and services, more revenue, more profit. While the word *more* can be an indicator of a growing business, it should not be the motivation or recipe for how one should go about starting and building a brand, a legacy, or a Great Company. The priorities, processes, and guidance that I will provide in the chapters here will be much more personal, inspirational, and lasting than any four-letter word could capture. *More* may be what happens at your business through the weeks, months, and years, but it will not be what gets you out of bed in the morning.

Do not doubt: Once you start your business, you will have moments of concern, second thoughts, or outright disappointment—that is all normal. Some days, you will feel like you are walking on a high-wire tightrope with flames shooting up around you and people yelling and demanding answers to their questions. Other days, you will be trying to figure out your next move, or you will find yourself having to do something unpleasant or completely outside your wheelhouse. When you start a business, sometimes there isn't anyone else who can do those unpleasant jobs; therefore, you must handle it. Operating a business means learning about necessary rules, regulations, and red tape that do not appeal to most people. The good news is that you don't have to do all the mundane work right away. If you are smart and fortunate, you can postpone some of those unpleasant tasks until the company is larger, and then you can use the great power of *delegation* to have someone more qualified handle the messy chore. One of the key tenets is that there is a right time to do the right things, but most things do not need to be done right away. Learning the rhythm of your company while making decisions to help it grow at the right pace will make it enjoyable for you and your employees, as well as help keep you sane.

Think about your startup as if it were a child, perhaps a newborn. As an infant, the company needs specific types of nurturing. As the company grows, you can teach it many things to take care of itself, and it will teach you things back. When your company is a teenager, you will need to provide different guidance and coaching, but it will do many things autonomously. How you set it up while it is a small child will determine how your company behaves as it goes through adolescence, just like any teenager. Someday, it will become an adult, and you may need to decide whether you continue to live together, or you turn your company loose to thrive and explore the universe on its own, via an Exit.

Most thrilling of all, starting and operating your business means that you and your cofounders are in charge. 100 percent. In. Charge. Success will happen because of what you decide and what you do and how you operate the company. The joy is pure, but the anguish is equally real and raw. You don't have anyone to blame. No "boss" or a big corporation or bureaucracy to blame or take the credit. To be clear, starting and operating a business isn't for everyone. But for those with grit, optimism, and background to succeed, it is the most rewarding, exhilarating opportunity in the business world. Nearly everyone needs to have a job to sustain themselves and their families. Why not do something that you love, with people you respect, to create something unique and important to your employees, your customers, and the world?

As you build your company, it will go through phases. I recommend keeping these phases in mind as you build the company, and it reaches certain milestones:

- **Phase 0**: When you have no revenue, and you're just figuring out how to proceed. During phase 0, you should keep the company small, preferably just the founding group. Moonlighting is OK during phase 0.
- **Phase 1**: When you have started to receive revenue and have sufficient income to support the business through 3 months of operations. At this point, you can start bringing on critical, high-impact employees.
- **Phase 2**: As the company grows and has sufficient revenue stream to support operations for 6 months. At this point, you can expand and hire additional employees to grow the business.

- **Phase 3**: The company is self-sufficient, and you can take long vacations without worrying about the health of the organization. This is the ultimate goal.

Salaries are by far the largest expense of running your business. Once you hire an employee, you are making a longer-term commitment to them and their families to keep them employed. The strategies I lay out in the chapters here will emphasize holding off on hiring until you have a need for the employee AND your business can afford them.

In *Chapter 1*, I will walk you through some of the things you should consider before starting your business, including your timing and passion for the endeavor. As you can imagine, starting a business is both hugely rewarding and occasionally exhausting. But if you have passion aligned with your efforts, it will feel more like an adventure than a job.

Solving a real problem, identifying what product or service people really need, and creating your own private market without competition, is the focus of *Chapter 2*. We will investigate how to avoid entering a crowded market, and how to create a totally new market where your product will shine.

Chapters 3 and 4 will dive deep into building the fabric which will become your team, starting first with building a lasting vision for your company that is memorable to customers, along with a fertile culture which enhances employee happiness and performance, all of which lead to stronger company performance. Major points of focus will be building a passionate leadership team coupled with the best possible core group of employees to get your company through the formative months and first year or two.

In *Chapter 5*, we will get serious about your business plan and review 14 different sources of capital, many of which do not have to be paid back or dilute your ownership. I will introduce strategies to help you gradually move into more serious forms of capitalization, so that you can retain ownership of your company as long as possible.

Fleshing out the operations, processes, equipment, and facility to run your business is the focus of *Chapter 6*, and we will start to put some teeth into the estimated cost of operations for your company, to help you determine whether the product and market you've identified is going to be economically viable.

Chapter 7 outlines the process to "soft launch" your business, test the waters, and gather customer feedback on your proposed product or service. The focus here is to not just to build sales, but more importantly learn from customers to help you optimize your product or service.

Since cost, pricing, cash management, and cash flow are such prominent reasons for business success or failure, we will devote *Chapter 8* to dividing the financial management of your company between accountants and yourself. The accounting team will handle the heavy lifting and day-to-day financial management, but you as the leader of your company will develop some tools to help you keep your finger on the financial future well-being of the organization and proactively avoid financial issues.

In *Chapter 9*, I will share a few tips and tricks that I and other business leaders have found to be useful in helping you grow and maintain a happy, engaged workforce. In addition, I will share a few tales of caution to help remind us of all that things can go wrong, but the longer one waits, the worse the problem will become.

We will evaluate a couple of business scenarios in *Chapter 10* and outline some methods to help you and your management team stay in control and grow your business logically while minimizing the risk of going bankrupt.

Finally, in the *Epilogue*, I will share a variety of ways that you might sell your business or pass it on to family members, when the time is right.

When George, Steve, and I started our company, George decided to call it "Blue Canyon Technologies" and I will refer to it throughout this book as simply "BCT." At that time, we each had between 10 and 20 years of experience in engineering of various kinds, and specifically in the field of satellite and space instrument design and manufacturing. But we really didn't know anything about starting and running a business. This is the book I wish I had on my bookshelf when we started BCT. Our first office is shown in Figure I.2.

During the early years at BCT, we did not grow. We couldn't generate any sales or even any strong interest. Then we slowly learned how to become relevant, and grew by leaps and bounds, sometimes too fast, eventually occupying seven different locations—each one bigger and better, and grew the company to more than 350 employees and over $100 million annual revenue. Most of the time, we improved through trial and error.

Figure I.2 Our first office space. Fairly modest but free!—We just had to buy a coffee occasionally so that the manager wouldn't kick us out

I have captured the key lessons in the chapters of this book so you can take advantage of our experiences. Through the course of it all, we had amazing successes and occasional setbacks. The satellites and products we built traveled to Mars; went into orbit for NASA to explore climate change; were launched for the Department of Defense (DOD) to protect our country; launched for universities and other commercial companies to help each of them perform their research or build their business. BCT won the American Institute of Aeronautics and Astronautics Small Satellite Mission of the year award in four consecutive years. The company was recognized on the Inc. 5000 list in 2021 as one of the fastest-growing privately held companies in the United States and was awarded the "Best of 2020" award by SpaceNews. In 2020, the company received the Tibbetts Award from the U.S. Small Business Administration, recognizing BCT as a company that exemplifies the best in Small Business Innovation Research achievements.

We provided good health benefits, generous leave policies, and 401K programs for our employees and their families, helping them in turn become successful parts of their communities.

But it wasn't all free beer and no cops (an expression we used at BCT for something really nice). We also endured attempted lawsuits, a few disgruntled employees, and some product issues with understandably unhappy customers. Most of those problems could have been avoided if we had used the strategies in this book. But through it all, we persevered, fixed what was wrong as many times as necessary until it was right. When it came time for the company to pass on to its new owners, there were 15 commercial companies and investment organizations fighting for the opportunity to acquire BCT.[2]

It was, as they say, *The American Dream*.

Your journey will be different, it will be a combination of what you start with and what you and your team make of it, enabled by the market, your customers, fate, timing, and the decisions you make. But of the thousands of choices you will make, there are many easy answers and ways to maximize your chances for success. There are also ways to minimize the likelihood and impacts of failure and still be able to spend time with your family and friends.

There is a popular assumption that to build a successful business you will have to work nights and weekends and sacrifice your free time, hobbies, and family. You will be *more* successful, and much happier, if instead you take time off, recharge yourself, and *do not* spend all your time at work. Building a successful company is a marathon, not a sprint. Happy, rested founders make good decisions. Tired, cranky founders make mistakes. Sometimes really bad mistakes as we will learn later. Additionally, we found that taking time off and letting your mind wander creates opportunities for inspiration which won't occur if your nose is always pressed to the grindstone.

You should recognize before you start into this adventure that many business startups fail, and that is OK. Unfortunately, many entrepreneurs are devastated by the process, and for some of them their lives are eternally impacted. But it doesn't have to be that way or a miserable experience for you. There are strategies to improve the chances of success, and improve the experience for you, the founder, your employees, and your customers.

Among our founders at BCT, we had three failed previous business startup attempts. We learned something from each previous failure, and statistically if you've previously failed in a business startup, you are substantially more likely to succeed on the second attempt, and twice as likely to succeed on the third attempt! Failure won't occur right away. Statistically, the second year of operations is the most challenging to survive. Because starting and running a business is a marathon, the #1 thing to focus on is preserving your cash and any capital you raise as long as possible. As shown by Forbes Advisor[3] in Figure I.3, different industries have different failure rates by year. The best advice I can offer to you, the entrepreneur, is to grow slowly, listen to the market, be responsive to what the world tells you, buckle up and enjoy the ride!

As we will discuss across many chapters of the book, timing can be a critical determinant of success or failure. We started BCT in 2008, amid the Global Financial Crisis. Many people told us it was terrible timing, but in retrospect, it was ideal for a few reasons. Due to our strategy, we didn't drain our savings, sell out to venture capitalists or institutional investors to build our company. Instead, we built slowly and conservatively. Budgets across the space program were tight, and our offering of a low-cost, high-performance solution helped many organizations continue to launch missions in spite of the financial challenges of the time.

Another fortuitous piece of timing was that the technology we needed to be successful in our venture had been developed recently; we just had to figure out how to make it work in space.

But most of the things we did were just the right things to do and have been done by successful businesses for centuries. Not always the splashiest, front-page headline, massive IPO darlings, but successful companies providing valuable products and services where the employees are happier, and the founders can sleep at night.

You will learn when to do things, when to wait, and when to bet big (but never bet the farm), and when to admit there's a problem and you need to change course. It may very well be that RIGHT NOW! Is the time you should start your business. But one thing is for sure, in the immortal words of Warren Miller about learning to ski, "If you don't do it this year, you will be one year older when you do." Time keeps moving, and if you keep waiting to pursue your passions, you may miss

Failure Rates by Industry and Year of Operations (Forbes Advisor 10/23/2024)

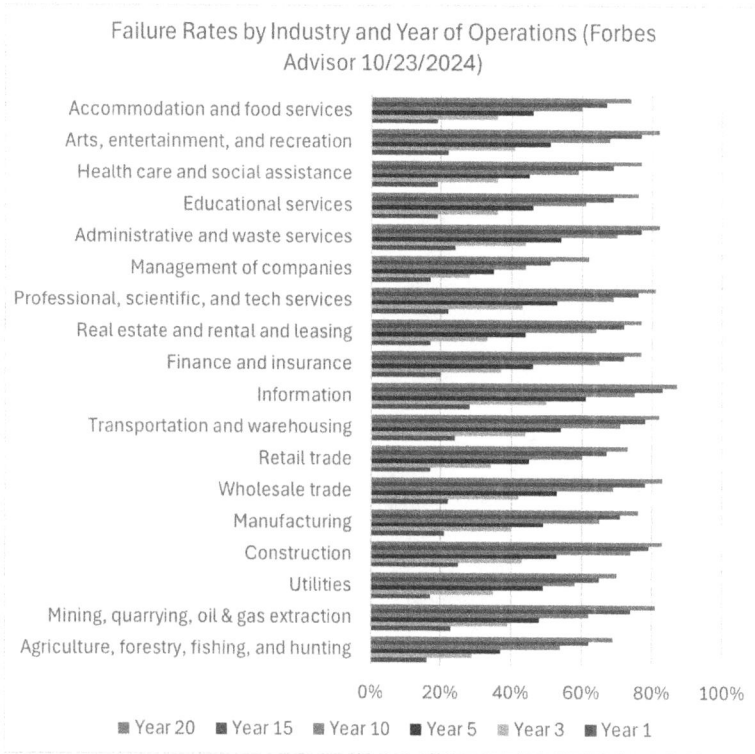

Figure *I.3 Failure rate of businesses by industry*

opportunities as time passes. Today could be the best day to start your new business and build your dreams, and whether you start now or later, I will help you along the way.

> *Your work is going to fill a large part of your life, and the only way to be truly satisfied is to do what you believe is great work. And the only way to do great work is to love what you do. If you haven't found it yet, keep looking. Don't settle. As with all matters of the heart, you will know when you find it.*
>
> —Steve Jobs

CHAPTER 1

Why Start a Business? Why Now?

If you are going to be doing something in life, spending thousands of hours per year at it...why not do something you love, something you are passionate about, and do it with people you enjoy working with? If you are currently in a frustrating, boring, or stifling job, why not do something about it? You should be happy and proud of what you're doing!

Why did Steve Jobs and Steve Wozniak start Apple? To make gobs of money and dominate the world of personal technology? No, they started Apple because they were having fun with technology and enjoyed working together. Honestly, those are much better reasons than anything monetary or status related. The friendship of Wozniak and Jobs heralded a new era in personal technology that would end up redefining the workplace and home environment around the world. But when they got started, it was just to enjoy what they were doing. I suggest you follow their example with whatever you enjoy.

Apple is typically one of the most profitable on the yearly Fortune 500 list. But is profitability the most important aspect of what makes Apple iconic? If you asked Apple employees, they probably will not even mention profitability, but they'll tell you a lot about how they love their work. How they feel motivated to work on cutting-edge technology in an innovative, inclusive culture. They'll likely share their passion for the brand, and how much they appreciate having a healthy work–life balance. If you ask diehard Apple consumers, they may gush about the usability, innovation, and creativity they feel when they use Apple products. All these things, not just financial performance, are part of the calculus of whether an organization is just a job or a Great Company.

There are as many reasons to start a business as there are entrepreneurs. All successful businesses can look in the rearview mirror and explain why their time was right, the message was perfect, the recipe was on point, and the success was just a result of all those great things coming together. Perhaps it was the team that made it all possible. We will dive into what your business might be, and how it can be positioned to be successful, in Chapter 2, but for now, let's just focus on you and the concept of starting a business, and look at a few different definitions of "success," then we will dive a little deeper into your situation.

Take the example of Ben & Jerry's Ice Cream. In addition to being a huge economic success, the company is consistently cited as one of the best companies to work at for a variety of reasons. It is a positive work culture, and the company emphasizes social responsibility, sustainability, inclusion, and activism. They host fun corporate events including ice cream tastings (of course!), and they have an on-site Ghostbusters team to investigate paranormal activities in their reportedly haunted office space. There is even a "flavor graveyard" at their factory in Vermont, where retired flavors are memorialized with tombstones and epitaphs to celebrate their legacy! By my definition, Ben & Jerry's would be a success even if it were barely profitable.

Before we consider what your company is about, why do YOU want to start any business? If your answer is "to make lots of money and buy an island in the South Pacific," well then, you should return this book for a refund. Statistically, most founders make less money running their business than if they'd stayed at their old job, especially during the first 5 to 10 years. Becoming rich is neither an actionable plan nor a worthy mission statement as you start defining your company. In fact, if getting rich quick is your only motivation, it will inevitably lead you to make some horrible decisions which you and your employees will ultimately regret.

If, on the other hand, you want to "change the world like Apple did" you might be on to something. But...back up a few steps. While your company may indeed end up changing the world, such change will be due to the innovation and value which you create with your team.

One universal principle that you will find is that most successful companies exist because they solve a problem for somebody (usually lots of somebodies) OR create a new product or service which is compelling enough for customers to change their habits. Lives are made better (at least in somebody's perspective), safer, or enriched in some way because that organization exists. If you believe that you have an idea that is going to solve someone's problem (ideally someone who can be identified as a "customer") then you're on the right track. We will get into this in more detail in Chapter 2.

To be completely honest, there is not a perfect answer to the why question, it is usually personal and may also be inextricably connected to the "why now?" question. One thing that we will visit from time to time in the chapters of this book will be your goals (personal and for the business) 5 years and 10 years from now. Whatever those goals are, don't get locked into when they should occur, but do hold onto your goals. Reality has a way of surprising us in both good and bad ways.

Most successful entrepreneurs are passionate about what they're doing. Their passion makes them excited, innovative, and dedicated to bringing their best effort to the company. Wozniak and Jobs just loved to tinker with any kind of electronics. Before they started Apple, they would play pranks on friends, like rigging up a painting of a hand showing the middle finger to suddenly be displayed during a graduation ceremony. They experimented with their technological know-how to build little "blue boxes" that made it possible to make long-distance phone calls for free, and made a call to the Vatican that nearly got them talking to the Pope.[4] Wozniak and Jobs were creative guys who loved what they were doing and had fun creating electronic gizmos. They were able to turn their passion into a successful business, so it never seemed like work.

In the minds of successful entrepreneurs, there is an opportunity to do something better or cheaper, provide some innovation, or best of all, provide a quantum leap from today's solutions. Contrary to popular opinion, successful businesses are not always started by people who are the most knowledgeable, most educated, or most influential people in their field. Oftentimes, the successes come from people who make a connection in an "ah ha" moment, or they are just "wired differently," they approach problems with unusual solutions, or they are excellent at fostering a great culture and leading those ultrasmart, influential people to excel in new ways or new markets. Do not be concerned about not being an expert, focus instead on being a visionary. Visualize what is possible, then gather a great team which includes some experts, and lead them to create the future.

Timing can be important, too. Today's great idea might have been last decade's dog, or an idea may not be possible until some future event. As an example, I started a software business around 1990 which I called "Placement Plus," with the concept of accumulating people's resumes in a computer database, along with various corporate career postings. This was a few years before the Internet became mainstream, so my business model relied upon a subscription service where companies would snail mail their job postings to me once a month and pay a small fee to be included in my database. I wrote a computer program that performed searches on the database to match a job seeker with any relevant opportunities. Rounding out my fabulous plan, job seekers could then purchase my software and database (and even purchase an ongoing subscription where I would mail them updates on a computer disc every month!). My idea was similar to career posting and search service websites like Indeed.com and Monster, but sadly my idea was premature and never went anywhere (Kudos to my wife for supporting me in that effort, and not ever making me feel bad about my first failure).

Indeed.com was acquired by Recruit Holdings of Japan in 2012 for a rumored $1 billion. In 2016, Monster was acquired by Randstad for approximately $430 million. So, my idea was a good one, but the technology had not been developed to support the necessary operations yet. When I tried to get information from companies, I did not get even a single response from the hundreds I contacted. Clearly, not only do you have to have the right idea, but it needs to be *at the right time*. For now, this concept will be left as "Why Now?" Why is now the right time for your business, as well as for you?

A right time example is Amazon.com, which began when Jeff Bezos, a former Wall Street executive, noticed the rapid growth of the Internet. Bezos had been observing the evolution of the Internet since the 1980s and waited until 1994 when the time was right to create an online bookstore. His belief was that the accessibility of the Internet coupled with a vast inventory would transform the retail industry. Bezos was patient and waited nearly a decade. He started Amazon from his garage in Seattle and chose to focus on books because the market was vast and had the potential for significant online sales. After writing a business plan, he used $15,000 of his own money and about $300,000 in funding from his parents and launched Amazon.com in July 1995.

The Amazon website offered a wide selection of titles, leveraging the Internet's ability to "stock" more books than any physical store. Bezos emphasized customer service, creating an easy user-friendly experience that encouraged repeat business. Word of mouth quickly helped Amazon gain traction, and it became known for its extensive inventory and innovative features, like user reviews and content previews, and the ability to "loan" books purchased on the Internet to friends and family.

In 1997, Amazon went public, and the company gradually expanded its product offerings beyond books to include music, electronics, and eventually everything from clothing to groceries. Bezos's vision was to create "the Earth's most customer-centric company," and he continually reinvested profits into expanding Amazon's capabilities, including logistics and technology.

This example of Jeff Bezos and Amazon.com provides an excellent starting point for the timing discussion. Suppose Jeff had tried to start Amazon in the early 1980s when he first had the idea? It would never have worked, because the Internet was years from being ubiquitous enough to support his ideas. On the other hand, suppose Jeff had waited longer for some reason (maybe he wanted to raise more money, or he had some sort of long-term family issue to worry about), and one of the executives at Walmart had a brainstorm one day and put the idea into place first? Amazon.com would not have become a household name with a market valuation of over $2 trillion.

As you grow your business, there will be times when you have nobody to turn to in your organization to ask, "What should I do now?" Millions of entrepreneurs have faced that situation and persevered. It isn't about knowing everything, it's about being comfortable not knowing and figuring it out, with some help. My partners and I at BCT found ourselves in those situations often during the formative years of the company. Sometimes it was questions from state and federal regulatory agencies, or tax questions, environmental health and safety questions, employment regulations, and on and on. To help cope, we developed a network of advisers and mentors that we could query (pro bono), and we became expert researchers. It's likely that in the coming years, AI could provide very valuable "business partner" support to you when you encounter these types of challenges. The important question is whether you and your leadership team are comfortable in situations where you don't know the answer, but you have the opportunity to learn?

Experience in a relevant field for what you are about to undertake is also extremely important. Knowing what the world considers the acceptable product, state-of-the-art solution, or best user experience is important. Understanding the going price, margins and cost of providing the service or product is crucial. Regardless of what type of company you are starting, you need to know what is currently available, the strengths and weaknesses, how customers feel about the current situation, and what might be possible. Knowing how much customers pay for the current solution, and how much they might pay for something better is beneficial as well.

Domain-specific knowledge, the kind of knowledge you get from working in an industry, gives you a *superpower* which many people don't appreciate, especially when starting a new business. Your superpower is that you likely know the dirty little secrets of the industry, like which companies are on the rise, which are struggling, and what factors are holding them back. If you've been paying attention, you know what works well, what is outdated, and with some imagination you can visualize what the future might look like. Use your superpower to conceive new solutions, services, or ways of doing business that solve problems or alleviate pain points for customers.

For example, if you were working in the insurance industry and had access to risk data, you might notice that people in the military or employed by the federal government are statistically safer drivers and thus present a lower risk to insure. That was the initial business model for a company named GEICO, founded in 1936 by Leo Goodwin and his wife Lillian.[5] Leo had previously worked in the insurance industry in San Antonio, Texas. As he became experienced in the field, he learned how the industry worked, where money was made (insuring safe drivers), and how it was lost (insuring risky drivers). By targeting low-risk drivers, Leo and his wife eliminated a lot of the ways that money was lost. They started the company by offering "direct" sales to low-risk military and government employed drivers, bypassing agents, which also helped lower rates, which, in turn, enabled the company to grow steadily. GEICO didn't open any regional offices until 1948, when it also expanded to offer insurance to nongovernment employees. Over the years, GEICO diversified its offerings and expanded into other types of insurance. It became well known for its memorable advertising campaigns, including the iconic gecko and the "15 minutes could save you 15% or more on car insurance" slogan. By the late 1990s, the company had become one of the largest auto insurers in the United States, prompting an acquisition by Warren Buffett of Berkshire Hathaway in 1996.

That "prior knowledge" superpower was important to us at BCT as well. All the founders and early employees of the company came from large organizations in the satellite industry. We had been designing and building spacecraft and instruments for NASA, the Department of Defense, and research organizations. Traditionally, that type of work is high risk, with uncertain costs and technical outcomes, a situation which hadn't changed much since the dawn of the U.S. space program in the 1960s. Much of the uncertainty and technical risk is unavoidable, because the satellite or instrument being developed was one of a kind, built for the first time for that government or DOD mission. Because the satellite was the first of a kind, it took a long time to design, analyze and build, which meant it cost a lot of money. Because it cost a lot of money, customers wanted to have extensive analysis and testing performed before it launched, to make sure it would work on orbit. More analysis and testing meant more costs, but there was always uncertainty because of the complexity of the designs and the uniqueness. The state of the industry was essentially a spiral that equated to the more the mission cost, the more time and effort should be spent on it, which in turn made it cost more, until the budget was used up and finally someone in authority decided that it was time to stop analyzing and launch the satellite.

Due to all that uncertainty, it became commonplace in the industry that many programs would be executed on a "cost-plus" basis, whereby the contractor accumulates costs for labor and materials, and sends invoices to the government periodically for reimbursement, along with a marginal profit of typically 6 percent or 8 percent. The government eventually receives their satellite, the contractor gets paid and makes a small (less than 10 percent but guaranteed) profit. Perfect, right? The problem is that unlike the U.S. Government, commercial aerospace contractors are usually for-profit organizations, with shareholders who expect an ever-increasing return on their investments. This situation sets itself up to evolve over time such that it is in the contractor's shareholders (and thus the board of directors') best interest to *increase* the complexity of the satellite or service, so that it costs the government more, and the contractor makes more profit because of the guaranteed fixed percentage. Worse yet, this cost-plus mentality rewards the contractor for becoming *inefficient*. I'm not saying these tactics were intentional by the contractors, but they were the natural result of an economic system that doesn't have any strong mechanisms to reward efficiency, favor simplistic designs, or reduce costs. That cost-plus mentality indirectly rewards the company that is inefficient almost to the point that the customer cancels the contract, but not quite.

Many large aerospace contractors had been thriving in this business model for decades, since the space program heyday of the 1960s and 1970s. By the time our team at BCT was starting our company, we had seen enough of the waste to know that we could provide a disruptive innovation to the marketplace, by providing standardized satellites, "mass produced," and tailored to meet the government's specific needs for their custom mission. I place quotes around "mass produced" because we typically manufactured in batches of five or perhaps 20, depending upon the product, but that was still significantly cheaper than one at a time. In addition, our approach paid for the cost of development on the first satellite of a kind, and the only recurring cost to future customers were the manufacturing and test costs. Most importantly, by having a standard set of designs which we provided to all our customers, BCT was able to have high confidence in the on-orbit success of our products, thus lowering the risk to NASA, the military, or our commercial customers. It turned out to be an innovative breakthrough which has in turn benefitted our country, scientists, soldiers, and many other commercial companies worldwide.

I used the word "disruptive" above, and it's important to emphasize in this chapter the power of some business opportunities. You can also substitute the word "multifaceted" in some instances. The word "disruptive" is probably overused and not well understood. The point is that when a business has multiple ways that it improves upon the current status quo, it is significantly more likely to be successful than if the innovation is singular. In the case of BCT, our strategy reduced costs, it also reduced the technical risk for the customer. Because our systems were smaller and lighter than traditional spacecraft, they were cheaper to launch. Because of the standardization, we were also able to employ a technique developed in the software world called "spiral development" where each iteration of our designs involved setting a new objective for better performance. We would make a few design improvements, perform some risk analysis and testing, and then evaluate the results and fold in lessons learned. Using this method, we could effectively stay ahead of our competition with minimal investment, a huge difference from the large aerospace contractor model where every satellite was a fresh "start from scratch" design.

If you have been an entrepreneur before, you have some idea about what you're getting into. But if you haven't started a business before, you may be wondering what it will be like. On the plus side, you will have freedom and autonomy to pursue your passions, create an impact on solving a problem or helping society, and be able to take satisfaction from building something from scratch. You can establish a flexible working environment which complements your personal life and leave a legacy of your accomplishments. If you enjoy meeting interesting people, learning a wide range of new skills from marketing to finance to leadership, and potentially creating a financial nest egg, then entrepreneurship may be a great opportunity for you.

There will be some degree of financial instability along the way, long hours and the potential for burnout, some unpredictability in your future, and the ever-present risk of failure. There is a very high risk of negative impacts to your personal life, vacation schedule, and time with your family. Following the guidance in this book will provide methods to minimize these impacts, but they cannot be eliminated entirely. Once you start your business there will be significant pressure to succeed, find customers, overcome competition, and keep your employees happy. None of these challenges are insurmountable, and some individuals enjoy the challenges and revel in the progress of their company. I can attest that it is an experience unlike anything you will encounter as an employee of any other company. Starting a business doesn't mean you must stay with it forever. It's fine to leave when the time feels right. Enjoy your work while it lasts, and if it stops being fun or your priorities change, it's OK to move on.

If you still aren't sure about your readiness and aptitude to become an entrepreneur, consider some ways to better understand yourself and how you might fare:

- **Self-Assessment Tests:** Personality tests like the Myers-Briggs Type Indicator (MBTI), the Big 5 Ocean test, or the DISC assessment can provide insights into your traits and preferences related to entrepreneurship. I personally recommend the Big 5 Ocean test. Several online sites offer testing.
- **Reflect on Your Traits:** For example, resilience, risk-taking, adaptability, and strong problem-solving skills. Reflect on how you handle challenges, uncertainty, and decision making.
- **Evaluate Your Passion:** Are you passionate about the idea or field of your potential business?
- **Seek Feedback:** Talk to friends, family, or mentors about your strengths and weaknesses. They might offer valuable perspectives on your readiness for entrepreneurship.
- **Explore Your Experience:** As mentioned above, relevant experience may be your superpower. Not only knowing how to do things but knowing what not to do can be a game-changer.
- **Network with Other Entrepreneurs:** Engaging with people in your same boat can give you insights into their journeys and help you assess whether you will be comfortable with the challenges and successes. Many cities and universities have websites and meetings to facilitate entrepreneurial growth.

My Big 5 Ocean personality test identified me as an "ENTJ." Famous ENTJ people include Jim Carrey, Steve Jobs, Harrison Ford, and Margaret Thatcher. ENTJ people are extroverted and gain energy from engaging with the external world. They are assertive, decisive and confident, often taking charge in social and professional settings. ENTJs enjoy interacting with people and are natural leaders, guiding others toward achieving common goals. They are outspoken and enjoy debates and discussions to challenge and refine their ideas. All of that sounds perfect for an entrepreneur and founder of a startup, right? Well, not quite. What the Big 5 test revealed about my weaknesses was more insightful. *Apparently,*

I have an intolerance for inefficiency, and I get impatient and frustrated by lack of progress. Even worse, I can be overly critical of myself and others, and I often struggle to recognize and respond to the emotions of others. Topping off my weaknesses, I am (according to the report) prone to taking risks without fully considering the consequences. Some of those weaknesses are real deal-killers for a solo entrepreneur and company leader! Fortunately, I had great partners with strengths to balance out my weaknesses.

Everything we will discuss in this book goes better with friends, partners, co-owners, or whatever you'd like to call them. The people who lead the organization may evolve, expand, or contract over time, but the company will benefit from people who are figuratively in the trench with you shoveling and sharing the experience. Partners provide a sane sounding board to bounce ideas off, different perspectives to help identify rational solutions during crises, and bring different skill sets and industry contacts. If you can make each other laugh and talk each other through a disagreement to a mutually agreeable conclusion, all the better. Ideally, a group of founding partners have complementary, not identical skill sets. There are many skills required to build and grow a business. If all of the partners are highly skilled in one domain, there will be friction and the potential for disagreement about the right way in that area, coupled with a gross lack of experience in other equally important areas.

I had the privilege of partnering with George, Steve, and later Dan at BCT. Each of us brought unique strengths and areas for improvement to the table, but our shared passion for the industry, the company's potential, and its eventual success was a unifying factor. Our complementary personalities and skill sets facilitated smooth collaboration, and even during disagreements, we viewed them as opportunities to improve the company.

George possessed a natural vision and inspirational leadership that fostered confidence necessary for his role as CEO. Steve led the design team with precision, consistently demanding high standards of excellence and performance from himself and the entire organization. Dan's deep industry knowledge and innovative approach to solving customer problems significantly contributed to steering the company in the right direction. My expertise in business systems, manufacturing, testing, and automation enabled me to construct the infrastructure required to turn ideas into working hardware. While we all hailed from the same industry, we had unique contributions to facilitate complementary innovation with minimal friction. The complementary nature of our skill sets is what I refer to as "Leadership Diversity."

The founding team felt that we could make a serious difference for our country for both NASA science missions and Department of Defense missions. We wanted to save money for the taxpayers, provide a superior solution to what was available from traditional suppliers, and enable missions which wouldn't have been possible without our innovations. We had an inkling that we were onto something special, but it took a lot of work to make it a reality.

We were optimistic but always kept options open such that if everything went to hell in a handbasket, we could wind up the company and go back to our old jobs. The founding team made a commitment that we would never take out a crushing amount of debt but always leave a way to fold up the company and walk away if the worst happened.

Our overarching goals for the company were to create an organization where employees were empowered and knew they were important to the company's success, and everyone could have a good time while working hard. In an industry that predominantly employs white men, we took pride in the number of women and the extensive racial diversity of our workforce. We didn't strive for diversity; we just hired the best candidates available, period. These mindsets influenced the culture and made BCT a more rewarding, enjoyable place to call home for 40+ hours per week.

BCT products enabled other companies to become possible, and those companies in turn created jobs, and new products which made discoveries about the world and our universe. Some of our products helped address global warming, and helped defend our nation from adversaries like North Korea, Russia, and other totalitarian states. BCT products have traveled to the moon, asteroids, mars, and many are orbiting the Earth making discoveries about climate change, the universe, and what the bad guys are doing. The company continues to provide innovative solutions to the small satellite industry spanning scientific research to national defense.

My most notable achievement in retrospect is that we provided rewarding employment, a fun culture, and salaries to hundreds of people in our state and across the nation. As a "primary employer" (meaning that our revenue came from outside the state) the money we brought to the community was a big driving force in not only employing our company, but also employed hundreds of people at companies that supported BCT. Our employees were able to buy houses, pay for doctor visits, buy groceries, put kids in daycare, and pay for meals at local restaurants. In total, thousands of people were employed by the money that our startup brought into the community.

You should spend some time thinking about what you would like to be doing in 5 or 10 years. What would your ideal day, week, and year look like? Who would you work with, and where could you recruit new talent as the company grows? How will you entice them away from their current jobs, and retain them? Everyone you hire should enhance the company to make it better. The first ten people who join your company will have the largest impact on the future of your endeavor. In the next chapter, we will explore how you can go about finding a great idea for your company.

Never give up searching for the job that you're passionate about. Try to find the job you'd have if you were independently rich. Forget about the pay. When you're associating with the people that you love, doing what you love, it doesn't get any better than that.

—Warren Buffett

CHAPTER 2

Identifying a Problem and the Opportunities

In Chapter 1 we focused on you, the potential entrepreneur, and your motivation and qualifications to begin a startup company. We also discussed the advantages of taking this journey with a complementary partnership team. As promised, in this chapter we will dive into what sorts of business you (and hopefully your partners) might want to start, or if you haven't made up your mind yet, how you can go about finding and validating different ideas. The following chapters will discuss how to build out your team, set up the operations of your business, and eventually launch your business. But for now, let's just focus on business or product ideas that separate you from the competition. In this chapter, we will provide a framework to help you visualize whether your business will battle among competitors or preferably operate without competition. If you already have a business concept in mind, you can use this chapter to review the merits and perhaps tweak your plans if necessary. So, let's dive in.

Remember from the introduction that the #1 reason for business failure is "poor product–market fit." What does this mean, really? It means that the company failed to identify what the market really needed or failed to respond to market feedback and make corrections. So simple, yet so many businesses fail due to this reason, along with reason #2, "running out of money," which I would argue is just another way of not having product–market fit. If your product is good, and you can find a way to produce it economically, then you will not run out of money. But I'm getting ahead of myself. Let's look at ways that you can figure out what the market really needs and not become a part of this statistic for failure.

Thomas Jefferson said, "I'm a great believer in luck, and I find that the harder I work the more I have of it," and he has been proven correct time and again You will also experience this phenomenon throughout your journey of building your business. But I am going to give you another thought to complement those fine words of Mr. Jefferson, "There's no substitute for experience." What this means in our context is that as you go about your life, working in your current job and when you are starting your business, nothing you encounter will help you make innovative decisions as much as your own experiences. Good experiences are helpful, but painful experiences are better!

If you have personally experienced a problem, worked in a company with problematic products and services, or bad culture, inefficient systems, or low morale, you know that feeling, and you should apply those feelings to imagine a superior new business opportunity. Similarly, as a consumer, if you have ever experienced a product or service that was surprisingly good or bad, you should fold those experiences into your plans for how to craft your future.

Very simply, businesses succeed if they are solving a problem for someone or some organization, that is the simplest definition of good "product–market fit." Good startup companies identify the pain that someone or something is enduring and endeavor to create a business out of solving that problem. Some academics will tell you in their books that you as the leader of your company need to be able to **predict** the changes in the market. That sounds mysterious and awesome! If only it were really that easy. As we will explain shortly, the key to being a very successful business leader is **creating** a change that results in an entirely **new** market!

The importance of solving real-world problems for somebody or some organization cannot be overemphasized. Fortunately, almost anything can be made better, or improve someone's health, education, or welfare. Here's a random list of business types. Take a moment and think about how each one solves a problem or makes someone's life better.

- Web Development Agency—Specializes in creating websites for clients.
- Landscaping Service—A business providing lawn care and landscaping design.
- Food Truck—A mobile kitchen serving a variety of cuisines at different locations.

- IT Support Services—Offers technical support and troubleshooting for businesses and individuals.
- Photography Studio—A service offering professional photography for events and portraits.
- Home Cleaning Service—A company offering cleaning services for residential properties.
- Robotics Engineering Firm—Designs and manufactures robotic systems for industries such as manufacturing, health care, and logistics, integrating AI and automation technologies.
- Telemedicine Platform—Offers virtual consultations and health services through online platforms.
- Software Development Company—Creates custom software solutions for various industries.
- Health Informatics Consulting—Helps health care organizations manage and analyze health data.
- Medical Billing Services—Specializes in billing and coding for health care providers.
- Financial Planning Firm—Offers personalized financial advice and investment strategies.
- Accounting and Bookkeeping Services—Manages financial records and compliance for businesses.
- Biotechnology Company—Specializes in using biological processes for medical and agricultural innovations, including gene editing and synthetic biology.
- Blockchain Development Company—Provides solutions for decentralized applications and smart contracts, focusing on enhancing security and transparency in transactions.

Obviously, "solving a problem" can be expanded in many ways, for example: Provides something desirable, resolving financial or health problems, or providing a service for a task that some people just don't like doing and would rather pay it done. All of these are viable business categories, clearly. Approximately 500,000 new businesses with plans for payroll are started each year in the United States. There are many opportunities for entrepreneurs in essentially any field.

The point of this review is that you need to start thinking about why any given organization exists. Does a Food Truck business provide food for people on the go? Well, yes, but what we'd like to start thinking about is that people, especially in modern urban areas, are very busy and don't always have time to drive or travel to a sit-down restaurant. In addition, a large number of drive-thru fast-food chains have come under criticism for serving unhealthy, mundane meals. People crave variety, and many people try to maintain a healthy diet, but they don't always have a lot of time for high-quality restaurant options. This is one of the reasons that the number of food trucks in the United States has *doubled* over the past decade, and it is estimated that there are now over 35,000 food trucks nationwide. People need to eat, and they don't have much time, and they'd prefer to have an enjoyable healthy option that they can feel good about. These food trucks are solving this problem and taking revenue away from the mega-chain, assembly-line processed-food purveyors.

In Chapter 1, we discussed how important it is to have at least a modest amount of experience in the industry where you're considering your startup. Whatever that industry may be, take some time now to consider what is problematic or what do people wish they could have or do? If you're passionate about your area of interest, you likely have already thought about completely new, unheard of methods or solutions to common problems or tasks.

If you were living in an urban area before 2009, your public transportation options were limited and largely consisted of buses, taxis, and if you were in a larger metropolitan area, perhaps trains or subways. At that time, people automatically accepted these solutions and worked their way around the city as best they could. Nobody considered that there might be a better option, even though plenty of people complained. Buses could only go on designated routes and at specific times, and the safety of the ride could at times be questionable. Taxis were great to get from airports to major hotels, but outside of that route (for example to the suburbs) they were not a very convenient solution. Trains were the high-volume, more efficient and usually more reliable version of buses. But there wasn't a good solution for a passenger who needed to get from random point A to point B on his or her schedule safely.

While attending a conference in Paris in 2008, Garrett Camp and Travis Kalanick struggled to get a taxi after a late-night outing. They became frustrated and imagined what it would be like to merely summon a car from a smartphone at the touch of a button. They created a simple app to run on their phones; used their own cars for transportation; and asked friends to drive for them to prove the concept out. They started the business in San Francisco and called it "UberCab" at first, then shortened it to "Uber." Today, it (along with Lyft) are a ubiquitous transportation solution in over 500 cities worldwide,[6] with annual revenue over $30B. Equally important, over 5 million driver "partners" enjoy the lifestyle and freedom of being an Uber driver.

The Uber founders, Kalanick and Camp, had backgrounds and passions which enabled their success in the establishment and success of the company. Kalanick grew up in the Los Angeles area and was interested in computers from a young age and had learned to write computer code by the time he was in middle school. He attended UCLA to study computer engineering but dropped out in 1998 to help launch the startup Scour, Inc. which offered Internet searching and file sharing, and was one of the first dot-com companies to enable users to share movies and music online. Although the company was successful, it was sued for copyright infringement and eventually filed for bankruptcy and folded in 2000. Kalanick's next startup was Red Swoosh, another company specializing in file-sharing technology, which he was able to sell in 2007 for Akamai Technologies for nearly $19 million. Camp, on the other hand, was born and raised in Calgary, Alberta, where he completed his bachelor's degree and Master of Science in Electrical Engineering in 2005. He created a personalized search engine portal called StumbleUpon with three of his colleagues.[7]

So, clearly both Kalanick and Camp had significant experience developing technology applications and web-based tools. They personally experienced the pain of being stranded in Paris on a cold snowy night. It was as simple as connecting the frustration they felt in that moment with the vision of a way to solve this problem for billions of future commuters and travelers. What they identified in that experience is a Blue Ocean opportunity, so called because of the work of W. Chan Kim and Renee Mauborgne in their international bestselling book "Blue Ocean Strategy."[8]

Blue Oceans and Red Oceans

The best way to understand Blue Oceans is to discuss Red Oceans first. Red Oceans are established industries where companies compete head-to-head to be the best, or battle for customers by undercutting each other on price, or attempt to win market share through minor strategic nuances or gimmicks like loyalty programs. A good example of a Red Ocean is the consumer beverage industry including the giants Coca-Cola, Pepsi, and Nestlé; hundreds of medium-sized companies that attempt to focus on specific markets or product types such as craft beverages and health drinks; and thousands of small, niche brands. There is extensive competition, and the market is described as a Red Ocean because the competitors are figuratively tearing each other apart in their attempts to gain market share and increase revenue.

Blue Oceans, in contrast, are defined by untapped market space, where demand for a product or service doesn't exist yet, simply because it is novel, innovative, or downright revolutionary. Looking back over the past century, imagine the state of transportation before the introduction of the automobile, or airplanes. Imagine the state of communications before cell phones, computers, and the Internet. The companies that were first movers into those fledgling industries had the opportunity to dominate, but in some cases the copycats were the survivors. Note also that over time, all significant Blue Oceans become Red Oceans as more and more competition enter the industry in an attempt to get a piece of the action. However, as Kim and Mauborgne highlight in their book, companies have the opportunity to renew their business and create other Blue Oceans. "Blue Ocean Strategy" is a good addition to any entrepreneur's library, and I highly recommend it. We referenced it extensively to guide the growth and success as we built BCT, but we also expanded upon it as I will explain later in this chapter.

The key elements of a Blue Ocean are:

1. **Uncontested Market Space**: An area where there is little or no competition, allowing companies to innovate and create new demand. Businesses operating in this space don't have to fight over the same customers because the market is essentially "unexplored."

2. **Value Innovation:** This is the cornerstone of a Blue Ocean Strategy. Instead of focusing on outperforming rivals, companies create value through innovation—simultaneously offering customers greater value while reducing costs. This creates a leap in value for both the company and the customer, making the competition irrelevant.

3. **Differentiation and Low Cost:** Blue Ocean strategies often combine differentiation (making something unique or better) with low cost, allowing businesses to break the traditional trade-off between quality and price that is typically seen in competitive Red Ocean markets.

4. **Creating New Demand:** Rather than focusing on existing customers in an existing market, Blue Ocean Strategy seeks to create new demand by identifying unmet needs or by finding new ways to make products or services more attractive to potential customers.

5. **Innovation and Growth:** Companies operating in Blue Oceans are focused on innovation—not just technological innovation, but in business models, customer experiences, or even distribution channels. This drives growth and allows firms to stay ahead of potential competition.

What I think is missing from the Blue Ocean Strategy concept yet is so extremely important to consider in this discussion, is *Passion*. Why pursue any opportunity, or build a company, if you aren't excited about it? Passion is a key element that we will weave into the discussion from this point forward. Passion also helps you hone in on a good market fit, because you care so much about it, and you are excited about the opportunities to create something better.

Does your business idea fit more into a Red or Blue Ocean? And are you passionate about it? To help you with this analysis, you might want to list out the competitors in your industry, or at least the closest you can identify within the industry. List out the significant factors over which the competitors attempt to differentiate themselves. For example, take the U.S. airline industry, with the four largest competitors of United, Delta, American, and Southwest, as shown in Table 2.1.

Obviously, there are a lot more factors involved in running a successful competitive airline than these factors, but evaluating performance,

Table 2.1 Comparison of major U.S. Airlines, 2023—Red Ocean

	United	Delta	American	Southwest
Fleet size	920+ aircraft	940+ aircraft	950+ aircraft	814+ aircraft
# of destinations	> 430	>290	>350	>110
Passengers/year	165 million	190 million	211 million	172 million
$ revenue 2024	$25B	$25B	$25B	$12B
Net income	$1.2B	$1.3B	$405M	$137M
Service model	Major airports, domestic and international	Major airports, domestic and international	Major airports, domestic and international	Major domestic airports and some point to point
Differentiator	International network, premium services	Good customer service, modern fleet, loyalty program	Global network and premium service and lounges	Low-cost model, no change fees, two free checked bags
Customer Selection Factors	Travelers typically choose based upon destination, budget, loyalty programs, and service preferences. In summary, if multiple airlines support a route, the customer chooses on price and loyalty			

financial results, and business model provide a relatively clear picture of the competitive landscape. At this point, I'd like to introduce a graphical representation to depict a cohort of various companies along two axes as shown in Figure 2.1.

So, we contrast the cost of operating the business (as the *x*-axis) versus revenue generated as a percentage of the cost of operations (as the *y*-axis). To take it a step further, one could also consider the *Value generated* as a proxy for %revenue, since the function of a business is to make money. So, in this manner we have a way to characterize how much value a company is creating, thus we can visualize whether companies are uniquely special or just competing for market share with each other.

Obviously, all four of these airlines are in a battle for market share, without any one of them being clearly different or providing unique value. Delta, American, and United are closely huddled together, with Delta being a slight profitability winner (value generated). United is barely getting by, and Southwest is hardly making any profit at all even though their overall cost of operations is significantly lower than the other three. So,

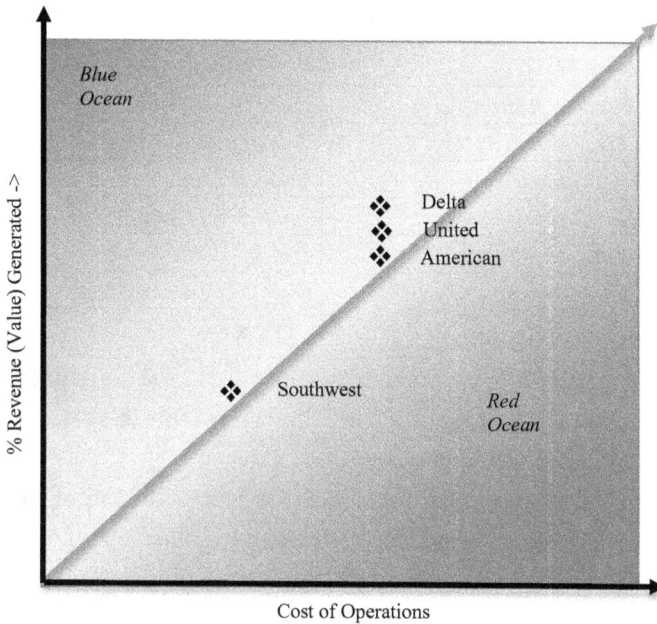

Figure 2.1 Value performance index major U.S. Airlines 2023

what really sets these three apart? Absolutely Nothing. Delta is managing to either be slightly more efficient, or has gotten lucky with some uncontested routes, but in any given year the figure could look largely similar with the four major airlines just making small moves as the tides of the economy and travel industry ebb and flow.

A good strategist looking for a Blue Ocean opportunity here would consider what is difficult or painful for travelers. Do you enjoy traveling on any of those four airlines? I hate the long process of getting to a major airport, the TSA security process, the long walk through crowded, noisy, often dirty terminals, the dehumanizing boarding process, and cramped seating onboard.

All those airlines operate from major airports under the same Federal Aviation Administration regulations, specifically Part 121, which governs operation of scheduled air carriers. As "Part 121" operators, they must abide by the same set of regulations which are implemented at airports with collaboration from TSA. Over time, most of the major routes have migrated into 20 "mega airports" in the United States.

Table 2.2 Red versus Blue Ocean factors for Airline Service

Red Ocean	Blue Ocean
Long process to get from parking to gate	Car to gate quickly
Onerous TSA screening process	Quick, minimal screening
Overcrowded large terminals	Uncrowded small terminals
Dehumanizing boarding by groups	Everyone boards simultaneously
Flights to mega airports primarily	Flights to convenient airports
Mostly economy "coach" service	Exclusively "premium" business class

Focusing on the pain points, what would need to be different to make airline travel more enjoyable? Table 2.2 provides some ideas that I think we could all agree would improve airline travel.

If you were able to offer those Blue Ocean factors as part of your airline, do you think you would have interested customers? Would you as a customer be more likely to choose such a solution for your travel needs, maybe even pay a little more? I know I would. As a matter of fact, I fly on such an airline whenever possible, an airline named "JSX." It operates smaller aircraft, with routes to popular destinations and often using smaller airports, all without the hassle incurred when traveling with the major airlines.

With JSX, the security process is greatly simplified, as they operate from private terminals which do not require TSA. Passengers are asked to arrive 30 minutes before departure, answer a quick questionnaire, and undergo a simple security scanning process, then they are on their way to their destination. Onboard, passengers are treated to free high-speed StarLink Internet service, complementary beverages including beer, wine, cocktails, or nonalcoholic options, and complimentary snacks. Pets are allowed to travel as well, although larger dogs are required to purchase a seat.

JSX was founded in 2016 by Alex Wilcox, who previously worked at JetBlue Airways as vice president of planning. He says that his time at JetBlue helped him gain insight into the airline industry, particularly how to build a business model that focuses on both customer service and efficiency. Prior to his time at JetBlue, Alex worked at Sabre Holdings and Cendant Corporation, both of which operate travel and tourism services and software solutions. As you can see, Alex's experience spanning airline operations and travel software gave him the tools to not only understand the strengths of the various industries, but also their weaknesses and opportunities to create a Blue Ocean business. Fundamentally, JSX has created a *new* market, so that they don't have to compete with the Red Ocean companies. Alex didn't predict the future of the airline industry, he created it.

To be clear, JSX has no interest competing head-to-head with the Red Ocean airlines, and because JSX operates outside the "Part 121" regulations, they legally cannot. Some critics of the business model cite concerns about safety and security, because JSX operates as a "Part 135" carrier, which is termed "commuter and on-demand" operations, aka "charters." They cannot operate with more than 30 passenger seats, for example, which limits their revenue as well as their costs, as the smaller Embraer 135 and 145 which have lower acquisition and operating costs than the Boeing or Airbus manufactured aircraft operated by the larger Part 121 airlines. But the key here is that most passengers don't know or care about part 121 or 135, they care about getting from one city to another as quickly and comfortably as possible!

What this exercise has done is identify the major components of the Blue Ocean Strategy, simply defined as the "Value Proposition": What is it that customers want, and they are willing to change their habits or spending, to acquire? Although financial estimates are not available for JSX, it is notionally depicted in Figure 2.2 illustrating the Value provided, and the separation from the other companies.

Red Ocean companies get locked-in to a constrained definition of their industry and accept the status quo as an immutable fact. They will ask questions such as, "How can we increase market share over our rival?" "How can we reduce costs or increase efficiency?" or "How can we defend our market share?"

As you may have guessed, although Southwest Airlines is a Red Ocean company now, it created a Blue Ocean in the late 1960s and early 1970s by creating a then new market: Offering low fares, short fights, quick turnarounds, and free baggage. Strategically, they only operated one type of aircraft, the Boeing 737, which allowed them to minimize the costs for training, equipment, and documentation compared to their competitors who operated a variety of aircraft, each requiring specialized tooling,

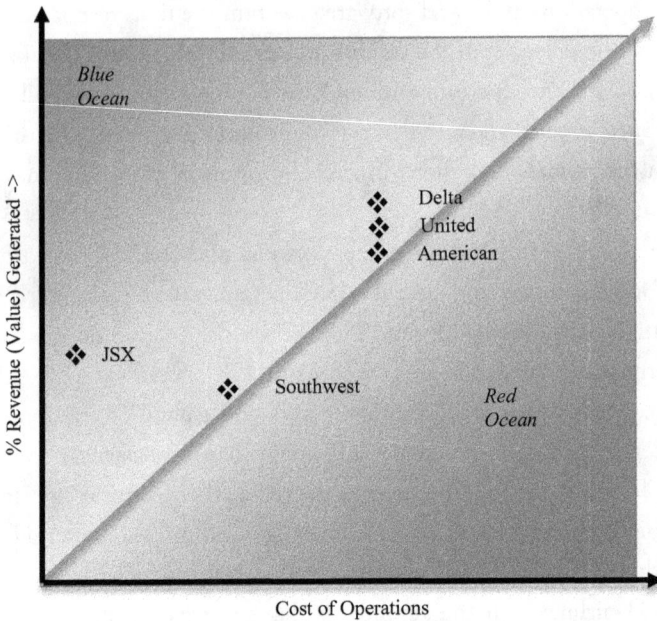

Figure 2.2 Value performance index including JSX as a Blue Ocean

training, and support. Perhaps most importantly, Southwest introduced direct "city to city" routes, at a time when the other airlines were operating old-school, traditional "spoke and hub" routes, meaning that many travelers had to first fly to a major "hub," then switch planes to continue on a "spoke" to their destination. These factors combined to greatly reduce their actual operating costs while simultaneously improving their market appeal to many travelers. They could reasonably sell tickets at lower prices than the competition and still achieve a healthy profit margin. In addition, the company implemented a customer centric "fun and friendly LUV" brand, allowing flight attendants to deliver quirky announcements and making flights feel more relaxed and enjoyable. Employees enjoyed the collaborative and fun culture and opportunities for advancement coupled with stock options and profit sharing.

Southwest's open seating policy was viewed for decades as a flexible and efficient way to board, but recent announcements have indicated that Southwest may discontinue open seating in order to conform to the rest of the industry and align with customer preferences. In other words, Southwest is succumbing to market pressure to more fully join in the Red

Ocean! As pointed out by Kim and Mauborgne, Blue Oceans are not permanent. Competitors arrive to partake in the action, customer needs evolve, technology advances, and new Blue Oceans are discovered. One of the keys for your business once you become successful will be to avoid stagnating but continue to refresh your Blue Ocean.

Identifying Red Ocean industries is straightforward. When people discuss companies comparing them to their competition, the discussion will be about pricing, efficiency, marketing, and customer loyalty.

Identifying a company which has created a Blue Ocean is easy as well, because the discussion will be about new features, services or experiences, market disruption, and unmet needs (solving pain). There won't be extensive dialog about competitors for Blue Ocean companies, because there aren't any competitors. A key tenet of Blue Ocean companies is that they disrupt the status quo with new business models, leveraging new technology, new distribution channels, or novel ways of organizing resources to create a unique customer experience which is viewed as valuable enough for people to change their habits. We discussed Amazon earlier and the amazing success of online retailing which is familiar to any online shopper. But the other ways that Amazon built their Blue Ocean business included providing Amazon Web Services (cloud computing and storage services), subscription services like Amazon Prime which generate recurring revenue, and advertising which generates revenue through sponsored product ads and data-driven advertising services. In this way, Amazon truly has no competitors, because they've combined several independent businesses into a complementary suite.

A final example from history is from the automobile industry. In 1900 in the United States, there were about *200* distinct automobile manufacturers, mostly small operators, founded by inventors who were experimenting with various engines and body styles. Production was performed by well-paid, highly skilled craftsmen who took weeks to assemble each vehicle. Automobiles were unpopularly viewed by the masses as a toy for the very wealthy. However, in 1903, Henry Ford began experimenting with innovative design and production methods, including inexpensive, simple parts which could be assembled by relatively unskilled laborers; each focused on building one part or assembly operation. When the Ford Model T was introduced in 1908, it took 12 hours to assemble a single car, but as Ford continued to innovate his production methods, introducing the concept of an assembly line, he was able to reduce the production time to 93 minutes.[9] He was able to reduce his costs so significantly that he could sell the Model T for as low as $260 each[10] (about $10,000 in 2024 dollars). Such an affordable price point brought mainstream America into the automotive revolution. Another innovative move by Henry Ford was that he utilized profit sharing to help retain his employees, paying them $5 per day.

The Ford Model T, JSX, and Uber all demonstrate the intersection of *Passion, Value,* and *Commerciality* (PVC). The founders and CEOs all had a Passion for what they were endeavoring to bring to the market. The Value that all these examples bring to the marketplace is obvious: A Blue Ocean product which either solves a problem or provides significant value for a wide range of customers. Commerciality is the ability to produce those products at a price that is appealing to the customer with enough margin. Becoming profitable allows these companies to reinvest those profits to kindle additional growth and prosperity. This intersection of PVC is similar to the "hedgehog" concept introduced in 2001 by Jim Collins in his landmark book *Good to Great: Why Some Companies Make the Leap...and Others Don't.* But we're going to improve this concept by integrating the Blue Ocean, adding Passion.

To be successful, a company must have *Passion,* there must be a *Value proposition* for that opportunity, and the company must also create a *Different* and *commercially viable* solution. The Intersection of all four of these parameters is what we will define and utilize for the remainder of this book as the *Elite Icon* as shown in Figure 2.3.

Let's make sure this all makes sense. Uncontested market space means your product or service is different from the available solutions. You are operating alone, without significant competition. This allows you the ability to create value, make mistakes, and not be perfect yet still sell a product or service and stay in business long enough to figure it out. If the market space is busy (contested), then the company which can provide the product or service the cheapest or fastest will dominate, and it is very difficult for a newcomer to break in and be successful.

Commercially Viable means that the cost of the product at volume, including the expenses to get your business up and running, is less than

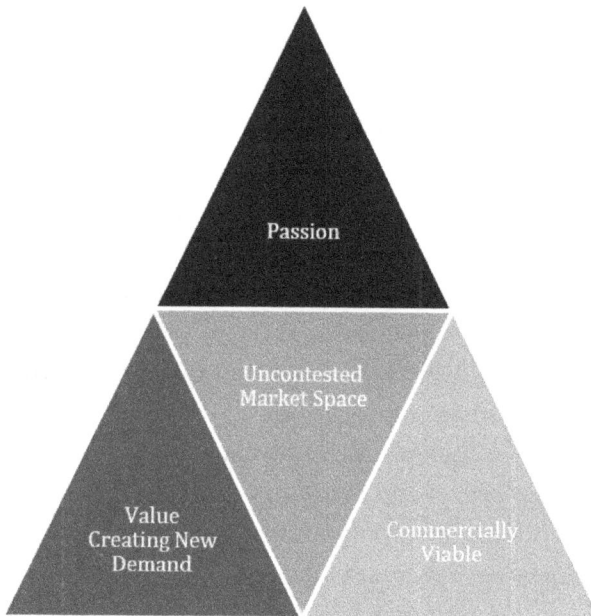

Figure 2.3 Elite Icon: The intersection of uncontested market space, your passion, value to the consumer, and commercial viability

the price that consumers will be willing to pay. Another words, with all costs considered, can you be profitable in 5 or 10 years?

Value Creating Demand is simply that people want your product, because it solves a problem or is desirable in some way. Is it innovative or does it uniquely combine desirable features to create something that people want but cannot currently obtain?

Passion is important because it will provide fuel and innovation for your team to create something special. If the only reason people go to work is to collect a paycheck, they have no passion, and they will not do anything innovative or valuable. Passion underpins everything!

In addition to these four factors, industry experience will help you when you're starting to navigate the waters and looking for ways to differentiate your company and create a true value innovation. If you understand the market, both in terms of the problems and opportunities, then you are well positioned to identify what Value means. Without experience, you are prone to *assuming* what is valuable, without *understanding* the customers' needs or pain points. Also, experience helps you understand the cost of providing the product or service, as well as what customers are typically willing to pay. If you don't personally have the applicable experience but have the passion, then surround yourself with innovative, open-minded individuals who *do* have relevant experience to guide your efforts to a solution which is truly valuable. Passion without experience may end up missing the target for Value Creating Demand as well as not being Commercially Viable.

There are some great examples of people who started fabulous companies with little or no industry experience, including Richard Branson who started Virgin Airlines (previously in music and media); Howard Schultz who started Starbucks (previously a salesman); and Sara Blakely who started Spanx (sold Fax machines). But they all enlisted experienced partners and mentors to help them learn about their industries.

If you have Passion for the industry or problem and can create a solution which provides *true* Value to the customer and can be delivered for less than the price customers are willing to pay, then you are well positioned to create that Elite Icon. Note again that we are not attempting to predict where the market is heading but rather creating something new and of such great value that the customers come to you in your uncontested market space! Powerful words for you to use in this phase of your company are "what if…."

Inversion Technique for Product Ideation

Once you do have an idea or some potential markets in mind, I'd like you to engage in a technique which is powerful to help you objectively assess whether it is indeed going to present a compelling value proposition: Inversion. Using Inversion technique, you will put yourself in the role of your customer, turn the problem around, and view it from their perspective. Do not focus on what you want to improve, and for a moment forget your product or service concept. Instead, concentrate on being the customer, and currently being in the place of buying the existing product or service. What do you dislike most about those options? Be as pragmatic and honest as possible. List out the problems, and then take it even a step further: What would make it *even worse*? How could you change it to be less reliable, less enjoyable, cost more, and be even less desirable. Sit back and reflect on these ideas. It seems silly, but by using the Inversion technique, you exercise your brain and challenge the concepts that make the current marketplace so unattractive. You free your brain to become more objective and counteract your personal biases. Have a cup of coffee or take a nap, then come back and imagine now a world without rules, what features, options, or characteristics can you imagine that reverse the problems? Do not let yourself be constrained by rules, laws, technology, or limitations of any kind. Just free-think and use your imagination. Using the Inversion technique is helpful to let you tap into your creativity without being constrained by the status quo; let it spark your creativity and unleash your imagination. Have fun experimenting with the Inversion technique.

Institutional Complexity Creep

There is a natural, pervasive phenomenon that may provide an opportunity for your company to carve out a niche, referred to as Institutional Complexity Creep. The observed results are that over time, business processes tend to grow increasingly complex and inefficient. There are several reasons that businesses follow this path, and the longer any business is operating, the more it tends to succumb to exhibiting these characteristics.

One of the factors is attributable to "the Iron Law of Bureaucracy," proposed by Jerry Pournelle, which states that in any system such as a company or government, there are two types of people: Those who work to further the goals of the organization, and those who work to maintain the bureaucracy itself.[11] Furthermore, if there is uncertainty about the future, there is a tendency for people to add complexity, which creates job security, increased budgets, and expanded authority. Cultural or regulatory influences can also add complexity, as organizations strive to comply with the latest rules or social priorities, showcase their corporate sophistication, maintain their power, or avoid accountability. In addition, when things go wrong in any given organization, there is a tendency to overcompensate by adding new layers of processes, controls, or oversight mechanisms to eliminate the chance of reoccurrence. Such additions are rarely removed, leading to a permanent degradation of the efficiency of the business.

Institutional Complexity Creep may provide an opportunity for your startup to create a new niche within an industry dominated by long-established, inefficient companies who have succumbed to the effects of Institutional Complexity Creep.

In Chapter 1, I talked about BCT's first attempt at an SBIR (Small Business Innovation Research) grant, which, to our surprise, we won. The grant was for developing a cost-effective small satellite. At the time, all of us were working in the satellite industry, so we were very familiar with the problems. The satellite market was dominated by large aerospace companies that provided custom-made, ultraexpensive satellites costing over $50 million each. On the other end of the spectrum, there were a few budget suppliers offering basic satellites for under $1 million. But there was a clear gap in the middle.

Our value proposition was simple: By applying innovative and modern design and manufacturing techniques, we could deliver a "low-cost" satellite (around $5 million) that would still offer strong performance, though not as sophisticated as the ultraexpensive models. We knew the industry well, and we believed our value proposition was compelling. Passion was high—everyone involved was a space enthusiast (OK, maybe, nerds), and excited about the technology and the chance to contribute to space exploration and national security. However, when it came to being commercially viable, we had no choice but to make a promise in our proposal. There were countless details to work out before it could become a reality. But we had discovered our "Elite Icon"!

What we didn't realize at the time was that the part of the proposal that we felt was the most compelling was actually not an Elite Icon, and it would be another 10 years before we would sell the product that we thought was the most exciting part of our proposal! We were extremely lucky, in that we wrote a very broad proposal which was awarded based upon things that we thought were somewhat interesting, but we listened to the market (the review team in the government) and built upon that first contract win to form our business and win more contracts by listening to our customers. Lesson learned: Be ready to pivot from what you think your customer wants to what they really want.

As depicted in Figure 2.4, we successfully identified a Blue Ocean opportunity, we were passionate about it, and we believed it was economically

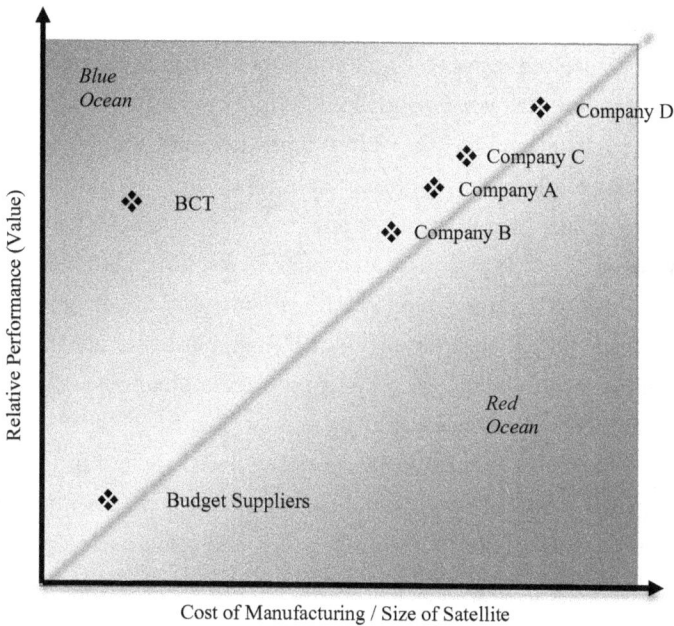

Figure 2.4 U.S. satellite suppliers (2010)

viable, so it qualified as our Elite Icon. It was up to us to create that new market. The larger companies routinely went head-to-head for massive, multi-hundred-million-dollar or billion-dollar contracts, and tended to win them alternately (meaning no one company dominated, they just fought it out in their Red Ocean). Our introduction of a very capable, yet affordable smaller satellite was innovative and of great value to the U.S. Government and other customers who were always struggling under tight budget constraints. Disruptive? You bet!

Timing is something we haven't discussed much, yet, but in this instance, it bears mentioning. The miniaturization of electronics parts, along with improvements in volume manufacturing methods which occurred in the 1980s and 1990s, were both fundamental enablers of what we promised to deliver at BCT. The large satellite providers were still using time-proven (1960s and 1970s era) large electronics and traditional manufacturing methods (highly skilled craftsmen hand building one-of-a-kind satellites). We embraced the innovations which were introduced by commercial manufacturers when they developed modern commercial electronics like flatscreen TVs and cellphones to market. If we had attempted to create our Elite Icon before 1980, we would have failed miserably, because the ultrasmall, super high-performance electronics parts hadn't been invented yet. Essentially, we created our Elite Icon by leaning into the latest technology innovations to differentiate our products from the established old-guard companies in our industry.

Once we won that grant, we thought we were hot stuff. We assumed we were full of magic pixie dust and would be winning a lot of contracts, so we started making more proposals for various grant opportunities. Fortunately, we did not start hiring a bunch of employees or spend lavishly on facilities or equipment. We proposed the development of astronaut exercise equipment (we knew nothing about astronauts, and almost as little about the science of exercise, being geeky engineers) and our proposal was rejected. We proposed the development of underwater unmanned vehicles (we knew about space, not underwater) and again our proposal was rejected. The simple truth is that when we attempted to identify Value differentiators about concepts which we didn't really understand, our ideas were not appropriate and sometimes were downright nonsense. We failed because we did not understand the pain of the users, nor the value system of those industries, or what would really be innovative. If we had been former astronauts or naval submarine officers, or even hired consultants who were, we might have been more enlightened and successful in identifying Value.

All in all, it was nearly 3 years between our first contract win at BCT and our next contract win. It took a lot of trial and error to figure out what we needed to be doing better. And tight belts. We worked to spend as little money as possible during that time frame, while we worked to figure out what the customers needed.

Learning how to identify a Value differentiator and create an Elite Icon were critical steps between dreaming and ultimately becoming a Great Company, but that wasn't all there was to it. Not surprisingly, it takes more than just thinking up a good idea to become a successful thriving business. If at all possible, you should keep your company in phase 0, with just you and the other founders working at the company, until you have confidence in a strong product or service which you believe fits the definition of an Elite Icon. Bringing on more people to potentially start developing the *wrong* product will only waste money and create tension among your team. Making that mistake is one of the reasons businesses fail. They commit early to the wrong idea, and it is a poor market fit, and they run out of money before they can figure out the right market fit. Those two reasons are listed as the top two reasons a startup business fails. Keep the team small, develop your ideas, test them out if you can and fold in the feedback. If you absolutely must build a prototype product or service in order to test the waters, we will discuss how to go about that in Chapter 7. The strategy here is to accept the fact that it is going to take some time and maybe a few iterations to get everything right for your product, the team, the operations, and everything else. By keeping the team small and agile, you will save whatever money you do have and be able to make as many attempts as possible to finally figure out the right product or service, and how to deliver them to your customers. If you get it perfectly right on your first try, congratulations!

In the next chapter, I will introduce the concept of the company Myth, which is a key part of your road to attracting customers, generating revenue, and becoming a viable growing company.

"Success is not the key to happiness. Happiness is the key to success. If you love what you are doing, you will be successful."

—Albert Schweitzer
Nobel Peace Prize Winner (1952)

CHAPTER 3

Creating Your MYTH

myth

noun

a popular belief or tradition that has grown up around something or someone. Especially: one embodying the ideals and institutions of a society or segment of society

According to Yuval Noah Harari, author of *Sapiens: A Brief History of Humankind, Homo sapiens* developed the ability of imagination around 70,000 BCE. With this development, humans came to dominate the world. Not because they were stronger, or faster, or bigger. Humans dominated because they were the only living thing that could cooperate flexibly in large numbers. Other animals could communicate simplistically, but not with the imagination and ability to talk unique to Humans. For example, large groups of humans could now develop a plan to hunt large animals, overcome other competing species, and respond to climate changes with abstract plans and collaborative "what if" style thinking. For example, "What if we create barriers and make loud noises to drive all of the animals into a confined space or over a cliff?" Harari also describes how this "imagination" ability of ours enables us think about things that exist purely in our made-up consciousness, including gods, nations, money, corporations, human rights, and future events. Harari describes how all large-scale human cooperation systems—including religions, political systems, trade networks, and legal institutions—owe their emergence to *Homo sapiens'* distinctive cognitive capacity for fiction. While these imaginary constructs are not tangible, they have immense power because people collectively act as if they are real. In some cases the fiction may be better than reality.

In this context, we refer to these types of "shared fictions" or "imagined realities" as *Myths*. Not to be confused with another definition of myths which entails an ancient story of supernatural beings, ancestors, or heroes that serve as a fundamental type in the worldview of a people.

OK, so what do "Myths" have to do with business? Myths are a fundamental building block of creating any successful company. In the business world, the Myth is a blend of reality, selective storytelling, and marketing strategy. Early in the life of any company, the myth will be mostly (or even entirely) fictional, in fact if may be solely reflective of the vision of the founders. The Myth will describe what you *wish* the company to become.

Your Myth will become synonymous with your company, whether we are talking about the world interacting with your company externally, or your employees operating within your company. If your Myth is a lie or an extravagant impossible dream, it will not work. To be effective, the Myth must be credible, attainable, and resonate throughout your employees and customers.

When you develop your marketing strategy, seek to raise capital, or are describing your new company to friends when you go out to dinner, your Myth will be the basis of your discussion. Just like the ancient *Homo sapiens* of 70,000 BCE, you will use your imagination, supported by the reality of the world around you, to develop this all-powerful Myth.

Let's take a look at a couple of well-known companies and unravel their Myths. Apple Inc. has always cultivated a powerful mythos which have helped to foster a near cult following both among consumers and employees. From the inception of the company, the management team at Apple portrayed that the company was a revolutionary innovator of computers, music players, smartphones, and wearable technology. The "reality" portion of the Apple Myth is that the company has indeed consistently been at or near the forefront of groundbreaking technical innovations (whether as the leader or a close follower is not critical to the myth).

The shared fiction surrounding the Apple I and Apple II computers is that they brought personal computing into the home, which is partially true. Similarly, the story around the iPod and iTunes is that they single-handedly saved the music industry from legions of media pirates such as Napster, and thus *created* the digital music revolution. Finally, the iPhone is presented as the device that *changed* the mobile phone industry, leading the shift away from Nokia flip phones and Blackberrys, and into an era of touchscreens, full-featured apps, and mobile Internet access. Over the course of time, Apple has also woven into these myths the narrative of "Privacy Guardian," with technical features and policy details which include not "monetizing" user data. The myth here is that Apple cares about its users' privacy more than other companies such as Google and Facebook, which are often criticized for exploiting user data.

All these stories are at least partially based in reality and help support the Apple Myth, and perhaps inflate and romanticize the products themselves and the role of Apple within the industry. A powerful subtheme within these stories is one of Apple being the "underdog" versus the evil competition, with Steve Jobs standing up to fight against the corporate establishment. Apple's early marketing often framed the company as a brand "for the misfits" or the "think different" brand.

Ironically, Apple is now a massive corporation with complex business practices and slick, futuristic retail locations such as the one shown in Figure 3.1. The corporation has implemented aggressive pricing strategies, which have occasionally had significant and debated effects on the technology ecosystem and the global market. Thus, any myth that Apple is an underdog has long ago expired, but during the early days of the company, such myths enabled the company to attract and retain legions of loyal customers. Such customers have religiously acquired new Apple

Figure 3.1 Typical Apple retail location

products as they are introduced, sometimes waiting overnight or days in advance. For many Apple Fans, waiting in line was part of a cultural experience, whereby consumers became part of a community of like-minded individuals, no longer felt like misfits, and anticipated each product introduction as a reason for celebration. The Myth makes Apple more than just a collection of personal technology products.

From a product standpoint, Apple portrays itself as the "Premium, Quality Brand" representing elegance and sophistication. The company spends extravagantly during development to achieve a specific "superior" user experience, including the look and feel of the products as well as the attention to detail in the unique product packaging. As my cofounder George observed, opening a new Apple product is akin to opening a special holiday present, complete with visually and tactile pleasing boxes and wrapping. In addition, the "Apple Ecosystem" Myth promises to enable seamless, intuitive interaction between computers, smartphones, and wearable devices, a claim which no other brand can replicate. Just spend a bit of time on the Apple website to feel the multiple facets and layers of their Myth. Likewise, the commercial, customer-facing retail outlets convey a feeling of advanced technology, sleek design, and cool vibes.

For employees within the company, Apple offers a culture of intensity, creativity, and innovation, all set within an environment that values collaboration, inclusion, and excellence. The attraction for many employees is the opportunity to work on groundbreaking technologies and be part of a company with a global impact, but the intensity, long hours, and work pace prove to be excessive for some employees, despite a corporate commitment to a healthy work–life balance.

Within the Myths of Apple, Inc. you can likely see some realistic facts, as well as a healthy measure of fiction and the results of millions of dollars of marketing. Can a new cell phone really make you feel better about yourself? Or is it just an electronic box? Can it make you feel like you are part of a community of people who "get you"? The results indicate that the Myths created by Steve Jobs and Steve Wozniak, and cultivated by thousands of employees ever since, are sustainably powerful and appealing to millions of dedicated consumers worldwide.

Pragmatically, most modern smartphones have similar capabilities, and an argument could be made that other brands provide superior performance and features at a lower price point than Apple products. But once that emotional connection has taken hold and created brand loyalty, the level of attachment between the consumer and the brand is nearly unbreakable.

In contrast, review the Myths of Blackberry, a smartphone manufactured by Research In Motion (RIM). The Blackberry was introduced in 1999 and by 2009 commanded a market share of approximately 50 percent of U.S. smartphones. The Blackberry Myth was that it was the ultimate device for productivity, and it was "Your Office in Your Pocket" (is that really a good thing?), and that it was "virtually indestructible" and secure enough for government and business. In other words, Blackberry was quite practical and very boring, and essentially had no Myth that would appeal to mainstream consumers. Admittedly, the target market for Blackberry was "Professionals, Not Consumers." The problem with that strategy was that buying decisions were made by employees within government and industry (aka "Professionals") who were also "Consumers," and ultimately those consumers wanted to buy products they liked. By 2014, Blackberry's market share had dropped below 5 percent, and they stopped manufacturing phones in 2016. The hardware was licensed to some manufacturers, but they were unable to release new models, and the brand faded into obscurity. The lack of a strong Myth wasn't the source of Blackberry's demise, but it was a symptom of a company which relied solely on the technical excellence of a single product.

Companies with a strong Myth, one which resonates throughout the employee base and extends to loyal customers and would-be customers, have proven to be much more resilient over time and through adversity. Recall some flop products from Apple including the Newton, Apple Lisa, G4 Cube, and the Hockey Puck Mouse among others. Most of these products failed because they had reliability issues, lacked key features offered by competitor's products, suffered from poor marketing, or they were just plain dumb ideas. But few consumers abandoned the brand, even after acquiring one of these products. The Apple Myth includes "Innovation" and "Think Different" and apparently sometimes it's OK to fail.

Obviously, the Myth must be well communicated throughout your workforce in order to be effective. Giving your employees the opportunity to dialog on the Myth, and help craft it as well, can provide excellent feedback to perfect the Myth and make sure it resonates with people outside the echo chamber of the leadership team. Strong adoption of the Myth will also serve as a guiding star for your employees whether they are conversing with prospective customers, developing new products, or navigating a crisis. In essence, your employees need to believe in the Myth, not just be fed a story.

Myths can help a company through a crisis, as well. In 2006 Google leadership made a controversial decision to launch a censored version of its search engine in China. Censorship was required to comply with the Chinese government's strict laws. The Chinese government required that search results be filtered to exclude politically sensitive content, such as references to the Tiananmen Square massacre, pro-democracy movements, or any content critical of the Chinese Communist Party. Google agreed to comply with these censorship requirements in order to access the expansive Chinese market, which was seen as a major growth opportunity.[12] Greed won out over the company ideology (Myth).

However, the decision raised ethical questions and created cultural friction. Many people criticized Google for compromising its core values of openness, transparency, and freedom of expression. Google's stance of prioritizing access to information was directly at odds with Chinese censorship laws. At the core, the decision to expand into the Chinese market and abide by the government's censorship requirements violated the Culture and Myth of Google. In 2010, Google and Gmail were the victims of a cyberattack which they believe originated within China. As a response to the attack, and to better align with their cultural values and Myth, Google transitioned their services to Hong Kong and removed the censorship features. Eric Schmidt, the CEO of Google at that time stated, "We have made a decision that we would stop censoring our search results and we would prefer to shut down the Chinese operations if we cannot find a way to comply with our principles." Any company that operates contradictory to its myth or culture will eventually be self-correcting, or else compromise on their values.

At BCT, we developed our Myth over the years through trial and error, because we really didn't know what we were doing. We were a bunch of geeky engineers, after all. While we did know a lot about designing, building, and operating spacecraft, we were totally in the dark about utilizing a Myth to build a brand. However, we did observe that some companies stood out in the marketplace and the reason they stood out was because they were able to convey an appealing image to their customers or the public which aligned with their company products, culture, passion, and ethos.

What we eventually ended up with for the BCT Myth was that we were "Enabling Space Missions to Expand the Frontiers of Science and Defense" through innovation and standardization. Our Myth included a focus on making space more affordable, lowering the complexity of space-based missions, thereby making it possible for the first time for many organizations to participate in space exploration and data collection. In a way, the Myth could be considered as an inspiring narrative of overcoming the traditional cost and complexity barriers in space exploration, opening new opportunities for innovation and data collection in space. Like the Apple Myth, we contrasted our tiny company against the mega aerospace companies like Boeing. We assumed the role of brilliant innovators fighting to lower costs and bring space access to the little guys, or at least save money for the taxpayers.

Internally, we fostered a culture of innovation, responsibility, activism, and inclusion. A healthy work–life balance, generous compensation and benefits, as well as flexibility to work remote, take maternity and paternity leave, and feel like part of a family of like-minded individuals were all hallmarks of the company. In the next chapter, we will expand on how these Myth factors play into recruiting and retaining a great team and fostering your culture.

During the early years, our failure to codify a Myth pervaded almost all aspects of the company. When potential customers, prospective employees, or investors asked about the company, we would describe our amazing products. For example, we would launch into a highly technical discussion of how our ball bearing technology made our wheels spin smoother and at lower power and made them more reliable. Or we would cite the field of view of the star tracker, and how many stars it could track and at what angular rate. It was all very technical, factual and meant very little to the customer, employment candidate, or investor. They would respond with a noncommittal "that's very interesting" to avoid having to continue the discussion, and we would be left feeling empty, as if we'd missed something important.

Imagine it is 2007 and you're shopping for your first cellphone. You step into the Apple store and ask about the just introduced iPhone. The salesperson tells you that it has the option of 4 GB or 8 GB of storage, a 3.5 in. display, and is powered by a 412 MHz processor. So what? While the technical details are important to what the device can do for you, most people don't know and don't care about GB or MHz. They care about how it looks, feels, works and, as we discussed earlier, all the intangible factors surrounding the Myth of the company that resonate with them personally.

The Rise and Fall of Theranos

A disturbing story worthy of review is that of Theranos, the Silicon Valley startup founded with a vision of revolutionizing blood testing. Elizabeth Holmes dropped out of Stanford University in 2003 to start Theranos with the ambitious idea of developing technology to quickly and inexpensively conduct a wide range of blood tests using just a single drop of blood, an innovation that would have revolutionized the health care industry.

Holmes cultivated an inspiring Myth, claiming to be working with major pharmaceutical companies as well as retail giants like Walgreens. She dressed in black turtlenecks, imitating Steve Jobs intentionally to help build an aura of superiority and entrepreneurial mystique. She recruited a board of directors including high-profile former senators and military leaders, continuing to build the Myth that Theranos was legitimate and credible. At one point, Theranos was valued at $9 billion.

The engineering team at Theranos built a prototype blood testing machine called "Edison" which was supposed to analyze tiny amounts of blood using a technology known as microfluidics, enabling health care professionals to detect hundreds of diseases from a single sample. Unfortunately, the machine was horribly inaccurate. Instead of admitting the problems, Holmes and her leadership team chose to fake the data and hide the flaws from investors, doctors, and even employees. There were reports that employees who voiced concerns were silenced or fired, and a culture of secrecy and fear soon permeated every level of the company.

By 2015, the company had raised millions of dollars in funding from eager investors, but the Myth began to unravel when investigative reporter John Carreyrou began digging into the company after receiving a tip from a former employee. Carreyrou uncovered the company's internal culture of deception, and that the Edison device was fundamentally flawed. Theranos had been manipulating test results and lying to both regulators and the public about Edison's capabilities. In 2016, the U.S. Food and Drug Administration issued warnings about the company's practices, Walgreens and other partners ended their relationships, and the Centers for Medicare & Medicaid Services revoked the company's license to operate a laboratory in California. In 2018, Elizabeth Holmes and the COO Ramesh Balwani were indicted on charges of fraud. Ms. Holmes was convicted on multiple counts of fraud and conspiracy in 2022 and began serving an 11-year prison sentence in 2023.[13]

Theranos crafted a bold vision, but the technology was fundamentally flawed. The company's leaders were more focused on maintaining the illusion of success than on solving real technical problems. I blame it on raising too much capital early and overcommitting to unproven technology. Once the company was deeply invested in a bad design, they fell into the trap of trying to buy time in order to create a miracle and save the day. What if they had created a minimum viable product (MVP) early to validate the technology before making vaunted promises to customers and investors? Making matters worse, the culture became toxic due to the coverups and lies. Instead of fostering transparency and open discussion about the challenges the company faced, Theranos cultivated an environment where dissent was silenced, and employees were pressured to ignore or cover up problems. The Theranos story is a dark chapter from the heyday of Silicon Valley success stories.

The Elevator Speech

A key application of a good company Myth is the "Elevator Speech." Imagine you happen to be going to a meeting at a conference where you hope to raise money to fund your new business startup. By pure chance, you board the elevator with none other than Ron Conway of SV Angel, a prominent Angel investment firm that has invested in a wide range of successful businesses including Google, Facebook, PayPal, and Airbnb. Ron is feeling amiable, and as you start the ride up in the elevator together, he asks you why you're at the conference. Here is your big chance, but it's only going to last for the duration of the elevator ride. How can you make an impression on Ron, describe your company in a compelling way, and pique his interest, all in less than 60 seconds? Any good Myth can be summarized, at a very minimum to the highlights, in such an elevator speech. You must make a significant, unique impression so that he wants to follow up with you to get more details.

Our elevator speech at BCT improved a lot over time as the company grew and evolved, but it always incorporated the facets of dramatically lowering the cost and complexity of space missions, by providing turnkey solutions which were simple to operate, in order to enable any organization to affordably and simply implement a space mission. If we had enough time, we'd emphasize that our customers didn't need to have any spacecraft experience, that our products were autonomous and reliable, as well as higher performing than any other spacecraft on the market. At one time, we even wove in the concept that our spacecraft were "the iPhone of spacecraft" to communicate that customers could develop apps to make the spacecraft perform different missions on orbit. It was a great marketing concept, but not practical or beneficial for most customers. Lesson learned: Sometimes you have to drop ideas that don't work out.

The reason that our Myth and our elevator speech worked well at BCT was because at that time in the industry, almost all spacecraft fell into one of two categories: Extremely complex and expensive ($50 million +) or very cheap and not useful for much. There was a vast gap in the marketplace for spacecraft that cost between $100,000 and $5 million dollars that could actually perform reliably and conduct some meaningful scientific research or military mission.

Plenty of companies like Boeing, Lockheed Martin, and Northrop Grumman were dominating the space industry with huge teams of engineers who designed, manufactured, tested, and launched highly complex, one-of-a-kind spacecraft for large government organizations like NASA and the Air Force. Because each spacecraft was custom designed for the mission, they took typically years to design, build, verify, test, and launch. Once on orbit, the operations were so complex that the organization that built it was often the only one that could operate it, leading to a fat operations contract for the contractor to charge the customer for years to come.

Thinking about the pain points, the spacecraft industry at that time was characterized by the "haves" and the "have nots." The "haves" were the U.S. government or large commercial companies with deep pockets and proven business models. Those were not our customers. The "have nots" were all the other, smaller organizations within government and industry that had a need for a space mission or a good idea but not enough money, know-how, or credibility to make it happen. These were our customers!

Enter BCT, with a vision of affordability, simplicity, and reliability. Our Myth also wove in factors such as "standard off the shelf products," a key factor once those products had been launched and we had actual proof that they worked. One of our earliest customers was the Jet Propulsion Laboratory (JPL) in Pasadena, California. They contracted with BCT to provide two small spacecraft systems for the MARCO mission (Mars Cube One) which was designed to demonstrate the use of small spacecraft for interplanetary exploration. The two spacecraft flew in formation with the InSight lander, which was launched in 2018, traveled from Earth to Mars, then descended into the Martian atmosphere, and landed on the surface. It was a very successful mission and effectively demonstrated that even small satellites could play a crucial role in space exploration. However, long before the mission was launched, essentially once we had inked the contract with prestigious JPL as a bonafide customer, BCT had instant credibility as a small satellite provider.

Our first meeting with JPL was humble to say the least. At that time, we were a group of seven or eight hopeful engineers, renting a small 1,200 square foot office space in a business park in Boulder, Colorado. When the JPL team arrived at our office, we didn't even have enough chairs for everyone to sit down at the same time! We had one whiteboard to draw pictures and we used a TV for projecting our company overview and product concepts. But the JPL team took a chance on us and gave us a small contract which helped fund the company growth and propel us on to bigger opportunities.

So, how do you go about creating your Myth? You're going to have to look at the big picture, combine the facts of what your business is going to provide, with some emotional and esoteric details which align with what you perceive is your market niche. Take some time to review any relevant companies or competitors in your marketspace and identify a few things that you believe differentiate companies within that space. If we review the airlines from Chapter 2, we find an interesting situation as shown in Table 3.1.

Reviewing what sets JSX apart helps craft the Myth for this company. The focus should be on what makes the company different and cast it in a positive light which will appeal *logically* and *emotionally* to customers, employees, and investors. One potential myth that could be crafted

Table 3.1 Expanded comparison of Red Ocean versus Blue Ocean Airlines

	United	Delta	American	Southwest	JSX
Fleet size	920+ aircraft	940+ aircraft	950+ aircraft	814+ aircraft	~ 50
# of destinations	> 430	>290	>350	>110	>20
Passengers/ year	165 million	190 million	211 million	172 million	500,000
Price point	Moderate	Moderate	Moderate	Low	Higher
Service model	Major airports, domestic and international	Major airports, domestic and international	Major airports, domestic and international	Major domestic airports and some point to point	Smaller convenient airports
Differentiator	International network, premium services	Good customer service, modern fleet, loyalty program	Global network and premium service and lounges	Low-cost model, no change fees, two free checked bags	Car to gate quickly, premium "private-lite" service
Wasted time walking, security screening	Time-consuming	Time-consuming	Time-consuming	Time-consuming	Quick
Hassel factor	High	High	High	High	Low
Onboard perks	Limited, buy à la carte	Limited, buy à la carte	Limited, buy à la carte	Limited, buy à la carte	Free drinks, snacks, and Starlink Internet

around the JSX business model is that "for a premium price JSX provides a private jet-like experience, similar to that typically reserved for the ultrawealthy and elite: private terminals, quicker check-ins, luxurious seating and a more streamlined, hassle-free experience. It positions the airline as a luxury service without the luxury price tag, appealing to people who want the *status* and *experience* of flying privately but are not willing to pay for a full private jet charter."

This myth helps JSX craft an image of exclusivity and sophistication—one that sells a dream to its customers. Even though JSX's service is not *actually* private, the myth is that it offers "exclusive" access to something better than traditional flying. It's a myth that allows JSX to charge a premium and create customer loyalty based on perceived value rather than on a traditional, purely commercial airline model. The Myth permeates the JSX website. The myth works because it taps into people's desire for status and luxury. Even if the reality is that JSX operates semiprivate flights on regional jets, the shared belief in the story of luxury and exclusivity still convinces passengers that they are getting something special. This myth makes flying JSX seem like a more desirable and aspirational experience, much like owning a luxury car or staying at a five-star hotel. There is also at least a perception if not an actual convenience and savings of time. Emotionally, the Myth appeals to the target customers, making them feel special, like they are receiving a VIP experience.

Employees at JSX report that they enjoy their work environment, especially in terms of company culture, work–life balance, and the focus on customer service. JSX is seen as a great place for those who value a more personalized, premium airline experience, as well as for employees who appreciate a smaller, more intimate company culture compared to the larger, more impersonal structure of major airlines. So, in part, the employees engage in the Myth as well that they are part of something more exclusive and different than mainstream traditional airlines.

Although it is still privately held, it is reported that investors in the company include GSO Capital Partners (a division of Blackstone Group), as well as billionaire investor Bill Gates. There are also reports that JSX has secured both equity and debt financing. All these factors indicate that the Myth of JSX is compelling enough to convince major investors to engage and finance the company.

When crafting your Myth, it needs to be believable to industry experts and credible to customers and investors. It needs to be inspirational and maybe even aspirational but not a bold-faced lie. Credibility is key for a good Myth. A background in commercial airlines helped Alex craft his business model and Myth, without saying anything preposterous which could destroy his credibility on day 1. He had firsthand experience of the pain and suffering endured by the big airlines' customers: long delays, crowded flights, busy, dirty terminals, and so on. To enable his vision, he became familiar with the FAA regulations which govern the operation of larger airlines (Part 121) and the loopholes which he could exploit with a business model conforming to the more relaxed commuter airline regulations of Part 135.

Much like Alex Wilcox, Steve Jobs, and Steve Wozniak, you have your own unique life experiences to draw upon. What have they revealed to you about your industry? Have you spotted an uncontested market niche? Do you know of potential opportunities that would allow you to create your own Elite Icon like Alex did with JSX and the Steves did with Apple?

When it comes to raising capital or finding investors, it will also be important to be able to convey the Myth of your company succinctly. In some instances, you may need to be able to simplify the Myth a bit or provide some background to help people who are not in the industry understand the Myth in context and be able to translate it into terms which work for them. Raising capital and securing investors is about numbers, plans, and contingencies as we will discuss in Chapter 5, but it is also largely about building trust and a common framework, all of which builds off the Myth.

The final thought to conclude this chapter is regarding artificial intelligence. AI is somewhere between the latest buzzword for the next boom–bust cycle and the next major revolution: The AI Revolution. Suffice it to say that many companies will create Blue Oceans and weave their Myths very tightly around AI technology, and in many cases, it may become the de facto driving force of innovation within entire industries. How you choose to incorporate or ignore AI in your business formation might be a critical step.

Branding is not merely about differentiating products; it is about striking emotional chords with consumers. It is about cultivating identity, attachment, and trust to inspire customer loyalty.
                                                                —Nirmalya Kumar

CHAPTER 4

Creating the Team and Culture

In the early days of BCT, we were writing proposals to the government as part of the SBIR program that would essentially provide us "free" money in return for performing innovative research and analysis. Our primary goal was to build the business without going broke or losing control to investors, even if it meant growing slowly, very slowly. Our philosophy was that Great would not happen overnight, it would take time and patience. We would write a proposal in response to a question from a variety of government organizations, outlining what we might investigate and how it might be of benefit to someone somewhere in the country, and if a government official in some office somewhere reviewed our proposal and liked it, we'd get selected and get paid up to $100,000 to do the research and analysis and provide reports. If our subsequent research and report showed promise and appealed to the government, we could earn a follow-on contract worth up to $750,000. This program is still operating, and awards billions of dollars of funding to companies in technology, health care, agriculture, education, manufacturing, energy, and consumer products, to name a few. We will dig into these opportunities extensively in Chapter 5.

The success rate of these proposals (in other words what percentage of applications are awarded) is fairly low, and varies significantly of course depending upon the nature of the problem and proposed solutions, but typically is around 5 percent. As engineers, George, Steve, and I were able to calculate that meant that we would probably need to submit around 20 proposals before we might get funded, so we started writing proposals. Much to our surprise, our very first proposal was selected for award! Once we got over our shock, we wondered how we were going to work on the project, since we were all still moonlighting at the time. The right way to moonlight is to get permission from your current employer and fill out any applicable paperwork. Do not attempt to sneak around the rules. We were surprised to discover that our current employers were agreeable, as long as we filled out the applicable paperwork completely.

Fortunately, since there were three of us, we were able to divide up the work, collaborate via a shared documents portal online, and each work from our homes during nights, early mornings, and weekends to perform the research and write our reports. That work eventually turned into a very successful series of contracts and products for satellites that are orbiting Earth right now, exploring the universe, performing scientific research and protecting our country.

Success in that effort—and winning contracts—would have been impossible for any one of us alone. Working as a team of three didn't just triple our capabilities; it multiplied them many times over, more like tenfold. The synergy of collaborating with people you enjoy working with, drawing from diverse perspectives, and balancing resilience—where one person pushes forward while another takes time to recharge, made all the difference. Here's how our Leadership Diversity played out.

George was our CEO, although he was never one to demand to have that title. He was a visionary, and was often able to redirect our organized engineering brains to see possibilities beyond what we would normally consider. He was a consummate professional, was passionate about making it a fun and enjoyable place to work, and somehow managed to also represent BCT to customers and investors with diplomacy and character.

Steve was our CTO—chief technology officer, with a background in instrument and space hardware design. He was always passionate about how amazing our products and company were, and pushed everyone around him to be creative, innovative, and considerate. Steve has always been a person who can walk into a room full of strangers, start talking to them about something highly technical and confusing, and make it fun and educational for everyone involved. He'd tell a few corny jokes along the way, which in some way helped him be more approachable and believable at the same time.

Dan was the late addition to the executive team, but he was certainly a very important addition. Before Dan joined the company, one of our other engineers (Gary) who was working part time, declined our offer to join the business full-time. He said, "You don't have the right team yet." He was right, even though as founders we weren't seeing it. We thought we just needed more people, but the truth was that we needed the *right* people. Dan was the right person at the right time. Part chief marketing officer, part technology wizard, part spell-caster, Dan was also amazing to watch with customers. Brilliant does not do Dan justice. His flavor of brilliance is that he can connect multiple seemingly unrelated pieces of information together to arrive at a truly innovative conclusion or solution. He also had a knack for creating catch names for our products, and most of the products still in production today were named by Dan.

I was the *behind-the-scenes-making-things-happen* piece of the leadership team, and what I could provide was essentially the operations, processes, facilities, and equipment selections to turn our ideas into hardware. I knew from my prior employer how a company could run, how manufacturing and test could be performed, and what typical methods were used in those operations. I was dubbed the COO—chief operating officer—and I figured out how to turn ideas into hardware ready to be launched into orbit. Most importantly, I knew from my previous employment that the industry status quo was inefficient, and how things could be done better, more efficiently, and with fewer people in order to reduce costs and improve quality.

We often joke that Dan dreamed up things that George then sold to customers, which Steve figured out how to design, and I figured out how to build. It was much more complicated than that, but in the early days, there were only about 10 people altogether in the company, and we worked together quite well. The Leadership Diversity of our team allowed us to maximize each person's strengths for the good of the company without suffering the consequences of any individual's weaknesses.

Regardless of how you build your leadership team, and how many people you decide to have in the inner circle, I urge you to seek out people who you enjoy being with as well as people who can wear many "hats," meaning they can take on a variety of roles in the company. Your journey as you build your organization will be more likely to succeed and be much more enjoyable (and survivable) if you are traveling with good companions.

If you are committed to starting and building your company as much as possible without outside investment, then it is even more crucial to build a leadership team of generalists who can fulfill as many roles as possible. In the case of BCT, we each carried as much of the burden as possible, while we stayed in phase 0: no revenue, minimizing expenses and just figuring out what the customers wanted and how to provide it.

For example, George not only led the company as the CEO but also developed marketing materials, handled company incorporation and business issues with our lawyer, crafted our strategy, and spent endless hours scouring the Internet looking for new business opportunities, and calling potential customers. His primary goal was to identify Elite Icon opportunities and help guide the rest of us in that direction. He felt that his primary purpose was to find revenue opportunities and win them to fill up our bank account.

I focused on developing seamless computer systems to tie our design tools together with our production software, wrote a very basic but functional set of business system documents, worked on building up our facilities and equipment, and I too spent endless hours scouring the Internet looking for new business opportunities. My primary goal was making the company look and act like a full-fledged aerospace manufacturing company.

Dan focused on product ideation (what could we develop that would be a Value Differentiator?), new business development, design, analysis, and being brilliant. He spent a lot of time traveling to talk with potential customers to find out what they needed and affirming that whatever they needed, we could create it! Dan's primary goal was to convince our customers that we were credible and simultaneously convince the rest of us on the team that we could create what he envisioned and had already told the customers we could provide.

Steve spent his time supporting all of us with beautiful CAD (computer-aided design) renderings that made our product visions look realistic. He also helped us develop a cadre of nearby machine shops, optical companies, and other suppliers that would become the backbone of our production capabilities for years to come. Steve's primary goal evolved over time from creating beautiful renderings of our products to leading the teams who performed the actual design and analysis to make those products become reality.

We also cultivated a core support network which we came to rely upon extensively to help us get through those formative years. For example, George had a family relationship with a corporate attorney who helped draft our operating agreement and handled legal matters. I developed a strong relationship with a local real estate agent who was always on the lookout for our next set of larger offices, helping us keep costs down by finding ultra-affordable yet aesthetically pleasing options which would fit our needs until we outgrew them as well. Negotiating leases with short (1–2 year) terms or simple exits helped us move up when we needed to without incurring financial penalties.

We also developed relationships with local incubators which helped us gain credibility and get introductions to potential customers and mentors. Some of our mentors we found ourselves, some were sent to us from the incubator. While none of them were intimately familiar with what we were trying to do, they each provided at least one great nugget of wisdom.

For example, we had been operating for about 5 years and at that time had decided that George would be president, and Steve and I would both be vice presidents. One of our mentors asked us if we felt like that was the best we could do for titles, and we honestly hadn't thought much about it and we were all too damn polite to argue much about titles anyway. This mentor thought our lack of titles was confusing and suggested that we select titles which were more "active" and would convey a sense of structure and responsibility. Once we thought about it a bit, we recognized that when we introduced ourselves to investors or customers, we spent a lot of time explaining our roles. Once we adopted CEO, COO, and CTO, the customers understood it and seemed to have more confidence in our company leadership structure. Lesson learned: Confused customers won't do business with you. Oftentimes, the key with customers is to build credibility.

Finding and Attracting a Great Team

As you do begin to expand your team, leverage your networks: Consider interviewing past coworkers, people you have interacted with as customers or suppliers in the past, even friends and neighbors who might be qualified. Even if the match does not work out, those people may know other qualified candidates who would fit. Ask people you know for references and keep in touch with your network. The key is to identify individuals who are great performers, fill a need for your company at that point in the evolution, and will positively enhance the culture. While statistics vary, the success rate of hiring new employees that work out productively tends to be cited at around 50 percent, and the rate of hiring somebody who is really an outstanding success is below 20 percent. The cost of hiring the wrong candidate is staggering, in terms of lost productivity, lost revenue, and collateral damage. Anything you can do to improve your odds is helpful, hiring people you already know and trust is the best strategy available.

Jessica Stillman, at Inc.com discussed a quote from Elon Musk regarding leadership and employee selection. Here's the quote:

> *Every person in your company is a vector. Your progress is determined by the sum of all vectors.*
>
> —Elon Musk

Ms. Stillman then identifies a writeup performed by Dharmesh Shah, HubSpot founder: *The less mathematically inclined might be scratching their heads trying to remember whatever they learned about vectors back in high school algebra. But fear not, even if you're terrible with numbers, you can put this principle to work. A vector, Shah explains, is nothing more complicated than a measurement that captures both the magnitude and the direction of something. It tells you not just how much progress a thing is making but in what direction it's making it. What do vectors have to do with managing people? Everyone on your team has both a magnitude of impact (how much they achieve, like how many lines of code they write or sales they close) and a direction of that impact (what feature they're working on or sector they're selling to, for instance). Mediocre leaders focus a lot on the magnitude of their people's contribution, i.e. how to level up the skill and effort of their team, so they get more done. Musk's quote reminds us that's only half the battle.*[14]

As this points out, you not only want people who are good at what they do but will "pull" or "push" in the right direction, *helping* the team, not creating a distraction or hurting the team by working at cross-purposes. Each employee should be recruited and hired at the right time in terms of the growth of the company. Some fledgling companies, flush with Venture Capital funding, proceed to hire a complete OrgChart full of all positions before any product or service is defined. Those companies then have people sitting idle, or worse yet creating busy work for themselves and their coworkers, waiting for their point in time to become useful. Instead of that path, hire only when you or your employees really feel the pinch of a missing role. And even then, be careful to hire and mentor the person to align their "vector" to point in the right direction. Have you ever wondered why Geese fly in a V-formation when they migrate? When each bird flaps its wings, it creates an uplift for the bird behind it. By working together in this small, efficient formation, they increase their range by about 70 percent compared to flying solo! Small groups of geese stay tightly coordinated, communicate constantly through honking (encouragement), and support one another. If one goose falls out due to illness or injury, two others accompany it to help it recover.[15] Staff your company like a flock of geese.

Lay out a timeline of what you expect to happen and when as the company grows, and list what sorts of personnel will be required at each stage and hire accordingly. Adding too many people too early will not only waste money, but they will also create extra hoops (bureaucracy) that will impede progress of the minimalist team. Keeping the team as small as possible through this early growth period will make them efficient and focused on the critical activities.

In each position you seek to fulfill, identify what you are seeking in terms of education, skill set and experience: Do you need a "Tall-Skinny" employee, or a "Short-Wide" employee?

"Tall-Skinny" employees are experts in their field, and you bring them onto your team because they bring world-class knowledge or skills to enable your organization to create that Elite Icon. But not every employee needs to be an expert Tall-Skinny individual, indeed most do not.

"Short-Wide" employees are typically generalists who know a little about a lot of things, but not too much about any one thing. Their scope of knowledge is broad, and the perfect Short-Wide employee is one who likes to expand their knowledge and is not afraid of doing research to learn about new things, as well as listening to the wisdom of the Tall-Skinny wizards. These are the people who get things done in your company!

Certainly, your company type and industry will have some bearing on the types of employees you hire, but overall, you will benefit most if you have a high ratio of positive attitude, energetic, Short-Wide employees and a few Tall-Skinny employees who specifically address your Elite Icon opportunity. At BCT, we found the ratio was about 10:1 for Short-Wide to Tall-Skinny employees.

In addition to the qualifications of the employee, consider workplace personality types as defined by Indeed.com[16] in Table 4.1.

Most organizations benefit from a balance of different personality types to create symbiotic relationships and avoid toxic overload of other

Table 4.1 Workplace personality types (Indeed.com)

Type	Characteristics
Analyst	An analyst is a neat and organized employee, who prefers to work within a designated structure. They have determined their best working methods and like to maintain them. Consistency is important to an analyst and unannounced changes that disrupt their approach to the day, week, or year may cause conflict. Avoiding surprises is helpful with Analysts.
Climber	Ambitious person who is often eager to advance their career as quickly as possible. This can be beneficial around the office, as they are often willing to take on additional work to make a positive impression. Monitor a Climber to make sure they don't cause morale problems by undercutting other employees.
Illusionist	Excels at making it appear that their contributions are larger than is actually the case, by giving their responsibilities to others and seeking shortcuts with their own work, then claiming responsibility for the final product. Avoid hiring if you can weed them out during the interview process.
Individualist	Will often prefer to handle their specific responsibilities in their own way. Individualists also often prefer a hands-off approach to management, allowing them to work how they prefer and you to judge them based on the results of their work. A skilled and trustworthy individualist can be a great asset. Note: Prone to becoming a Busy Burt if you let them.
Motivator	Believe in pushing themselves and others to accomplish as much work as possible. Sometimes this can lead to the motivator overstepping boundaries and offering motivation the recipient did not ask for and does not believe is helpful. Note: also prone to becoming a Busy Burt.

Type	Characteristics
People Pleaser	Prioritizes being liked by as many people as possible. This may mean the people pleaser helps others regardless of how much work they have of their own. This can generate positive relationships and allow them to help other staff, but it can also have detrimental effects if they take on too much, are overly insistent when coworkers do not need help or avoid addressing an issue because they don't want to cause a problem.
Perfectionist	Show acute attention to detail and can deliver impressive final products. However, focusing too much on perfection can lead to delays in delivery, and their high standards may also cause unease for other staff if the perfectionist is obtrusive into their fellow employees' work and responsibilities.
Performer	Loves to be the center of attention around the office. They are often talkative and quick to advertise their contributions. They often will also seek to garner attention in nonwork conversations. The performer may be one of the more popular members of the staff, as they are often very gregarious, however, there is potential for time waste and some staff to be put off by their personality and talkative nature.
Worrier	Someone who often appears anxious about the work they are delivering. A worrier requires consistent validation to assure them they are meeting expectations and delivering satisfactory results. When you identify a worrier on your staff, it's important to work to build their confidence. As a worrier reduces their anxiety, they may become more independent and produce higher quality work without second-guessing their actions.
Upward Worker	When talking with senior staff, an upward worker behaves much like a people pleaser, while interactions with others on staff may resemble a personality type like the motivator or the perfectionist, offering advice and criticism freely. This personality type can cause morale problems and should be addressed by management as soon as possible.
Plus two bonus types which I think Indeed overlooked:	
Negative Norman	This person always emphasizes the worst-case scenario, drawing coworkers into their pit of despair, or engaging in irrational arguments about all the things that are going to go wrong and eventually bring about disaster. You have to purge Negative Norman as quickly as possible.
Busy Burt	Usually starts out as an Individualist or Motivator. As they take on more work, they focus on quantity rather than quality. Busy Burt may be a product of your environment if they receive too many competing assignments and can't keep up. The sudden appearance of one or more Busy Burts is an indicator of an overcommitted company. You can help them recover.

traits. Most of the types identified by Indeed can find a place within the organization, with the notable exceptions of Negative Norman, the Illusionist, and the Upward Worker. Our general tactic during interviews was to ask specific questions about the applicant's actual contributions on their resumes (which were occasionally too impressive to believe). Asking specific questions, then drilling down into the next layer of detail and so on will often expose the Illusionist or Upward Worker for what they are. Busy Burts are most often a product of their environment when your company takes on too many divergent challenges and becomes overloaded. You have to fix the problem to help Burt.

Every business owner has horror stories about hiring employees that not only don't work out, but they cause problems. The employee that keeps picking fights with coworkers, or the employee you find in the middle of the day in his car in the parking lot downing a bottle of booze. Or when you get a visit from the local police department, and one of your employees is escorted away, never to be heard from again. The number of things that can go wrong is extensive, and frankly when you're hiring strangers, there is only so much that you can do to assess an individual's work ethic, professionalism, or even whether they're flat out lying during the interview. Checking references is crucial as well as a background check service which will pay for itself instantly when it helps you identify one problem employee before you hire them. In November of 2023, Forbes reported that 70 percent of workers have lied on their resumes.[17]

Once you have a diverse leadership team in place, you should evaluate and agree upon an ownership model that works for your situation. In our case, our decision was that we wanted the company to be employee-owned as much as possible. Therefore, the structure that we adopted was that we all had equal shares at the beginning, and then as we decided to bring on more employees, we gave each of them shares as part motivation, part reward for taking a chance on a new venture. Over time, we decreased the number of shares that each new employee got so that early employees maintained a higher percentage of ownership, since they had taken more risk and had more time to make an impact. As a founder, it may become difficult to part with ownership to the employees. Consider, however, that you are asking these individuals to take a significant risk in their career and sacrificing a secure position at their current employer.

The Case for Employee Ownership

Giving employees ownership in the company provides a potential long-term reward which partially offsets the risk of joining a startup company. In fact, the types of personalities which thrive and benefit a startup the most will easily understand the risk–reward situation, because they are, by nature, long-term, opportunistic thinkers. Among the leadership team, our question was "would you rather own 30 percent of nothing, or 10 percent of something Great?"

The option of Employee Ownership has significant appeal to the prospective employee for a couple of other reasons, as well. First, in years when the company is profitable, some amount of profit should be distributed to all the owners in proportion to their ownership percentage (profit sharing). Especially if your company is a "pass-through" entity such as an LLC or S-Corp, the company tax liabilities will be passed through to all of the owners, and your accountant should generate a K1 for each owner to record their share of the profits and losses. In years where the company suffers a loss, those events are reflected in the K1 as well, generating a tax write-off for the employees. Thus, ownership has significant short-term appeal to employees looking for additional income or a potential end of year "bonus."

Second, there is a long-term appeal for employees owning stock in that if there is ever an "event" (sale of the company, stock sale to a holding company, acquisition, etc.) then they could be rewarded with a significant payout. Many of our employees viewed this as an excellent retirement possibility.

A third reason that Employee Ownership appealed to employees was that it gave them "skin in the game" where they felt that their performance on the job directly contributed to not only the financial well-being of the company but also their own and their families.

Finally, if you elect to raise capital via an ESOP (Employee Stock Ownership Plan) as I will outline in Chapter 5, the employees will be able to invest in the long-term financial performance of the company, giving them a real opportunity to create something akin to a 401K plan.

From your perspective as an owner, the concept of employee stock ownership has great appeal in terms of attracting the best talent, enhancing their involvement and engagement in the company that they own a little part of, and as we will explore in the ESOP section, a small stream of revenue which can offset the costs of running the business.

In addition to ownership, offering our employees great benefits was part of the attraction and often sealed the deal due to the "spousal dynamic." What we found was that intelligent, innovative people were naturally attracted to a startup culture and modern workplace vibe, and the opportunity to make a difference by getting in on the ground floor. The employees were sold on the job once they interviewed, met the team, and toured the cool facilities. But then they had to go home and sell the opportunity to their spouse, which often worked out well because we paid the employees fair and competitive salaries and offered a generous benefits package. The spousal dynamic was in play in many of our recruiting efforts and something you can consider in your recruiting efforts.

A Gallup poll from late 2023 indicates that the top five key factors which employees consider when deciding whether to take a job with a different organization are evenly matched[18] as shown in Figure 4.1 (actually, the

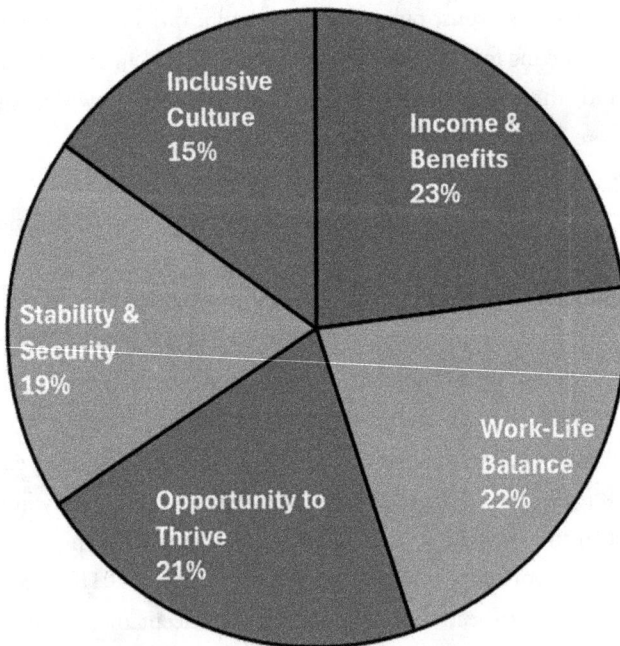

Figure 4.1 Gallup poll—Employee factors when considering an employer

survey included a sixth factor, which was related to COVID-19 mandatory vaccination policies which I've eliminated from the chart).

Joining a startup will probably impact "Stability and Security" negatively, so you as the hiring team need to *sweeten the pie* somehow to be seen as an overall better employer. Equity ownership, even a small number of shares, plus a combination of a fair salary, good Work–Life Balance, happy Culture, and an Opportunity to Thrive make a very attractive workplace for the type of employee you're seeking.

Culture

As you interview candidates, and make hiring decisions, think not only about skills and qualifications, but equally as much about personality and culture fit. Ask yourself: Do you want your company to be like Google, Zappos, Ben & Jerry's, or Wells Fargo pre-2016?

Google, for example, offers employees free meals, nap pods, on-site gyms, and a variety of creative spaces to foster an atmosphere of creativity and inclusion. Employees feel that they are working in a flexible, open work environment where they can feel safe to innovate and it's OK to learn from mistakes. The company actively promotes a culture of psychological safety where team members feel comfortable sharing ideas without fear of judgment. That sounds pretty nice, doesn't it?

Zappos is an online retailer of shoes and apparel that has built its culture around exceptional customer service. They strive to deliver a "WOW" experience to their customers, and employees are empowered to go above and beyond for customers without needing approval from supervisors. Internally, Zappos emphasizes employee happiness, a focus on fun and a variety of quirky company events. They have a unique "Offer" where new employees are offered a $2,000 bonus to quit after training if they don't feel like they're a good match for the culture.

Ben & Jerry's embraces a dual mission: making the best ice cream and doing social good. They offer employees opportunities for community engagement whether it's in support of racial justice, LGBTQ+ rights, climate change, or fair trade. Employees are encouraged to be openly political, active in the community, and become agents for positive change in society. Another great place to work.

Wells Fargo (pre-2016), on the other hand, faced widespread allegations of fraud, poor treatment of employees, and a lack of ethical leadership. The focus was on aggressive sales performance at all costs, leading to a toxic environment where unethical practices were normalized. Employees were often forced to create fake accounts to meet quotas, leading to a widespread scandal that resulted in legal and financial penalties.

I include the Wells Fargo example to illustrate that culture is a result of management and employee decisions and actions. We should assume that nobody in upper management at Wells Fargo set out to create a toxic and unethical culture (hopefully)! But that culture came about as the product of policies and actions performed by the leadership team. Setting in place unrealistic expectations for employees will usually result in high turnover rates, with the remaining employees left with no choice but to become "creative" and potentially unethical. There are many books about building culture for your team, but the universal truth is that a culture will evolve whether you attempt to create one or not.

At Google, Zappos, Ben & Jerry's, and Wells Fargo, the cultures are the result of a combination of features and policies put in place by the founders and executives. By actively telling each new employee about the unique company features, opportunities and policies, then reinforcing the instantiation of those traditions, the culture is built over time. It is not an instantaneous creation but takes nurture and time to take root, good or bad.

Although it didn't work out all the time, our target at BCT was for everyone to have interesting work, support from management and mentors, a 40-hour work week, and plenty of time for recreation and family time. We provided full health care benefits paid for by the company and tried to come up with fun thematic events to host in the company. Employees often would tell us that BCT was the best company they'd ever worked at (and that wasn't just what they said at raise time!). We knew that for our business to succeed, we needed to attract and retain a great team of intelligent, innovative employees, and allow them to soar.

We encouraged flexible work hours, an open and positive communication environment, and a work hard–play hard culture. We purchased a ping-pong table for the break room. We provided free snacks and drinks, and let employees vote for new drinks, snacks, and coffee types. When we moved to a two-story building, we seriously considered putting in a fireman's pole and a slide (at the suggestion of Charles, our chief fun officer), but it never worked out, unfortunately. Once we were in phase 2 (steady revenue, consistent growth), we spent a considerable amount of money to build a rooftop deck so that employees could go outside and enjoy the sunshine and a beautiful view of the mountains for breaks or lunchtime. Halloween costumes became a point of serious competition each year (as a grassroots, no-management-involved affair), to the point where voting and awards were given for the best costumes, complete with pictures posted on LinkedIn. A highpoint of the year is "Bring Your Child to Work" day, held annually where children young and old are encouraged to come see where Mom or Dad work, engage in some science and technology demonstrations, and learn about spacecraft.

In this discussion, I have intentionally blended policies, traditions, events, facilities, and purchased items to the culture description, because they all work together to cultivate the environment or vibe of your company. One cannot "dictate" a company culture per se. You can only put in place some policies, provide encouragement, and spend some money on things that are supportive of what you hope to happen, and let it grow. Saying that the company embraces "work hard–play hard" is just hollow BS if there aren't some actual activities or monuments (things that are bought or built) to support playing. Saying that your company values a work–life balance, then asking everyone to work every weekend doesn't ring true, either. It takes time, creativity, and collaboration between management and the employees to develop a good culture.

There is, of course, no practical way to measure the impact of a positive company culture, or to calculate the return on investment. But if you want to create and grow a company that you and your employees enjoy, then a positive culture is an essential requirement. Our experience at BCT was that the leadership team decided on a few items (the rooftop deck and "Bring Your Child to Work" day). We then consistently communicated an openness to adopt a fun environment and let the employees themselves figure out what appealed to them. The ping-pong table, Halloween costumes, coffee service, and snack programs were developed through employee collaboration. The cost to the company for those items was a few hundred dollars per year, essentially free. But...coming up with those ideas helped foster inclusion and boosted morale. Such activities bring shy employees out of their shell a bit, bring coworkers from differing roles closer together, and allow them all to become closer in non-work-related activities. I'm also very sure that having that type of culture convinced some key employees to join the team or stay with the team. Without those employees the company might not have been as successful. Calculate that ROI!

The Role of Bureaucracy

While your company grows and employs more people, those people will be performing their jobs according to written or spoken expectations, seeking to achieve the goals which you and your leadership team communicate to them. Both within your company and throughout the world in general, the life of humans has become more bureaucratic with each generation.

As Yuval Noah Harari points out in *Sapiens: A Brief History of Humankind*,[19] "The most important impact of script [writing] on human history is precisely this: it has gradually changed the way humans think and view the world. Free association and holistic thought have given way to compartmentalization and bureaucracy." Essentially, people have lost the ability to creatively imagine, as society and business have prioritized reading and following rules. In many of today's institutions and corporations, employees are not expected to think independently but rather to focus on following the rules and performing their role properly. Remember my story about how our moonlighting activities were approved by our previous employers simply because we filled out the paperwork properly? Nobody at those big corporations had the mindset to protect the human capital or prevent an upstart competitor; they were just following the rules as documented in the paperwork.

A major lesson we learned at BCT was that true innovation and disruptive improvements (improvements that are not incremental but revolutionary and unexpected) are the product of free thinking and combining concepts and disciplines which are not typically adjacent to one another. That's a lot of words to say: Sometimes you have to forget about the current market and products in order to imagine something innovative. By fostering a collaborative culture, with activities that created opportunities for employees from different departments to mesh and mingle, we created a fertile garden for new ideas and solutions to occur via random interactions. Obviously, some rules and processes need to be written down. But if the company "book of rules" becomes overly restrictive, it hampers creativity. Getting the right level of bureaucracy may take some experimentation: enough rules to avoid chaos, sufficient freedom to enable creativity.

Once you and your leadership team have established the Myth and planted the seeds of your desired culture, you will be well on your way to creating a Great Company. For your employees to feel empowered and successful in their roles, you need to provide them a MAP: Mastery, Autonomy, and a Purpose,[20] as described by Daniel Pink in his 2011 bestseller *Drive: The Surprising Truth About What Motivates Us.*

The MAP

Mastery in an employee's field or area of responsibility will come from a combination of experience and training. When your employees feel competent in their role, they are set up for success and will work with confidence, especially when their actions are guided by your company Myth.

Autonomy is perhaps the most difficult for managers to foster in their employees. Not all individuals are comfortable operating autonomously, but more often most managers have difficulty letting go and not micromanaging. Indeed, there is an overpowering impulse for us to guide the organization and every employee to make sure that everything is done properly. However, as your organization grows, it will become more and more difficult to maintain knowledge and control of every action. Most important of all, however, is the psychological messaging you send to your employees between micromanagement and autonomy. Micromanagement tells them, "I don't trust you and I think you might not be competent." Autonomy tells them, "I trust you and I know that you have the skills to succeed, and we have an understanding that you will consult with me if there's ever a need." Discussing autonomy and when to consult is a safe way to set the guardrails on a comfortable relationship for both parties.

Purpose is usually the simplest of the MAP principles to convey, but it does require cultivation by management. A clear discussion of each employee's role and responsibilities in the organization, and how it supports the mission and Myth, will provide a good foundation for the Purpose. Clearly communicating the Purpose in the context of a larger company objective is helpful for more senior and experienced employees.

Strategies you can leverage to support your employees and your company to achieve Mastery–Autonomy–Purpose within your company include:

- **Communicate the Bigger Picture:** Help employees see how their work fits into the company's overall mission and values. This can be done through regular conversations and team meetings where leadership connects individual roles to the company's vision.
- **Create Personal Purpose Statements:** Work with each employee to help them articulate their own purpose within the company. A purpose statement outlines how their individual work contributes to the company's success and aligns with their own personal values.
- **Recognition of Impact:** Regularly highlight how an individual's specific accomplishments help the company reach its objectives. This could be during performance reviews, team meetings, or informal check-ins.
- **Frequent One-on-Ones:** Regular check-ins with managers are a great way to keep the conversation open about an employee's role, growth, and purpose. In these meetings, discuss how the employee's contributions are aligning with their personal goals and the company's objectives.
- **Ownership of Projects:** Empower employees to take ownership of their work and contribute to decision making. By giving them responsibility for projects or initiatives, employees can clearly see how their role drives results.
- **The Power of "Why":** When communicating an employee's purpose, always tie it back to *why* the work matters—not just the

what or how. Understanding the "why" can turn a mundane task into something with deeper significance.

- **Invest in Growth:** Providing mentorship and professional development opportunities shows employees that the company values their growth and future contributions. It reinforces that their purpose is tied to long-term success and development within the organization.

- **Encourage Collaboration and Shared Purpose:** Build a workplace culture where the company's mission is consistently communicated and embraced at every level. Foster teamwork by reminding employees how their collective efforts align with a shared purpose.

- **Continuous Feedback Loop:** Regularly share constructive feedback to reinforce how the employee's work is aligned with their purpose. Make sure the feedback is specific and tied to their role within the broader goals of the company.

- **Celebrate Purposeful Wins:** Recognize milestones and achievements that directly relate to the employee's purpose and contributions to the company's goals. Celebrating these accomplishments can reaffirm their sense of purpose.

All put together, and supported by a strong culture and company Myth, these strategies will enable your employees to succeed and be most productive. The goal for you as a leader as well as all managers within your organization is to connect each employees' daily tasks to the company's broader mission and demonstrate how their contributions matter, something younger employees find exceptionally rewarding. Figure 4.2 provides an overview of how all these elements of an organization work together.

A couple of examples will help clarify all these elements. As I was preparing to graduate from the University of Colorado with a bachelor's degree in engineering, I began searching for jobs. Unlucky for me, I happened to graduate during a lull in the economy and companies were not actively hiring, so pretty much an employers' market. In full disclosure I was not a "Tall-Skinny" candidate, nor did I have enough experience to be a "Short-Wide" employee because I didn't have much experience. I was

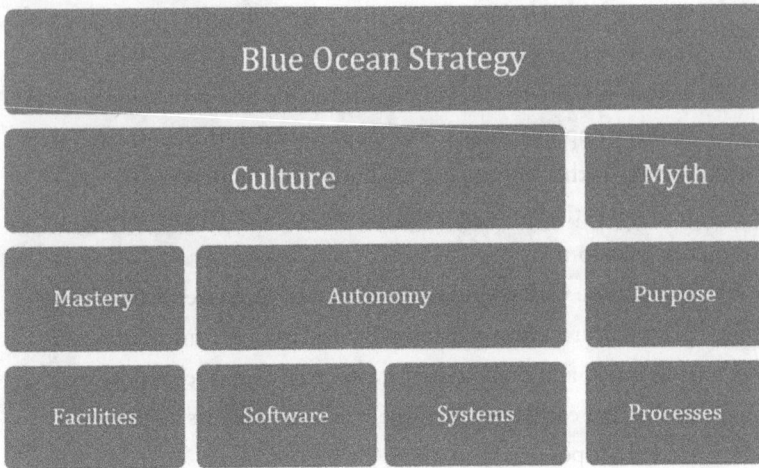

Figure 4.2 *Many factors come together to foster a Great Company*

at best an average student. I did manage to be invited for a number of interviews, and a couple of them stand out clearly as examples both good and bad as it relates to attracting a great team.

One company I interviewed with was a local startup developing technology for tracking biometrics (heart rate, respiration, calories burned, etc.) for exercise bikes. Nobody at the company took the time to explain why this was in any way special, innovative, or interesting. The team was small and seemed grumpy, and they were working out of a dingy, windowless warehouse in a run-down section of town. The salary was on the low end, and there would not be any benefits provided because of the added expense, explained the hiring manager/business owner. They just were waiting to get a big break, then they could compensate the employees better. To top it off, some of the employees I interviewed with asked if I was willing to get my master's degree (on my own dime and time) while I was working there, in order to bring more horsepower to the team? In summary, this opportunity was to work in a crummy facility where the startup company was struggling to make ends meet, for a low salary with little appreciation for what I could bring now, but more interest in me spending more time to help *them* more. I felt like I would be lowest-ranking person for the foreseeable future until the company managed a breakthrough, and nobody seemed optimistic or could explain why anything going on at the company would result in any sort of change in the outlook. It seemed like a dreadful place to work.

The second company I interviewed with was a robust supplier of aircraft to the U.S. Air Force, with full benefits and leave program, and an industry average salary. During the interview, I was shown a professionally prepared video explaining how important the company was to the U.S. defense, the innovative work being conducted, and how each employee was important to corporate success and national security. This company had a recreation center where many of the employees participated in softball, tennis, dancing, bingo, and a variety of arts and crafts activities. The hiring manager explained that I was coming in at an entry-level position but would have opportunities to experience different career tracks, advance through promotions, and would be eligible for tuition reimbursement if I wanted to pursue an advanced degree. Several people from the human resources group followed up after the interview to ask me what I thought about the opportunity and encourage me to join their team. I felt wanted, excited about the company, and felt that I would be doing important work.

Of course, I accepted the offer from the second company, and it turned out to be a very good choice. The first company didn't bother to make me an offer, and I was relieved that I wouldn't have to worry about declining what looked to me like a bad situation. I'm still wondering why they even bothered with the interview, but I'm sure they're long since bankrupt and just a minor entry on a few pour souls resumes.

Once you attract great employees, you will want to keep them around as long as they are working out well. In 2024, iHire conducted a survey of 1,544 people across various industries to ascertain why people leave their employers. As would probably be expected, respondents typically cited more than just one reason, but surprisingly, "Unsatisfactory Pay" was only cited in 20.5 percent of the cases, as shown in Figure 4.3.[21] The work environment, leadership, and work–life balance are all more important to employees.

This tells us that in order to retain the people that you have taken so much time to recruit, you should endeavor to avoid a toxic work environment, have good leadership and managers, provide a good work–life

% of Employees (1,544 respondents) Citing Factor

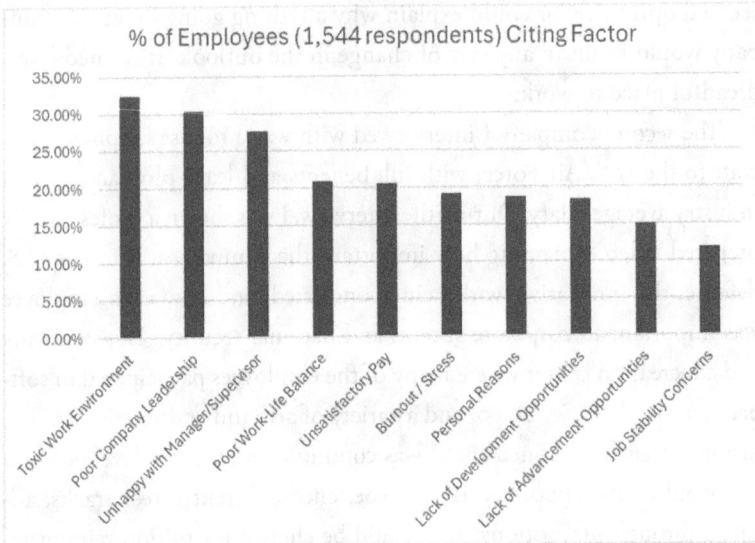

Figure 4.3 Reasons people quit jobs

Source: iHire. 2024. "Top 10 Reasons Why People Quit Their Jobs in 2024." November 25.
www.ihire.com/resourcecenter/employer/pages/reasons-why-people-quit-their-jobs-in-2024.

balance, and provide satisfactory pay. Not just one of those factors, but all of them should be addressed to create an attractive environment.

Our experience at BCT suggests that the way to achieve these goals was to keep the team small and empower everyone in the company to become part of the solution by awarding them even a small amount of ownership in the company. This ownership changed the dynamic from "us vs them" to "all of us together." The entire team felt like they were together to foster a healthy work environment and pulling together to create positive interactions throughout the organization. Simply put, awarding them shares in the company changed their mindset from "employees" to "owners." People mindfully worked to eliminate a toxic work environment, and felt like they were on the same page as the managers and leaders.

One final thing I would like to bring up with regard to building your team is a reference to Price's Law, a principle published by Derek J. de Solla Price (1922–1983), a British physicist and historian of science. According to Price's Law, there is an unequal distribution of productivity within any group or organization. It states that 50 percent of the work is typically done by the square root of the total number of participants. For example, in a company with 100 employees, approximately 10 individuals will be responsible for half of the company output. This concept highlights the tendency for talent and productivity to be unevenly distributed across various domains, including businesses.[22] I observed this phenomena at my various employers as well, although I did not have the data to determine that it was the square root of the number of employees! This concept is important for you to leverage to keep your team small while you are Staying Hungry. According to Price's Law, doubling the size of the team will only increase productivity by 41 percent, but it will increase the payroll expense by 100 percent. As much as possible, keep your team small with the best people you can find, and keep them happy!

To close out this chapter, we've described the unique opportunity you have as the business owner to plant the seeds and cultivate an amazing culture that is what you and your leadership team desire. You can then use that culture and an attractive compensation/benefits package to attract a great team. Most people are looking for a salary that is fair but doesn't have to be jaw dropping. Round out the package with a generous suite of benefits and as many perks as you'd like to add to capture and retain the best talent. Offering a path to company ownership in some format for these employees is a way to simultaneously attract those innovative difference makers and retain them for the long haul. As you formulate your strategy, you can use as many of these factors as you'd like to help build a great team which will, in turn, make your company successful.

It doesn't make sense to hire smart people and tell them what to do; we hire smart people so they can tell us what to do.

—Steve Jobs

CHAPTER 5

Getting Funded and Staying Cash Positive

There are two schools of thought when it comes to capitalization of a startup business: "Fully Capitalized" versus "Staying Hungry." Fully capitalized businesses have a flush bank account (millions of dollars ready to spend), with plenty of funds to hire a complete staff, lease a large facility, and setup operations to quickly transition to 100 percent operations. The Fully Capitalized path is appropriate for businesses which have a well-defined product, predictable revenue stream, and ready access to sales and distribution channels. In other words, if you know that your company is going to be profitable and have X revenue by the end of year 1, then 2X by year 3, and so on, then your company might be a good candidate for full capitalization. Being fully capitalized is a huge load off your mind as the founder, as you now do not have to worry as much about raising money and can focus on getting the company running right.

But what if you are still working out your product idea, you aren't sure how much it will cost to make, or how much sales or revenue you might be able to achieve on any given timeline? Then Staying Hungry is a better choice, because it will provide you and your team with more time to figure those things out.

Once you fully capitalize your business you are committed (to whomever provided the funds) to start making profits on their timeline. Remember the story of Theranos? That is a good example of a company that went the fully capitalized route too soon, and put the founders in a corner with millions of dollars sunk on an impossible product. By Staying Hungry, you and your team will be focused on the most important tasks and problems to get your company up and running efficiently. Once you know your product is viable, then you can get more aggressive with funding.

As I alluded to in Chapter 1, the goal of this book is to provide strategies for you to retain control of your company, grow it with a happy and engaged workforce, and not lose majority ownership. In other words, Staying Hungry, which is also called growing Organically. Toward those ends, the best source of funding to run your company is "free" (ish) money with no strings attached. Those sources of funds are plentiful, as in billions of dollars per year. Although the initial dollar amounts per award are modest, they are sufficient to start and grow any business. Free money should be your go-to first choice for capital. The worst source of funding is to completely drain your personal savings. Using some of your own money is OK, and in that scenario the goal is to use that personal money that you invest to start bringing in more money, then recycle that money to keep the business growing.

Some companies you might recognize which all grew organically without external investment, include Patagonia, Spanx, and GoPro. Spanx for example, was started by Sara Blakely with $5,000 in savings and a dream which grew into a billion-dollar brand. GoPro was founded by Nick Woodman with his savings and small loans from his family and eventually went the route of an IPO at nearly $3 million. Patagonia was founded in 1973 by Yvon Chouinard and grew organically and is still privately held with an estimated valuation of $3 billion.[23]

The allure of spending all your savings to run your company is powerful; you control the money, it's easy to access, and you just *know* that your new business idea is going to be Great! However, there are a lot of things that can go wrong, even if your idea is stellar. Completely consuming your savings could leave you without a safety net to fall back on, impacting your financial future for years. Who could have predicted the Covid-19 pandemic, which resulted in an estimated 100,000 permanent business closures in the United States?

What we're going to review in this chapter are ways to use some of your own money and use that to obtain money from other sources to help you grow the business yet stay in control. We will explore a graduated menu of 14 different ways to fund your business, with pros and cons for the methods, and when to leverage each type of funding. In general, I will present the funding opportunities ranked from "most free, fewest strings" to "least free, most strings" attached, under the assumption that your goal is to maximize your ability to maintain financial and executive control of your company for the long run. These methods may result in slower growth, but you retain control and you and your employees will benefit the most financially if there is an exit. If on the other hand your Elite Icon opportunity dictates that you accelerate into the marketplace immediately to maximize your potential, then you may need to elect funding avenues that can provide a big cash bomb quickly. For each funding avenue, we will evaluate the relative amount of capital you can raise, the speed of access, strings attached, and caveats or precursors.

But First—Your Business Plan

Before we can start talking about sources of capital, we need to discuss the business plan. If you haven't drafted one already, you need to document your business plan prior to going out in search of capital. This process of putting together this plan will also help you and the leadership team get everyone on the same page about how the company is going to operate, the goals for the business, and what to do when things go well or not so well. You need to outline your business goals, strategies, market analysis, and financial projections. The business plan is not something to be dreaded, it should be looked at as something fun and exciting, like planning out an itinerary and making reservations for a big international vacation. Have fun with the process and use it to fill in the assumptions that you and the other founders might have overlooked up to this point.

Executive Summary: The executive summary is often what potential investors or lenders first read, so make sure it's clear, compelling, and captures their interest. Include the key facts about the business such as name, address, location, and a summary of the business objectives, products and services. A quick summary of the market opportunity and the financing you're looking to raise (amount and type) will round out the executive summary sufficiently for busy investors to make the decision whether to keep reading or put it in the "round file" (trash bin). Therefore, make your executive summary great!

Company Description: Explain the business structure (LLC, C-Corp, S-Corp, etc.), the history of the company, business model (how revenue is generated), mission statement and vision, legal structure, products or services offered, and target customers. The main question you're addressing in this section is, *Why does your business exist?*

Market Research and Analysis: Provide charts and diagrams, along with summaries to demonstrate that you understand your market, customers, competition and industry trends. Here is where you should start describing the pain points being addressed, the customer needs, and how this opportunity is unique (a Blue Ocean). This section should convince the readers that you are knowledgeable and able to tackle the opportunity and succeed.

Organization and Management: Explain the structure of your business and the experience and qualifications of the executive team. Explain who owns the business, their responsibilities, and their qualifications. Include an organizational chart. List any advisers, board members, or mentors and their backgrounds. The goal in this section is to convince the reader that you are organized and have a qualified team capable of running the business effectively.

Products or Services: Explain in greater detail the offerings of the business, including diagrams, descriptions, the competitive advantages, cost of production, pricing strategy, and any research and development required. Your reader should be convinced that your product is compelling and has a good competitive advantage to succeed.

Marketing and Sales Strategy: We will get into this in detail in Chapter 7. In this section of the business plan, you need to outline how you will attract and retain customers, including which channels, what the sales process entails, and any additional details on pricing. Investors and lenders want to see a well-thought-out strategy for acquiring customers and growing your revenue.

Operational Plan: We will embark on this subject in Chapter 6, to include the logistics of running your business on a day-to-day basis, including how the facility operates, what operations are conducted where, how products or services are produced and delivered, as well as what tools, software, or hardware are required to run the business. Since those items may be the reason for your funding request, put as much detail as you can into these needs. Finally, provide a time-phased staffing plan (how many people, of what type, when they will be hired). This section should convey a solid understanding of the people, places, and things necessary to operate your business and fulfill the projections set forth in the prior sections. Make sure the numbers are consistent and credible.

Financial Plan: In this final section, outline the current financial health as well as the forecast for your business, showing that it will be profitable and sustainable. Include key components of the financials including startup costs, revenue models, financial projections for the next 3 to 5 years, and a projection of when you expect the business to start making a profit (break-even point). This is the final place to explain how much capital you need to grow (overall, how much at each phase), and how much you're asking for at this point. Investors want to know that your business will generate consistent revenue and have a clear path to profitability.

Funding Menu

In the next sections, we will review the different sources of funds. We will start with money that is essentially free, then progress to money that you must pay back and then finish up with money that you would get in return for giving away equity ownership in your company. As I outlined earlier, the more control of your company you can retain, the happier you and your employees will be. But there are times when trading equity for capital is unavoidable, and for those cases, I will provide strategies to help you maximize your chances of successfully retaining control and a happy workplace.

At BCT, we managed to organically grow the company from absolutely nothing to about $100 million annual revenue without ever progressing past loans and lines of credit. Yes, it is unusual, but it isn't impossible. The organic growth plan meant that we leveraged Grants,

Table 5.1 Menu of funding opportunities

Free Money	Money you must pay back	Trading ownership for money
SBIR/STTR grants	Friends and Family Funding	
State matching SBIR grants	SBA loans	ESOP—employee stock ownership plan
State and local grants	P2P loans	
Accelerator and incubator funding*	Bank loans	IPO—initial public offering
Crowd funding	RBF: revenue-based financing	
	Angel investors	Angel investors
	Venture capital—convertible notes	Venture capital and private equity

*Some incubators may ask for equity ownership.

Incubators, and a bit of bank lending to get started, then as the company started to sell products, we reinvested that revenue back into the company to help it grow. I recommend you follow a similar path if you can for your company, especially if you wish to retain control of the decision making and culture.

Table 5.1 provides a summary of the types of funding we will review in this chapter, including the Free Money options which will be discussed first.

SBIR/STTR Program

The Small Business Administration coordinates over $4B in funding allocated exclusively for small businesses, in a program named "Small Business Innovation Research" (SBIR) and "Small Business Technology Transfer" (STTR). I am constantly surprised that nearly all of the company founders I meet have never heard of this program which provides funding to thousands of companies each year. The funding is strictly off limits to companies with more than 500 employees. Your business must be an independent small business as defined by the small business administration (SBA), and it must be primarily American owned. The SBIR program operates in a cycle consisting of a "solicitation" release (government agency ideas, problem statements, pain points), followed by a short period for small businesses to interact with the government team, then a blackout period and opportunity to make a research proposal, followed by notification of award. The funding is broken into phase I (Proof of Concept), phase II (expansion of the research, proof of concept), and phase III (Commercialization).

Each phase has increasing levels of funding, and fewer numbers of awards. The STTR program accounts for less than 10 percent of awards, but operates similarly to SBIR, with the exception that the small business must partner with a nonprofit research institution such as a university or a federally funded research center. No more than 60 percent (typically) of the funding may be allocated to the nonprofit research institution, the remainder staying with the small business.

Over 5,000 awards totaling over $4B are made each year for companies addressing critical needs in topics such as aviation, agriculture, border security, climate, cybersecurity, education, forestry, health and life sciences, nutrition, renewable energy, space, and water safety, to name a few.[24] A random sampling of awards in 2024 included:

- Developing methods to counteract motion sickness
- Improving fruit juice concentration processes
- Using biomass waste to create biodegradable, noncorrosive road deicer
- Utilizing ultrasound for treating prostate cancer
- Detection of synthetic opioids (fentanyl analogs)
- Methods to increase catfish production in hatcheries
- Forest fire management using Infrared technology
- Tracking systems for equipment and assets on ships
- Development of wargaming simulations to include cultural effects
- Using AI to predict pesticide toxicity in support of food safety and quality
- Making palmtop computers accessible to individuals with mental retardation
- Development of virtual reality models of the Solar System
- Recycling of plastics used in the automotive industry

- Development of personal cooling systems for workers in hot environments
- Methods for screening newborns for hearing impairments
- Low-cost hardware for space propulsion
- Forecasting extreme weather events utilizing AI

Overall, in 2023, the SBIR/STTR program awarded $3.9 billion to 3668 companies (an average of $622,000 per company). The average company size was 42 employees, with 525 of the companies woman-owned and another 580 of the companies being "socially or economically challenged." Companies receiving awards are in all 50 states plus Puerto Rico and the District of Columbia.

SBIR Advantages: SBIR and STTR funding is what I call smart money. Smart because it is nondilutive, the customer has already identified the problem for you, and they will pay you to develop innovative solutions and create a commercially viable product. Nondilutive funding means that you receive hundreds of thousands or millions of dollars of funding, retain ownership in your company, and keep the products of the research. The government will usually retain a right to use the products of the research, but the goal of this SBA program is to help small businesses grow and develop new commercial products. Why wouldn't you want smart money to support your growing business? The government has already identified the problem, allocated money to help small businesses develop solutions (products or services), and as a taxpayer you are already funding this program.

SBIR Disadvantages: SBIR and STTR funding are a slow mechanism to infuse your business with capital. Participating Agencies post SBIR/STTR funding opportunities on a regular periodic basis throughout the year. Some agencies have multiple solicitations throughout the year, while others may only have one solicitation release each year. Once you identify a relevant agency to target, learn more about that specific agency's process. As you can surmise from Table 5.2, many of the opportunities are technical in nature, so if your background or business are not technical then

Table 5.2 SBIR/STTR program overview (2024)

Agency	Funding opportunities	Annual funds	Phase I	Phase II
USDA	Forests, Plant and Animal Production and Protection, Conservation of Natural Resources, Food Science and Nutrition, Rural Development, Aquaculture, Biofuels and Biobased Products, Small and Mid-Size Farms	$42M	$125k–$175k	$600k
DOC	Commerce technologies in support of the missions of the National Oceanic and Atmospheric Administration (NOAA) and National Institutes of Standards and Technology (NIST)	$15M	$100k	$400k
DOD	5G, AI/Autonomy, Biotechnology, Control and Communications, Cybersecurity, Directed Energy, Hypersonic, Microelectronics, Network Command, Nuclear, Quantum Sciences, Space, and more	$2.3B	$50k–$250k	$800k–$1.83M
DOE	Advanced Scientific Computing Research, Environmental Management, Fossil Energy, Biological and Environmental Research, Fusion Energy Science, Cybersecurity, Energy Security, Renewable Energy, and more	$315M	$200k–$250k	$1.1M–$1.6M
ED	Funds New Education Technology Products for Use by Students, or Educators, or those used by Infants, Toddlers, or Students With or At Risk for Disabilities, or Teachers in Early Intervention or Special Education Settings	$10M	$250k	$1M
HHS	Funds health, life science, and biomedical discoveries that could impact the lives of patients and their families	$1.2B	$275k+	$1.83M

(continued)

Table 5.2 SBIR/STTR program overview (2024) (continued)

Agency	Funding opportunities	Annual funds	Phase I	Phase II
DHS	Funds innovation supporting: Borders and Maritime Security, Chemical and Biological Defense, Critical Infrastructure and Resilience, Cybersecurity, Explosives Detection and Aviation Screening, First Responders, and more	$18M	$150k	$1M
DOT	Funds technologies in support of DOT Operating Administration: Federal Highway Administration, Federal Railroad Administration, Federal Transit Administration, and Pipeline and Hazardous Materials Safety Administration	$9M	$200k	$1M
EPA	Broadly funds technologies addressing Air Quality, Homeland Security, Sustainable Materials Management, Safe Chemicals, Land Revitalization, and Clean and Safe Water	$5M	$100k	$400k
NASA	Propulsion Systems, Flight Computing and Avionics, Aerospace Power and Energy Storage, Robotic Systems, Communications, Navigation, and Orbital Debris Tracking/ Characterization Systems	$174M	$150k	$1M
NSF	Funds almost all areas of technology and market sectors (with the exception of clinical trials)	$215M	$300k	$1.25M

Source: Courtesy of sbir.gov

SBIR/STTR may not work for you. Also, you will find that there are many businesses out there which subsist solely by competing and winning SBIR grants. These companies become "SBIR machines" with entrenched relationships in the government and well-honed proposal processes. They never commercialize any of their products or graduate out of the SBIR ecosystem. While that isn't how the SBIR grant program is designed to operate, those companies unfortunately continue to win many grants and soak up funding which could benefit other small startups.

Assistance: Local accelerators and support organizations are available in many states around the country to provide technical assistance and support identifying and applying for awards. Search for "SBIR L2M Lab to Market" for additional details.

Utilize the open question and answer period to interact with the government team and learn as much as you can about their problems, pain points, and any predisposition to particular solution types. It is a free chance to discover any hidden information which might give your proposal an advantage. The typical cadence of topic release and open dialog period is presented below by agency in Figure 5.1. You can determine what the review team is looking for, what exciting technology appeals to them, and determine if you have an alignment between their needs and your team's skill sets. The critical challenge in proposing SBIR topics is to present a credible solution which is high reward as well as high risk,

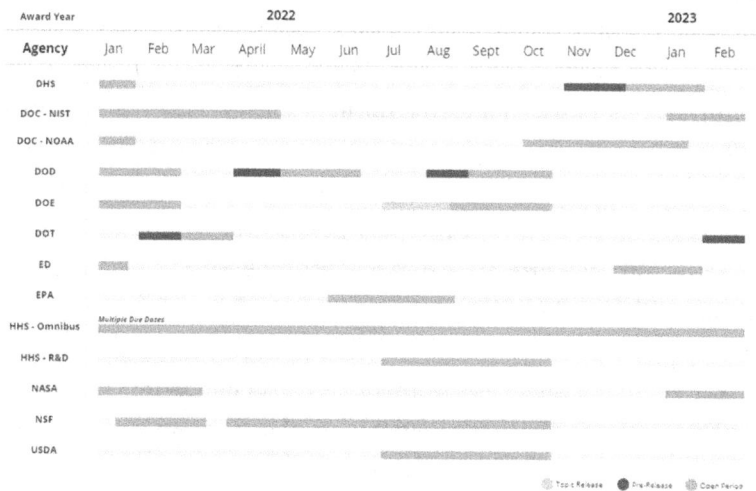

Figure 5.1 SBIR/STTR typical funding opportunity cadence—Courtesy sbir.gov

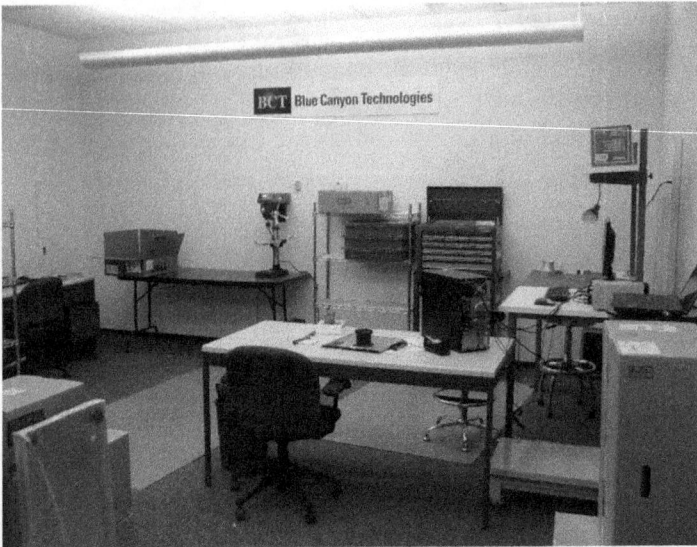

Figure 5.2 Circa 2010. BCT's Space "office" at a Colorado Technology Incubator (eSpace)

then needs the right amount of research and development to bring it to fruition. A bit of a tightrope walk to not immediately solve the problem, but show that the problem could be solved and that your team is the best team to receive funding.

Note that it is common for multiple companies to receive funding for the same topic in some branches of the government including the Department of Defense and Department of Energy. Table 5.2 presents a summary by government agency of amounts awarded per year.

Not only is SBIR/STTR funding free, but there is also a "partnership" trust factor which develops between the government agency and a funded company after the first successful contract. The agency is more likely to award additional contracts to companies that have performed previously (and produced good results). In fact, for the years 2011 to 2020, 57 percent of the companies received more than one award, 15 percent received more than five awards, and the overall most-awarded company in that time frame was Physical Optics Corporation of Torrance, California which received 731 contracts valued at over $250 million. Notably, that company is employee-owned, was founded in the early 1970s, and currently employs about 285 people. Obviously, they have made a solid business out of performing work for the U.S. government via the SBIR/ STTR program.

A benefit of the SBIR/STTR program is that the problems have already been identified by the customer, along with some discussion of the nature of the pain points and potential opportunities; the customer is going to give you money to develop strategies and potential solutions to this problem; and if they like your proposed solutions, they will give you even more money and never ask you to repay them. The potential award amounts are typically $100,000 for phase 1, $750,000 and up for phase 2, and even more for phase 3. Really, the question for you is: Why wouldn't you want to take advantage of this program?

Federal, State, and Local Grant Programs

For federal grants, check www.Grants.gov. For women-owned businesses, check www.AmberGrantsForWomen.com. Another national private grant is hosted by FedEx (search for FedEx Small Business Grants). In addition, many states offer a variety of grant programs, incentives, and funding opportunities aimed at supporting small businesses, fostering economic growth, and encouraging innovation. If you are pressed for time and are looking for help, you can enlist the aid of organizations like Grantify to help you raise money through grants. Grants you may be able to find in your state includes:

- General small business grants providing direct funding for business operations costs
- Grants for technology and innovation geared toward specific business sectors
- Grants for minority, women, and veteran-owned businesses (Minority Business Development Agency)
- Grants for rural and agricultural businesses
- Economic development and job creation grants
- National Association for the Self-Employed (NASE) growth grants
- Energy efficiency and sustainability grants

Grant Advantages: Grant funding is usually nondilutive much like SBIR funding, and unlike SBIR or STTR funding does not necessarily require any research and development. The range of grants is constantly changing and varies widely state to state. The goal of the grant programs is usually focused on economic development, so if you can describe or demonstrate job creation then you have an excellent opportunity to secure a grant. In addition, many states have matching grant programs which will add funding for companies that win SBIR or STTR federal grants, creating a multiplier effect for the federal grants, as summarized in Table 5.3.

Table 5.3 State SBIR matching programs

State	Matching program	Phase I match	Phase II match	Additional notes
North Carolina	One NC Small Business Program	Varies	Varies	Supports technology development
Oregon	Business Oregon	Up to $100,000	50% of federal award amount	
Hawaii	Hawaii Technology Development Corporation	Varies	Up to $500,000	Cap applies to phase II only
Illinois	Illinois Department of Commerce and Economic Opportunity	Up to $50,000	N/A	
Indiana	Elevate Ventures	Up to $50,000	Lifetime cap of $150,000	
Michigan	Michigan Emerging Technologies Fund	Up to $25,000	Up to $125,000	
Minnesota	Launch Minnesota	Up to $35,000	Up to $50,000	First-time awardees only
Nebraska	Nebraska Department of Economic Development	65% of federal grant	Up to $100,000	

State	Matching program	Phase I match	Phase II match	Additional notes
New Jersey	New Jersey Economic Development Authority	$25,000	N/A	Phase I, fast track, and direct to phase II federal awards
New Mexico	New Mexico SBIR Matching Grant Program	Up to $25,000	Up to $100,000	Competitive grant process
Rhode Island	Rhode Island Science and Technology Advisory Council	Up to $45,000	Up to $100,000	
South Carolina	South Carolina Research Authority	Up to $50,000	N/A	Matches up to 50% of federal awards
Tennessee	Launch Tennessee	Up to $100,000	Up to $300,000	
West Virginia	West Virginia Small Business Development Center	Up to $100,000	Up to $200,000	
Wisconsin	Wisconsin Economic Development Council and Wisconsin Center for Technology Commercialization	Varies	Varies	
Wyoming	Wyoming Business Council	Up to $100,000 (first time)	Up to $70,000 (repeat phase I)	

For more details, visit the respective program websites or contact the state agencies directly. States which don't match SBIR grants often have other grant programs which are advantageous to small businesses.

Grant Disadvantages: Funding amounts are typically more modest than many SBIR amounts, and many require cost-sharing or contributions from the commercial company, thus providing a real cost benefit to reduce costs or defray expenses but not providing 100 percent coverage for the project.

Assistance: State by state opportunities vary significantly. For your state of operations, you should consult:

- State Economic Development Websites, which will list grants and opportunities
- State Small Business Development Centers (SBDCs)
- Local Chamber of Commerce
- Government Grant Databases such as Grants.gov may provide federal or state grants

Accelerators and Incubators

Not all industries have incubators, but for those who do, you may be able to secure free office space, access to mentors, access to telecom services, maybe even a live person to answer the phone for you while you're at your day job. Some of the incubators operate pro bono, and some expect some equity in return for their contributions. By working with an accelerator or incubator, you may be able to receive guidance on developing a product, or help proving a market for it, receive technical or legal consultation, or find a mentor. Some top accelerators include:

- Y Combinator
- Techstars
- TechNexus
- Capital Factory (Texas)
- 500 Startups
- Seedcamp (European)

Be careful to select an accelerator or incubator that is aligned with your needs. Some accelerators or incubators can provide some level of funding but will typically expect to receive an equity stake. In addition, some organizations charge a recurring membership fee, which to me is counterproductive unless its justified and makes sense in your situation. As you may have deduced, Incubators are for companies with an innovative business idea, whereas Accelerators are for more mature startups that have developed a product concept but need help making it successful. Incubator space may be fairly modest, like what BCT used as shown in Figure 5.2.

Friends and Family Funding

My recommendation for your own long-term financial security is that you only invest an amount of your own money that you can accept losing entirely if the business fails. The same goes for any funds you receive from family and friends. Do not promise anything with regard to returns or appreciation. Do explain that this is a high-risk investment, and it might be wiser to take the money to Las Vegas and bet it at the roulette table. If your friend or family member is still onboard with helping you with cash, then proceed carefully and as if the money is your own. Consult with your CPA and Attorney to ensure the process is legal and does not trigger any tax liabilities. Note that you cannot have more than 35 individuals invest in this manner but, in practice, keeping it much smaller than that is more manageable.

First things first: take care of your own financial investment. For the sake of your family and long-term financial peach of mind, set aside a sizeable amount of your personal savings for "later" to help you get back on your feet in the event that things don't work out for your startup. Also, there may come a time when you will need to give your company a short-term line of credit to get through a cash flow problem. In summary: Do not invest all your money in this startup, set aside an "Emergency Fund."

If you have a situation where it makes sense to borrow from friends and family, I have two suggestions. Either borrow from them (structured as a loan) or allow them to invest with you (equity ownership). If you go the route of the loan, you should draft up a simple promissory note, including the amount, the number of months or years (term), the interest rate, and repayment expectations. Both parties should agree that they're satisfied and sign it. You should treat this obligation as if it were from a bank or any other creditor. Do not let your business become a family feud or create a rift in a friendship. Document the agreements, sign them, and update them if there are changes.

If you opt for the route of equity ownership, where the friend or family is investing in your company in return for shares, you should include them in the Cap Table to reflect their ownership alongside everyone else. You can work out the amount of ownership that makes sense, but just keep in mind several factors: First, you will be working diligently to make the company successful, while the investor is "passively" contributing money. While the value of your work is difficult to convert to a monetary value, the company will only be successful with your hard work. Second, consider how much their share could potentially be worth in the event of an exit. 3× or 4× is a great return, but 0.5× or 40× are unacceptable to one party or the other. Third, if you've already kicked in some of your own money, that gives you a reasonable multiplier to use to establish how much of a percentage they might own. Finally, consider an option where you buy back their shares at an agreed upon value if and as the company becomes financially successful. You can even create a buy-back schedule that specifies how much you will pay to buy back their ownership in 1, 2, 3, or 5 years. You can even consult the valuation tables in the Epilogue to provide some long-term projections of the valuation of the company, to help guide a discussion with your friend and family investors.

A key concept of organic growth is that as your company becomes cash positive, you reinvest the money to keep the business thriving and growing. Do not expect to get your money out quickly. If it happens that way, that will be great, have a big party!

Crowd Funding

Platforms like Kickstarter, GoFundMe or Indiegogo may allow you to raise small amounts of capital from many people. The amount of money you might raise will probably be modest, but a large degree of interest can support your efforts to raise capital elsewhere by demonstrating a strong demand for your technology, product, or service. The best opportunity to maximize crowd funding is through telling a compelling story or narrative, making a great video presentation, leveraging social media, and offering tiered rewards that are compelling and provide value. Be sure to explain why you are doing this project, what makes it unique, and why people should care.

Employee Stock Ownership Plan

Assuming you are onboard with employee ownership, an employee stock ownership plan is a modest but reliable way to generate some additional capital for your business operations, as well as providing flexibility for you and other members of the leadership team to maintain control, if that is your desire. In this method, the ESOP allows the business owner to sell small amounts of the company to the employees as shares on a yearly, quarterly, or monthly basis. You can even set it up to be a payroll withdrawal such that employees make regular contributions and receive stock in exchange. You will need support from an experienced business attorney and CPA knowledgeable in the process.

This shared ownership creates a bond between all of the owners of mutually aligned outcomes, enabling everyone to be on the same page and have additional motivation to go the extra mile. Getting the details of the ESOP plan correct is important to ensure it meets the requirements of the Internal Revenue Code. If your company structure is a pass-through organization such as an LLC or S-Corp, all the owners will receive K1 forms annually to reflect the profit and loss of the company.

A considerate owner will set aside enough cash at the end of the year to at least cover the worst-case tax obligations of the owners, if it is a profitable year. If the profits are significant, you can distribute additional funds as a profit distribution, or annual bonus, which is always very welcome at the holidays!

Bank Loans and Lines of Credit

Banks can provide you and your company with a temporary source of funds, without sacrificing any equity ownership. The adage for entrepreneurs is, "If you wait until you need money from a bank, you won't be able to get it." The problem is that when your company is struggling or in distress financially, your numbers will indicate that you are too high of a risk to approve a loan. You need to establish a relationship with a commercial bank and a banker you will know by name when your company is in good financial health. Reach out to at least two or three different banks and have a conversation with a business banker (make sure you are working with a bank that supports businesses not just a retail consumer bank). Commercial banks will adjust their risk and opportunity profiles over time, and some banks will be more agreeable to working with you. Having a conversation with two or three bankers will help you find out which bank might work best for your situation.

Once you have an established banking relationship, I recommend you work to establish a Line of Credit then exercise it routinely by making draws to support your operations, then paying it back on time. You need to demonstrate to the bank that you are a serious client and that your company can be relied upon to repay loans. Over time, as your business grows, you will be able to work with your business banker to expand the size and terms of your loans and lines of credit. The business banker is incentivized to maintain and grow his or her portfolio of commercial clients, and you should respect and foster your relationship with your banker. You may have to call them in a crisis someday, and a good relationship will facilitate funding much better than cold calling out of the blue when you haven't stayed in touch. Your banker will work for you if you treat them with respect and as a partner. However, this are some serious downsides to conventional bank loans.

Loan Is a Four-Letter Word

Before we dive into the different types of loans, let's review some of the risks associated with many loan types, so that you can prioritize which types of loan you pursue. Unlike personal loans, business loans will usually include restrictions called "covenants" which place certain requirements on the business and the major owners. For example, covenants can impose requirements on the company financial strength, how much liquidity you have on hand, how much leverage you have, and the net worth of the business. Covenants can also restrict what you spend money on, your ability to take on additional debt, any changes in management, establish minimum cash flow requirements, and even stipulate requirements around profitability. Violation of any of the covenants is grounds for the lender to recall the loan and require that you repay the loan in full immediately or face legal action and seizure of assets. Take for example Starsys Research Corporation which took out a loan for $6 million to facilitate growth. The loan included a covenant to remain profitable, something which the company had achieved for 10 straight years. However, when the company encountered some challenges and posted unprofitable numbers, the bank doubled the interest rate and required an immediate payment of $1 million. To make matters worse, if the company failed to make that payment or any other payment, the bank would chain the doors and take ownership of the company, seize the owner's personal assets, and sell the assets to pay off the loan.[25] In short, a couple of unprofitable months for Starsys led to the eventual financial collapse of the company. The founder had no choice but to sell his company to get out from under the loan or face bankruptcy.

The next difference between personal and business loans to small companies comes in the form of a personal guarantee from the owners of the company that if in the event the company is unable to pay back the loan, the owners will be responsible to pay it off. Almost every small business owner I have ever met took out a loan which included a personal guarantee once, suffered many sleepless nights, then swore to never do it again.

The last thing you want to get into is the "Nightmare Loan," which we nearly encountered during the early years of BCT. The Nightmare Loan scenario occurs when you take out a loan with a value commensurate with your potential incoming revenue. Then, if the company doesn't grow as fast as you'd anticipated, or any one of hundred other things delays the growth, you end up unable to make the monthly payments. The Nightmare happens if the company is unable to thrive, and you must shut down the business. At that point, you and the other founders (what the bank will call "co-borrowers" on the loan paperwork) will have to get other jobs to pay off the loan, in addition to meeting your normal financial obligations. For this reason, you want to limit the size of any loans you take out to the lesser of what the company can pay back without any new revenue, or the amount of your Emergency Fund.

Personal guarantees and Covenants will usually be stipulated for loans and lines of credit from banks. SBA loans and some peer-to-peer loans will include "lite" covenants requiring financial reporting and restricting how the funds may be utilized. Consider SBA loans the most "borrower friendly" and traditional bank loans the most hostile.

SBA Loans

Getting a U.S. Small Business Administration (SBA) loan is another way to secure funding for your small business without giving up equity, but the process can be competitive and requires a *ton* of paperwork

Table 5.4 Summary of SBA loan types

Loan type	Max loan amount	Average loan (2022)[26]	Typical use
SBA 7(a) loan	$5 million	$443,097	Working capital, equipment, real estate, refinancing
SBA 504 loan	$5 million (SBA portion), up to $13 million (total project)	$1,112,115	Real estate, large equipment purchases
SBA microloan	$50,000	$16,500	Startups and small businesses, working capital, equipment
SBA express loan	$500,000	$218,038	Working capital, inventory, faster approval
SBA disaster loan	$2 million	$2 million	Disaster recovery, property damage, lost income
SBA export loan	$5 million	$2,100,000	Exporting businesses, international trade financing

and hoop-jumping. The secret to getting an SBA Loan lies in positioning your business as a low-risk borrower and navigating the application process.

One thing that you might consider would be using an SBA Preferred Lender. Some lenders have a special designation as Preferred Lenders (PLPs). These lenders can make decisions on SBA loan applications more quickly and with less paperwork, speeding up the approval process. Use the SBA's Lender Match Tool on the SBA website to help you find SBA-approved lenders and PLPs that are well suited for your business. Table 5.4 presents a summary of loan types provided by the SBA.

Once you have narrowed down which type of loan to pursue, review the collateral requirements, personal guarantees, and covenants. Typically, SBA loans will stipulate how the loan can and cannot be used, as well as financial reporting requirements, but minimal other covenants. If you can navigate the complex paperwork and application process, SBA loans are the most favorable for small businesses.

Peer-to-Peer (P2P) Lending

Peer-to-peer (P2P) lending platforms connect businesses and individual investors, allowing businesses to borrow money without going through traditional financial institutions like banks. These platforms typically offer competitive interest rates and more flexible terms compared to traditional loans, as summarized in Table 5.5.

Table 5.5 Example P2P lending providers

Platform	Overview	Loan type and terms	Requirements
Funding Circle	Connects businesses with accredited investors who lend money in exchange for interest	$25k–$500k+ 6 months– 5 years 5–27%	Generally, requires businesses to have been operating for at least 2 years, with $150,000+ in annual revenue
LendingClub	Offers personal and business loans. Allow small businesses to secure loans from individual investors with fixed rates and predictable payments	$5k–$500k 1–5 years 7–35%	Businesses generally need to have at least $50,000 in annual revenue and be in operation for at least 1 year
Prosper	While Prosper is more known for personal loans, they do provide options for small businesses through their business loan marketplace	$2k–$500k 3–5 years 8–36%	Businesses need to show at least $100,000 in annual revenue and have been operating for at least 2 years
StreetShares	Offers financing specifically for veteran-owned businesses but is open to all types of small businesses. It offers both term loans and lines of credit funded through P2P lenders	$2k–$250k 3 months– 3 years 7–40%	Businesses should have at least $25,000 in annual revenue and at least 1 year in business
Upstart	Uses AI and machine learning to evaluate credit risk, which can sometimes allow for more flexible underwriting	$1k–$50k 3–5 years 8–35%	Generally requires 2+ years in business and $50,000+ in annual revenue

(continued)

Table 5.5 Example P2P lending providers (continued)

Platform	Overview	Loan type and terms	Requirements
Kiva	Allows entrepreneurs to raise small amounts of capital from a large number of backers, interest free	$1k–$15k 6 months– 3 years 0%	Focuses on social impact, so it's ideal for small businesses that may not qualify for traditional financing
Fundera Marketplace	They connect businesses with multiple lending sources	$5k–$500k 1–5 years 6–35%	Businesses generally need to have been in operation for 1 year or more and generate $50,000+ in annual revenue

P2P lending allows you to raise capital without giving up equity. Platforms like Funding Circle, LendingClub, and Prosper provide businesses with flexible, accessible funding options, while Kiva offers a more social, community-driven model with interest-free loans. If these loans make sense for your business' needs, compare terms across platforms, and work with several options then choose the one that best suits your growth stage and financial situation.

Most P2P loans will only stipulate how the loan can and cannot be used, as well as some minimal financial reporting requirements and conditions, making this loan type pretty attractive to most small businesses.

Revenue-Based Financing

Revenue-based financing (RBF) is also referred to as "Venture Debt" and it is a nondilutive alternative to traditional venture capital or loans. In RBF, businesses raise capital in exchange for a percentage of future revenue rather than giving up equity or taking on debt with fixed repayments. Several firms specialize in RBF and cater to companies that need growth capital but want to avoid dilution or long-term debt commitments. Typically, you may be able to raise $100k to $1 million, provided you have at least $10k to $50k in monthly recurring revenue. You will need to be able to demonstrate strong, predictable revenue. The financer will extract a portion of your monthly revenue to repay the loan, typically between

5 percent and 20 percent. Examples of companies that offer RBF include Lighter Capital, Capchase, Bigfoot, RevUp, and Clearco.

Unlike traditional loans and SBA loans, RBF does not typically include covenants but may stipulate some *conditions*. For example, your company revenue will need to be reported and audited, with minimum threshold requirements and limitations on the use of funds and restrictions on business actions which could jeopardize repayment of the loan.

In the following sections, we are going to cross over into methods which will dilute your ownership in exchange for capital. I recommend exhausting all the nondilutive options and making a conscious decision to confirm you and your partners are willing and ready to begin bringing in new ownership to the company via dilution. Once you cross over to these types of capital raising, it is difficult to "undilute."

Angel Investors

Angel investing provides early-stage funding where high-net-worth individuals (Angels) provide capital to startups or early-stage businesses in exchange for equity ownership or debt. This type of investment is often great for businesses that are too early in their development to attract traditional venture capital or bank loans, but it offers substantial potential for both the investor and the business owner. Now, contrary to what you read or hear in the media, most Angel investors are not providing huge sums of cash. In fact, the median check size written by Angel investors in 2017 was $35,255, as reported by the Harvard Business School.[27]

Angel investors are typically wealthy individuals who use their own money to invest in startups. Unlike venture capitalists (VCs), who manage pooled funds from multiple sources, Angel investors make personal investments in industries they are familiar with, or where they see high growth potential. Some Angel investors are part of formal networks or groups (e.g., AngelList, Tech Coast Angels) that pool resources to fund startups together. You should recognize that Angels are busy, and typically have many companies they are working with, so you won't get as much time from them as you might like.

Most individual Angel investors will invest between $25,000 and $500,000 in a single deal. The investment amount often depends on the stage of the company, the size of the opportunity, and the Angel's risk tolerance. The funding may be Seed and Early Stage (the first round of external funding to your company) or Equity (a larger amount in return for a negotiated stake in your ownership cap table) or Convertible Debt (a loan that can be converted into equity at a later date, typically during a future financing round.

Angel investors take on high risk by investing early in a business, so they typically expect a significant return on investment if the business succeeds. The return is usually in the form of equity ownership (a share of the company), which can appreciate significantly if the company grows and becomes more valuable. The Angel is repaid typically upon an exit event.

That exit might happen through acquisition by another company, an IPO if the company goes public and issues shares of stock to the public, or a secondary sale whereby the Angel sells their shares to another buyer.

Angel Investment Advantages

- Because many Angel investors are experts in their industries, they may be able to provide you with expertise, mentoring, or leveraging their industry networks to improve your opportunities for success.
- Angel investments are typically long-term (5–10 years), providing you with a reasonable amount of time to grow the business before any expectation of exiting or repaying the Angel. This can also turn into a disadvantage if the timeline doesn't work out well.
- Capital is generally available very quickly and can provide funding to operate and grow your business as you need it, avoiding the waits typical of SBIRs or Grants.
- In theory, Angels are less demanding than Venture Capital groups, because they have been in your shoes and appreciate the challenges of your endeavor.

Angel Investment Disadvantages

- Obviously, you are going to trade some equity (future value) in exchange for capital. The devil is in the details. If you can achieve an arrangement that still results in a satisfactory situation either when you exit, or the Angel exits, then great. Make some estimates of how the numbers could play out. Assume your estimates are wildly wrong, and make sure you are still OK with the result.

- Depending upon the structure of the agreement, you could lose some control over your business. Some Angels are very hands off, others want to make sure their investment is successful by helping you. That may be good or bad.

Angel Investment Process

- First, you will provide your Business Plan and a Pitch: The pitch deck should be concise and clearly communicate your idea to potential investors. Include your business model, financial projections, and how you intend to use the funds.
- Find Angel Investors: Attend pitch events, use online platforms (AngelList, SeedInvest), or network with Angel investors. Angel investors come from many different industries, so it's important to target individuals with relevant expertise or interest in your sector.
- Pitch and Negotiate Terms: Present your pitch to potential investors. Be prepared to answer questions about your business model, financials, and how you plan to grow. If an investor is interested, you will negotiate terms, including the amount of investment and the equity or debt stake they will receive in exchange.
- Due Diligence: Angel investors will often conduct due diligence to assess the viability of your business. This includes examining your financials, business model, legal structure, and market potential. They may bring in a team of specialists to perform a thorough review. This step may be a challenge for you and your leadership team, but it is crucial for the investor to make sure he's making an informed decision and to uncover any risks associated with the business.
- Agreement and Investment: Once terms are agreed upon, a term sheet is drawn up, outlining the specifics of the deal (investment amount, equity stake, voting rights, etc.). If the terms are accepted, the investment is made, and the funds are disbursed.

Angel investing may be a good fit for you to get some early-stage funding, allowing you to grow and scale. As I mentioned earlier, there is a lot more hype about Angel investors than there are real big-time investors. Most Angels limit their investment to smaller amounts, less than $100,000. The ones I met were busy with their own lives, and didn't really have a lot of time and energy to spare for yet another demand on their time. If you are lucky enough to get an invitation to pitch, you should give it your best with a well-prepared presentation, a solid business plan, and clear terms for the investment, because you will likely only get one opportunity. Investors are busy and see a lot of opportunities and they first sort into "investigate further" or "not pursue." However, if you are able to secure some Angel investing, it makes a great complement to other funding such as SBIR/STTR or Grants.

Shark Tank?

The odds of getting funded via Shark Tank are approximately 0.15 percent of all applicants. There are typically 35,000 to 50,000 applicants each year, and less than 100 of those applicants are selected for inclusion in the final TV lineup. However, while the odds are against, you, there are some considerations that may make this option worth the effort. For example, if your business is truly unique, has some solid sales or clear growth potential, and you are a charismatic presenter with a compelling backstory or business journey, your odds are significantly enhanced. The producers are not only looking for good business cases, they're looking for interesting people who will increase the show's ratings. The average funding received by successful presenters is around $250,000. However, the real benefit of Shark Tank is the massive marketing exposure and increased sales due to the "Shark Tank Effect" regardless of whether you secure a deal or not.

Convertible Notes

One of the first mechanisms you may encounter with Angel investing or Venture Capital is the offer for convertible notes. Convertible notes allow you to raise capital without setting an immediate valuation for the company, as the debt converts into equity at a later funding round, typically at a discount or with a valuation cap. Many venture capital firms, Angel investors, and specialized funding platforms offer convertible note financing. Your challenge in this scenario is to defend as high a valuation as possible, such that the dilution is minimized.

In a convertible note, investors lend money to the startup, which converts into equity in the future, typically during the next funding round. Here are some key terms that influence the funding amount:

- **Valuation Cap**: The maximum valuation at which the note converts into equity, offering investors protection against excessive dilution.
- **Discount Rate**: The percentage discount applied to the price of shares in the next round of financing (usually 10–30 percent).
- **Interest Rate**: The interest rate (usually 2–8 percent) is accrued on the loan, often converting into equity along with the principal when the note converts.
- **Maturity Date**: The date at which the note must convert into equity or be repaid. The longer the maturity period, the more flexibility the company has.

The flexibility of convertible notes allows startups to raise capital without committing to a valuation immediately, which can be advantageous in the early stages. However, the terms, including valuation caps and discount rates, play a significant role in determining how much investors are willing to invest. The ability to negotiate favorable terms can have a big impact on the capital a company can raise. Convertible notes are typically a gateway to Venture Capital.

Venture Capital and Private Equity

Venture capital (VC) is private equity funding provided to early-stage, high-potential, and high-risk businesses with strong growth prospects. The primary reason that Venture capital exists is to provide a high risk, high reward investment opportunity to speculative investors. The method in which that return is realized is by investing in many companies like yours, in the hope that some of them will be successful. But the primary reason is to make money for the client investors. Private Equity is a similar construct, just used for more mature established businesses that need more capital to grow to the next level.

Venture capital is typically invested in exchange for equity (typically 10–25 percent ownership) in the company. VC funding is most commonly associated with startups in the technology, health care, and biotech sectors, though it can apply to any high-growth business. Unlike Angel investing, which as we outlined above usually involves individual investors, venture capital comes from professional investors who pool their money into funds managed by VC firms.

VC firms are in the business of making money for their clients, and they are not necessarily in the business of helping you be successful beyond the extent necessary to meet their financial targets. Let's look at the numbers more closely, just to understand your company's place in the VC world. Venture Capital firms receive thousands of inbound company proposals every year. Of those, they will select less than 1 percent of the companies to include in their portfolio and provide funding. Of the firms included in their portfolio, typically around 10 percent will be successful, and less than 1 percent will be an ultrasuccessful "unicorn" like Uber or AirBnb.[28] The Venture Capital fund managers are playing the odds for their clients. Do you get the picture yet? They don't have a lot of time or charter to care about you or your company being happy, maintaining your culture, or pursuing your passion. They care whether you will be profitable. This is the reason I'm not a big fan of VC funding: It's very difficult to obtain, and actually being included in a VC portfolio starts to introduce a dynamic which makes it difficult to become successful: The high pressure to become profitable on the timeline dictated by the agreement. This scenario has tanked many potentially good companies by forcing them to commit all of their resources to an immature product or concept, before the details were completely fleshed out.

Well-known VC firms include Sequoia Capital, Benchmark, and Andreessen Horowitz. Within the structure of the VC there will be Limited Partners (LPs), investors who provide the capital to fund the investments and may include institutional investors, family offices, and wealthy individuals who invest in the VC fund. LPs are passive investors and don't make decisions about individual investments but receive returns based on the fund's performance. General Partners (GPs) are the professionals who run the VC firm and make decisions about where to invest the fund's capital. They actively source deals, perform due diligence, and guide the startups in their portfolios.

VC firms may be interested in investing at any stage of the company's growth, starting with seed rounds where they might invest $100,000 to $2 million. As the company's market position becomes clearer, additional rounds of funding may be conducted (series A, B, C, etc.) with capital amounts from a few million to hundreds of millions of dollars depending upon the situation.

VC firms make money in several ways, including through acquisitions or by taking a company public (IPO). If your company is acquired by a larger firm, or by third party investors, the VC firm can sell its equity stake, at a significant profit. If your company goes public via an IPO, the VC can sell its equity stake when the shares are listed on a stock exchange. In addition to the profits made from exits, VC firms charge management fees (usually around 2 percent of the fund's total assets) to cover operational costs. The VC investment process involves several steps but is like the Angel process in many ways.

Look for firms that have invested in your type of business in the past and might be looking for new opportunities. VC firms get inundated with inbound companies looking for capital, so it is best to get a "warm" introduction from a mutual connection if possible. This is an area where local incubators or state Economic Development Centers may be able to give your company assistance.

I also highly suggest that you protect yourself when working with Venture Capitalists by hiring and teaming up with an investment banking firm to represent your interests, or at least hire an experienced CFO who has participated in the VC process previously.

Retaining control of your company while working with VCs can be challenging, as they typically seek equity and a say in decision making to protect their investment. However, there are strategies you can use to maintain a level of control while working with VCs:

1. **Align Interests with the VCs**
   ○ **Clear Expectations**: Set expectations with your VCs early about your vision and long-term goals. When VCs understand

that you are aligned with their desire for growth but also want
to maintain control, you can often find mutually beneficial
compromises.

- ○ **Define Strategic versus Operational Roles**: Make it clear that
  you will remain in charge of day-to-day operations, while they'll
  focus on providing strategic guidance and introductions. This
  reduces the chance that VCs will try to take over operational
  control of the business.

2. **Negotiate Equity Terms Carefully**
   - ○ **Keep Dilution to a Minimum**: VCs often require a significant
     percentage of equity in exchange for funding. Negotiating for
     a lower percentage of equity dilution can help you retain more
     control. Start by understanding your company's current valua-
     tion and the value you're bringing to the table.
   - ○ **Set a Cap on Future Dilution**: Establish limits on how much
     more equity you're willing to give up in future funding rounds.
     This gives you more control over the long term, even if the com-
     pany needs additional capital.

3. **Seek Noncontrol Voting Rights**
   - ○ **Class of Shares**: Create different classes of shares with varying
     levels of voting power. This can allow you to retain more voting
     power even as you give up ownership. For example, common
     shares might give you full voting rights, while preferred shares
     (often held by VCs) might give them financial privileges without
     as much control.
   - ○ **Founders' Shares**: Some companies give founders special voting
     shares, also called "supervoting" shares, which allow them to
     maintain control over major decisions despite owning less equity
     than investors.

4. **Set Clear Governance Structures**
   - ○ **Board Control**: Negotiate the composition of the board of di-
     rectors so that you have a majority or at least a strong presence.
     VCs often require board seats, but ensuring you have a seat at
     the table and perhaps a controlling or veto power can help main-
     tain your influence.

- ○ **Veto Rights**: As part of the shareholder agreement, you can request veto rights on specific matters, such as company direction, significant financial decisions, and hiring/firing of key executives. This can give you the ability to block decisions that might negatively affect your company.

5. **Use Milestone-Based Funding**
   - ○ **Tranches or Staged Investment**: Rather than giving away a large chunk of equity up front, negotiate funding in stages or tranches, based on the achievement of specific milestones. This can help you maintain control and prove your business model, thus reducing the risk of large-scale dilution early on.

6. **Avoid Excessive Control Terms in the Deal**
   - ○ **Limit Veto Power**: VCs often ask for veto rights over major company decisions, but you should aim to limit these rights. For example, you could agree to a veto on decisions like acquisitions or major strategic shifts but keep operational decisions in your hands.
   - ○ **Control Over Exit Strategy**: Negotiate for a say in any exit decisions, like mergers or acquisitions. You can seek to ensure that any exit strategy aligns with your vision and values.

7. **Stay Engaged in the Company's Culture**
   - ○ **Leadership Role**: Maintain your position as CEO or in a key leadership role. VCs typically prefer a strong, experienced leader who can drive the company to success. Ensuring that you remain the public face and voice of the company can also help assert your control.
   - ○ **Company Culture**: Emphasize the importance of company culture and leadership vision. VCs may be more likely to defer to your judgment if they see you as a strong and trusted leader, especially in the early stages.

8. **Understand and Leverage Your Negotiating Power**
   - ○ **Have Other Options**: If you have multiple VC offers or can secure alternative financing, this gives you leverage in negotiations. It signals that you're in demand and aren't desperate for funding, which can help you negotiate more favorable terms.

○ **Show the Value You Bring:** Remind potential investors that your knowledge of the market, your customer base, or your product gives you strategic insights that are critical to the success of the business. This can help position you as indispensable, even to VCs.

9. **Be Prepared to Walk Away**
   ○ If the terms become too favorable to the VCs at the expense of your control, don't be afraid to walk away. A bad deal can jeopardize not only your ownership but also your personal vision for the business. Standing firm on control may lead to better offers in the future.

The key to retaining control when working with venture capitalists is finding the balance between securing the capital you need to grow and maintaining enough ownership and influence to stay true to your vision. You will need to be a skilled negotiator and communicator, clearly setting expectations and boundaries with your investors.

Statistically, only around 10 percent of VC-backed companies will be successful (meaning they return the targeted return on investment for the VC fund). The speed of growth will be faster for VC-backed companies, with the top 25 percent of VC-backed companies reaching $1 million of revenue in approximately 1.75 years. For companies which grow organically, using grant funding, self-funding, and loans, the top 25 percent reach the same revenue in about 2.3 years. But the growth pattern for organically grown companies is more linear and consistent, versus the rapid, sometimes difficult to control growth of VC funded companies.[29] This dichotomy in success patterns is attributable to a couple of factors in my opinion. First, the pressure to succeed for a VC-backed firm is quite high, and success is defined as "generate a profit substantial enough to reward the investors," which can lead to unsustainable growth strategies, committing to a product or service too early, and sticking with a bad idea too long. Second, the definition of success for an organically grown company is different: Success is meeting payroll, staying in the black, and maybe being profitable on some timeline. But as long as the bills and salaries are getting paid in the organically grown company, it is "successful." If the organization needs to pivot or take longer to capture the market or find the right niche, that is OK. Organically grown companies are also more resilient during economic downturns and other financial challenges than VC-backed companies.

Initial Public Offering

Companies go public for a variety of reasons, but the largest of those reasons is to raise capital and legitimatize the organization to world markets. Once the process is completed, the stock becomes much more liquid, and after any lock-up period employees may be able to sell their stock, thus satisfying a second reason for the IPO: rewarding employees with a potentially significant windfall. Going public also increases the ability of an organization to access additional capital through bank loans and other sources. The stock can also be used as an incentive to attract new employees, or it can be utilized to acquire other businesses. In some cases, the substantial publicity generated by an IPO creates a significant boost for the business, driving brand awareness and prestige for the company.

In the United States, there are typically between 150 and 250 IPOs per year, although some years may see 400 or more, including the banner year of 2021 which witnessed an astounding 1,035 IPOs![30]

Take one of the largest IPOs on record: Rivian Automotive Inc. (RIVN) which went public at $78 on November 10th, 2021, establishing a market value of $66.5 billion! That market cap was higher than GM, Ford, or Honda. That valuation made even less sense considering the company recorded a mere $1 million in sales and a net *loss* of $1.3 million in the quarter before going public. So, how, you ask, can a company which is not profitable, and has admittedly modest sales, be valued at over $65 billion? Expectation. The public, and investors at large, were ready for the next Tesla, from both a consumer and investment standpoint. When Tesla went public in 2010, the price was $17/share. Within a short period, the price dropped to around $1.50/share. Some savvy investors loaded up on the stock at that point, and if they were willing to wait until 2020, could have seen 100× or more growth in their investments. Rivian looked like the next Tesla, and the investor enthusiasm was downright exhilarating. It's impossible to calculate a valuation on a company with net losses (unless one is willing to accept that the company has *negative* value!). During a brief surge to $129/share, Rivian's market value was a whopping $127 billion! Since that time, Rivian stock has now settled into a more realistic $13/share, reflecting a market value around $13 billion, or about ¼ that of GM or Ford Motor Company.[31]

What these examples illuminate is that the IPO represents the potential for an absolute home run in terms of wealth generation. But it can be a volatile and risky process. There are several hoops and controls on the IPO which usually prevent founders from capitalizing on the initial investor hysteria. Assuming the founders of Rivian were subject to a 6-month lock-up period, they would not have been able to liquidate their stock until May of 2022, when the stock had fallen to about $28/share. Still not a bad deal, as the current price is less than half that price.

An IPO will take significant time and money to accomplish. In order to even qualify to be listed on the Nasdaq, for example, the company must have aggregate pretax earnings in the prior 3 years of at least $11 million and show at least $27.5 million in cash flow for the prior 3 years or have an average market capitalization over the past year of at least $850 million and revenues in the prior year of at least $90 million, or have at least $80 million in total assets plus $160 million market capitalization and stockholders' equity of at least $55 million.[32] As you can see, IPOs are for seriously accomplished businesses. Each stock exchange has different levels of qualification and focus, with a goal of curating respectable listings. Think of any stock exchange as a private club, with exclusive membership requirements, initiation fees, and ongoing obligations to maintain a positive listing status.

Once the IPO is completed, your company will be obliged to file SEC reports and keep shareholders and the market informed about the company's business operations, financial condition, and management, which will take a significant amount of time for the management team and result in additional costs. If those obligations are not satisfied, you may be liable for fines. The management of the company will now be scrutinized, and some actions will have to be approved by the shareholders. Finally, information about your company, such as financial statements and disclosures about material contracts, customers and suppliers, will become available to the public (including your competitors).[33]

If there is any chance that your company will follow the path to an IPO, you should start thinking early about the way the organization should operate, which standards you will need to meet for inclusion in each stock exchange, and the necessary infrastructure and reporting requirements. Contact an industry qualified Investment Bank to understand the expectations, costs (typically 4–7 percent of the gross IPO proceeds[34]), and viability of this path.

The Now and Later Problem

So, we covered 14 different sources of capital, and you may be wondering why so much emphasis on finance and raising capital? If you just grow your business slowly, everything will be all right, correct? Maybe. If your product doesn't take much time to produce, for example less than a month, or your profit margin is extremely high, then you are blessed. But if not, then pay attention to this next section: The issue is what I call the "Now and Later Problem," which applies to any company which is growing fast, takes some time to produce its product, and doesn't have high profit margins. As your company grows, you will need to expand to meet the demand, including hiring more employees, perhaps larger facilities, more equipment, additional computers and materials. You will purchase those items and hire those people *Now* and have to pay for them immediately, including salaries, insurance, taxes, and invoices for equipment. Then, you will be able to get increased revenue (to pay for the new items and people) at some *Later* date. How much later? There are three delays: Onboarding, Processing, and Payment. Onboarding includes the time to hire and train people, receive new equipment, configure new computers, and get new facilities up and running. Processing is the time delay between getting all of those things up and running, and when you are able to deliver the higher quantity of product or services to meet the increased demand. This processing time could be developing new services or products, manufacturing, or other activities that your company performs in the process of delivering the goods. The final delay is the time between delivering the product and receiving payment. Some industries operate on NET-30 (payment due in 30 days), some are Cash on Delivery. How long will Onboarding + Processing + Payment delays add up to for your company? For BCT it averaged 1 month + 6 months + 1 month = 8 months. During those 8 months, the company was operating at higher expense but not receiving higher revenues yet. Thus, the Now and Later Problem is not just higher costs, it is higher costs for some amount of time. The faster your company grows and the longer it takes to deliver the product to the customer, the bigger the problem.

Let's take a simple example: Suppose your company has $12 million a year in revenue with 20 percent gross profit margin and projected growth of 40 percent for the next year. In order to meet that growth, you need to staff up, buy more equipment, and expand your facility. For simplicity, we will assume that the costs go up by 40 percent as well, maintaining your 20 percent gross profit margin. The Onboarding + Processing + Payment for your situation is 6 months. In January you will begin the expansion activities necessary to grow and begin processing customer orders that are 40 percent higher than the previous 12 months, expecting to get paid in July (January + 6 months). For those first 6 months, your expenses are also 40 percent higher than they were in the previous year, so you will actually be operating at a net loss for the first 6 months until you can get paid. Putting some real numbers into play, your company had $1 million of revenue per month last year with $800k monthly expenses (20 percent net profit margin), and you plan to grow by 40 percent this year, your anticipated monthly expenses will now be $1.12 million through June, but with only $1 million of revenue per month, so you will need $720,000 in the first 6 months in order to cover the higher operating expenses until you can start to receive payment on the higher volumes. This problem only becomes an issue, incidentally, if your company is growing faster (%) than your Net Profit (%). Here are the equations:

$$\text{Net Profit} = \text{Revenue} - (\text{COGS} + \text{Operating Expenses} + \text{Interest} + \text{Taxes})$$

$$\text{COGS} = \text{Cost of Goods Sold}$$

$$\text{Net Profit Margin} = \left(\frac{\text{Net Profit}}{\text{Revenue}} \right) \times 100$$

As I mentioned at BCT, our year over year growth averaged about 100 percent (meaning we doubled in size every year), while our margins varied significantly but averaged 20 percent, and our "Now and Later" delay was 8 months. When the company grew in 1 year from $10 million to $20 million in revenue, our now and later problem was over $5 million. Where could we get $5 million? We had to scrounge from other revenue sources like grants, leverage bank lines of credit and work with customers for favorable (up-front) payment terms. As long as your profit margin % is greater than your growth rate %, you don't have to worry about the Now and Later problem. But if your product and company represent an Elite Icon, then your rate of growth is likely to exceed your profit margin, and you are going to need additional funding.

Funding Conclusions

There are a lot of different ways to fund your company and keep it growing. We've only covered the common mechanisms; some others exist specifically in niche industries. My suggestion to you is to leverage as many of the mechanisms as possible which make sense in your situation. The more styles of funding you leverage, the better your odds of making it through the formative stages of your business and achieving long-term, durable success. Keep in mind the time frames and amounts of capital you can likely raise.

The top of Table 5.6 summarizes the smart money, "Stay Hungry" options which allow you to stay in control of your company and grow it at your pace while you figure out if your product is great or not. You can also *shrink* the company, if you determine there is a need to pivot or make some serious changes. The bottom of the table lists the "Fully Capitalized" options which are appropriate once your company is well defined, including a proven product or service, end-to-end operations, a reliable revenue stream, known costs of production and minimal risk. Taking your company into the VC or IPO world too soon can result in a loss of control of the company for you and the other founders, as well as greatly increasing the risk of business failure. That doesn't mean your product idea wasn't great, it is just that once you are in bed with multimillion-dollar investors, they will want to see a return on their investment.

To help picture the assorted opportunities, relative capital availability, speed of access, and impact on your company, I have provided Figure 5.3. The red line is where you potentially cross over into losing equity as well as autonomous control of your company. To the left of the red line is the "Staying Hungry" zone where you are in control. Passing to the right of the red line is venturing into "Fully Capitalized" territory, where you will have large investors in bed with you. It's OK to go there, once you have

Table 5.6 Summary of funding mechanisms

Funding type	Relative amount	Time to raise funds	Challenges to complete	Loss of equity	Benefits
SBIR/STTR	$$–$$$	Long (months to years)	Must write a winning proposal	No	Market need and customer are already identified
State grant	$–$$	Medium (months)	Must demonstrate a need	No	
Accelerators and incubators	$	Short	Must align with the accelerator or incubator	Sometimes	May provide access to additional resources and mentoring
Friends and family funds	$	Short	Can strain relationships and create workplace tension	Sometimes	Easy to get, but be careful
ESOP	$$–$$$	Very Long	Must be legally conducted, managed and audited	Yes	Win-win-win: Funds company, motivates employees, long term exit strategy
Crowd funding	$	Short		No	Will get direct feedback from potential customers
Angel investors	$–$$	Medium (months)	Finding the right Angel and getting them to fund your idea	Usually	Funding plus potential expertise and industry connections
Bank loans and LoC	$–$$	Short	Need to establish a credible relationship before you get into financial trouble	No	Helps cash flow management and builds a relationship to support long-term growth

Funding type	Relative amount	Time to raise funds	Challenges to complete	Loss of equity	Benefits
SBA loans	$-$$	Medium to Long	Complex process with challenging requirements	No	May be lower interest rates than banks
P2P loans	$-$$	Short to Medium	Finding a lender can be challenging	No	May be lower interest rates than banks
Venture capital	$$-$$$	Medium	Extremely competitive (< 1% of companies accepted)	Yes	Large cash amounts, possibly industry help
IPO	$$$$$	Long	Extensively regulated, complex process, expensive	Yes	Adds credibility to your company and the opportunity for individual exits

Relative Amounts:
$—Tens of thousands of dollars or less
$$—Hundreds of thousands of dollars
$$$—Millions of dollars
$$$$$—Hundreds of millions of dollars

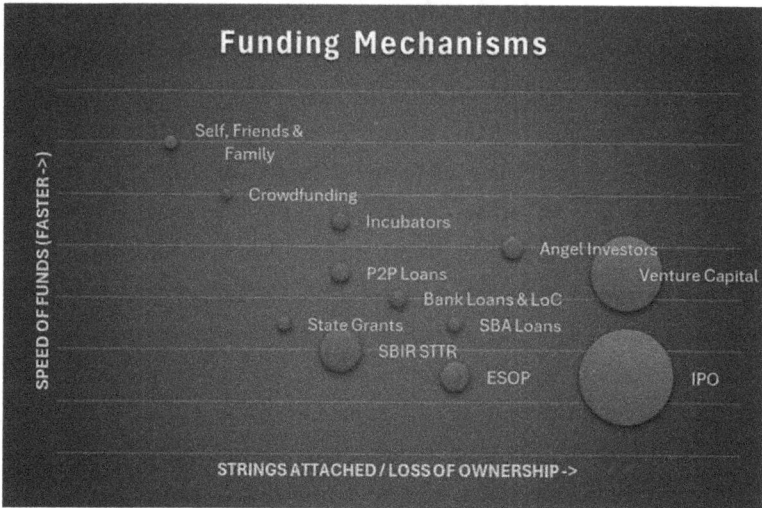

Figure 5.3 Comparison of funding mechanisms in terms of speed of liquidity, amount of funding to expect, and what strings may be attached

the details worked out and a plan to use the funds efficiently, become profitable, and not give up so much of the equity in your company that you lose control.

So, if you plan to get your business started *slowly and conservatively*, you could begin by leveraging a portion of your savings or some friends and family investment as a loan. Staying in Phase-0 (not paying any salaries yet, just a small group of founders, even moonlighting), you could establish a presence through setting up your website, building your company Myth, and developing some product concepts to spark interest. Proposing to some SBIR or STTR opportunities early gets a potential long-term funding mechanism in the pipeline, while you can start investigating the opportunities in incubators and state grants. As the company gets fleshed out, start the dialog with bankers to establish loans or lines of credit. Over time, and slowly in this process, you will be able to build your team and gradually add facilities. Yes, you will probably only experience modest growth and will be "Staying Hungry." If you can leverage this approach into a fully self-sufficient company, then you have avoided any dilution through outside investors and can fully retain ownership and control of your company. On this slow and conservative path, you will need to consider the need and methods whereby you can protect your Elite Icon concept from more aggressive interlopers while you build out the company.

On the other hand, you may need to pursue a more *aggressive* path: Start with an outstanding product concept, funded with a bit of self- and crowdfunding to establish interest, then approach an Angel Investor or VC firm with your Elite Icon concepts in exchange for convertible notes aka equity ownership. Upon securing the funds, you could then staff up more quickly, establish your facilities promptly, and make a big splash in the marketplace to capture maximum market share before competition can sprout up. You could delegate the task of securing other funding (SBIRs, grants, loans, and incubator funding) to one of your employees while you and the leadership team run the company on the capital you secured from the VC or Angel investors. On this path, you've sacrificed some ownership and control but minimized your time to market and may be able to dominate a Blue Ocean with your Elite Icon and have higher revenue and a larger, more lucrative company than if you had followed the conservative self-funded, bootstrapped approach.

The path you choose will be a combination of your and the leadership team's desires, and the market opportunities and time criticality of what your business product or service entails. Either path can work, as well as many other combinations. The key is to utilize as many of the available funding mechanisms as possible such that you are not reliant upon a single source that could choke or kill your business if it dries up or hiccups for some reason. Remember the biggest reason for failure: "running out of money, cash flow, and other financial problems." Leveraging multiple funding avenues and only spending when necessary to propel success will maximize your monthly bank balance and stretch your funds as far as possible.

At BCT we utilized self-funding, a lot of sweat equity, organic growth and SBIRs to get started, with low-cost facilities at an incubator. We used our limited funds to develop a few commercial products which we were able to sell in small quantities to bring in more revenue, attract additional interest from other customers, and help keep the company going. All companies should expect to reinvest early revenue to keep the momentum going and perpetuate more growth. Next, we expanded into state grants and established loans and lines of credit with a couple of banks. Before we had loans and lines of credit, we had to drain our savings and leverage personal home equity lines of credit from time to time in order to make payroll. Those were frightening times because if the company had not recovered, we would have been left unemployed, without savings, with a loan to pay off without income from the company (The Nightmare). My wife was very trusting and supportive through those events, and thankfully it all worked out OK.

Hopefully, this chapter has given you a good overview of potential capital sources, advantages and disadvantages of each, and enough information to proceed onward to put together a plan to fuel your growth. You will find that startup companies have a voracious appetite for cash, and keeping the checking account full ahead of cash needs will become a full-time obsession for at least part of the leadership team. The best advice I can provide is to not spend money purchasing anything or hiring anyone earlier than necessary. Once you commit to hiring someone or purchasing something, the money is as good as gone and whatever it is you purchased or whoever you hired needs to start helping bring in revenue.

As we will discuss in the next chapter, you can be extremely tactical in how you build out your team, facilities, and equipment to maximize the amount of time your company can operate and grow.

The future belongs to those who believe in the beauty of their dreams.
—Eleanor Roosevelt

CHAPTER 6

Building a Great Railroad

The time has come to dive into the nuts and bolts of the company structure and operations. This chapter will discuss the company legal formation and operating agreement, business systems including software and hardware that your employees will use to perform their daily work, the importance of the right level of bureaucracy, what to do versus what to buy, and overall, the vision of your company as a living, breathing, growing organism. We will also dive into facilities considerations, and what factors you should consider when evaluating potential locations and amenities. Just like a railroad, you want your company to run smoothly, like it's on polished rails, whether you are there directing traffic or away raising capital or on a well-deserved vacation.

The #1 principle which you should follow in setting up your business operations is *Preservation of Capital*: Do whatever you can to build out as complete and capable a company as you can imagine, using as little cash as possible, but do not be stingy on what you decide to fund. This may feel like a contradiction, but the subtlety is to choose carefully where you spend, and when it will have influence on your success. If spending a bit more will measurably increase your odds of success, then go for it! Ideally, you can quickly build out a fully operational business, with processes and systems to facilitate the work and an inspirational website and robust social media presence. All this which is impressive to customers and fully capable of delivering products and services—with money prioritized to the things that will accelerate your journey to becoming cash flow positive. Most likely at this point, you are operating in phase 0 (no revenue, no capital) or phase 1 and have some capital raised and perhaps even some modest revenue. But overall, the imperative is to demonstrate credibility to the outside world, including customers and potential employees. First the company must become a legal entity in whatever municipality and state you will be operating. Typically, it should take about a week to accomplish the steps to become a bonafide business entity.

Legal Formation

For basic situations, you can form your company yourself as an LLC by simply visiting your state website for Department of Revenue, generally looking for "form a new business" or "register a business." Each state's particular process and regulations will vary slightly, but overall, the process is for you to provide the registration information, pay a nominal fee annually or biannually, and receive a certificate of good standing and registration. While this is a simple 5-minute process in some states, other states are significantly more complex.

If you are not sure of the process, it is time to add an important member to the team, a paid by the hour Corporate Attorney. Look for law firms and interview corporate attorney candidates with experience and practice in entrepreneurship, small business and corporate law, employment law, lending and finance, and ideally industry experience similar to your business. While your attorney will certainly be able to assist with the details of registration of the business with the state as I outlined above, the more critical services they provide will start with drafting an Operating Agreement. Your needs for legal support will grow over time as your business becomes successful. Some business attorneys will work at a reduced rate with small business startups in exchange for a small amount of equity ownership on the cap table. It never hurts to ask if such an arrangement is acceptable.

Once you or your attorney have completed the state registration process, you can then obtain a Federal Employee Identification Number (EIN), the tax id for your business, consisting of nine unique digits assigned by the IRS. The web portal for obtaining the EIN is fairly straightforward and it takes about 15 minutes to obtain your tax id. You will use it for tax filing, opening any bank accounts, and obtaining any necessary licenses.

Boom! With a website visit to your state Department of Revenue and the IRS.gov website you have successfully registered your small business.

The most important part is the aforementioned Operating Agreement, which will document the key features and rules of your business' ownership structure. The Operating Agreement is one of the most critical documents you and your team will create, essentially spelling out how the owners will interact on legal matters and how changes to the company legal structure can be performed. Make sure the document addresses

- Member's ownership percentages. This is often referred to as the "Cap Table" meaning the table that specifies how much of the capital each owner owns as a percentage. It is often more convenient to reference a separate list of spreadsheets, especially if you plan to add ownership members later or envision employee ownership.
- Managerial powers and duties of the ownership group, often called the "Board of Directors." This section will define who can make what decisions, how managers may be replaced, appointed, downgraded, or upgraded.
- Profit distribution guidelines. How and when (upon what events) profits may be distributed. In most cases, the best summary for this section is "when the Board determines to distribute profit."
- Procedures to address disputes within the Board if they occur. You need a method to part ways as founders if things aren't working out.
- Options for one member to exit and sell his or her shares. You need to create an exit in case one of the founders needs to leave for professional or personal reasons.
- Procedures for company events like buyouts, liquidations, joint ventures, rollups, and other exits.

The Operating Agreement defines the founders' responsibilities, their authorities, financial distributions, and how to manage changes to the ownership group. Just like good fences make good neighbors, good operating agreements make good founders. If a dispute arises between the owning members, a strong operating agreement provides a prearranged method to resolve the dispute. On the other hand, if the operating agreement is weak in defining methods of resolution, the situation can degrade quickly and leave all parties in limbo. I know of at least one company that failed to have an operating agreement to define how the owners could resolve disputes and allow an individual exit. The process to separate the company became akin to a divorce proceeding with a drawn-out legal battle. Save yourself time, money, and headaches by addressing all these considerations in your operating agreement.

Next, let's put company ownership into the equation as we think about how we attract and retain great employees. The reality of career mobility in the twenty-first century is that employees have unlimited opportunities to pursue different career paths through remote, in-person, or hybrid arrangements. From your vantage point, you have to accept the fact that each of your employees can build a career with any number of different employers, so why should they stay with your company for the long run? *The Wall Street Journal* reported in December 2024 that "more than half of 20,000 U.S. workers surveyed in November said they were watching for or actively seeking a new job."[35] This reflects the opportunistic nature of today's employees. Who can blame them if they are staying aware of potential better opportunities to build their careers?

In Chapter 4 we discussed why employees might choose to join your company, including the company Myth, which hopefully appeals to your employees emotionally and pragmatically. The question is: Do they feel good about what your company is doing, and do they believe in your mission? Culture can help create an environment where employees feel safe, valued, and part of something important, even part of a work-family. What else can you offer those employees? All the things that we discussed in Chapter 4 affect employee satisfaction including the salary, benefits, culture, and employee ownership. But many of them will take great satisfaction or be frustrated by how the company runs—the Operations.

It makes a lot of sense that employees are interested in how the business operates and how they will fit into the daily operation and execution of your enterprise. These are the things that they are going to be doing for ±40 hours per week. Simply put, is your company a place that is fun and interesting to work at, where employees feel empowered and capable of doing their job well? Or is it a place where the rules, systems, and equipment get in the way of productivity? The next section explores this topic.

Business Operations

Business Operations = Converting customer needs into delivered products or services in return for money.

In a Retail business, the operations could be summarized into "Marketing" (putting ideas in front of potential customers), "Sales" (converting the customers interest into an order), "Buying" (obtaining product from suppliers or wholesalers), "Shipping" (delivering the purchased product to customers), and "Service" (all the support required to ensure smooth operations and customer satisfaction). In a Manufacturing business, the operations of "R&D" (developing new products), "Manufacturing" (building products), and "Test" (verifying product quality and conformance) could be added. All of those are the operations that define how your company runs.

Underpinning these top-level operations will be functions including "Accounting" (keeping track of money and assets), "Human Resources" (managing and developing people), and in some industries other operations such as "Quality Control," "Supply Chain," and others. Overall, how these suboperations all weave together will make your business either succeed or fail. Always start with the big picture, keep it simple, then add only what is necessary to complete the job.

Consider the day in the life of any one of your employees: They arrive at the workplace, record their arrival, enjoy a cup of coffee, check in with some colleagues, and begin their day. Through the course of the day, they will interact with each other, with customers, with management, and in many industries spend much of their time interacting with computers and machines to get their work done. What objectives should you have for these employees? Obviously, you would like them to be effective and efficient. You would like them to keep your customers happy, secure new revenue opportunities, control costs, and deliver the product or service of your company. And of course, you should want them to do it with as much Autonomy as possible. If you and your leadership team spend substantial amounts of time each day explaining what needs to be done, or how to do it, that indicates that your operations are not enabling autonomy. Such a situation spells frustration for all parties and indicates you have not built a great railroad yet.

How you and your management team structure the operations of your business will have a profound effect on the culture, employee satisfaction, bottom line profitability, and overall success of your new business. In day-to-day activities, the operations are what employees live and work with. If the operations are confusing, your employees will be confused, which will frustrate your customers. If the operations are innovative and efficient, your employees will be as well. When employees socialize with friends and family and are asked, "How is your new job?" the heart of the answer will come from business operations and culture. Both reveal much about the health of your growing organism.

Let's further consider the operations as being manifested into four constructs that you will utilize to build the operational foundation for your company: processes, software, equipment, and facilities. The goal is to create a system where these four pieces work together efficiently and seamlessly so that the employees enjoy their work, and the high-quality product or service is delivered with minimal cost or delay.

Processes

Business Processes are defined as structured, interrelated tasks or activities that you design to achieve the goals of your organization. They provide the building blocks of how work gets done by your employees in the context of transforming inputs (customer orders or desires, plus materials, additional information, and human effort) into outputs (such as finished goods, services, or information). This is the "value creation" which equates to why your company exists, and why it is special. Good processes are goal oriented, structured, and repeatable, cross-functional, and optimizable for improvement or adapting to changes in the marketplace. Most importantly, processes are documented in writing or pictures, such that employees can reference them (autonomously) to understand how their work should be performed and how it relates to other's work.

Take for example the Processes of a Starbucks coffee shop: There are processes defined and documented by the company to describe to employees how they should greet customers, how orders are taken and entered into the store's point-of-sale (POS) system, and how beverages should be prepared. Additional processes define how the kitchen and barista stations (equipment) operate, how foods are stored and prepared, how inventory is managed, as well as how employees are trained in those processes, hired, terminated and how their performance is evaluated. There are documented processes for accounting, store cleaning, how the store should appear, and how the equipment should be maintained. Who knew coffee could be so complicated? Not surprisingly, Starbucks is known to have a highly organized and detailed set of processes, a fact that has enabled the company to expand to over 80 countries with approximately 40,000 stores globally and annual revenue over $30 billion. The processes ensure that each store operates seamlessly and efficiently, that employees can quickly learn and repeatedly perform their tasks, and most importantly that customers anywhere in the world can order a caffe latte and expect to receive the same drink whether they are in Cleveland or Bangladesh. The processes ensure that each store operates seamlessly and efficiently, that employees can quickly learn and repeatedly perform their tasks, and equally importantly that customers anywhere in the world can order a caffe latte and expect to receive essentially the same drink whether they are in Cleveland Ohio or Bangladesh. Because of those processes, customers and employees are generally satisfied with the Starbucks experience, regardless of which side of the counter they stand.

Processes have always existed in businesses, originally as oral descriptions where experienced masters taught their apprentices how to work in their trade. With the advent of writing, some companies chose to document those processes on paper, while other companies preferred to rely on verbal communication and freedom of innovation. Around the middle of the twentieth century, standardization of operations became a focus for some international standards groups, and in 1947 the International Standards Organization (ISO) was formed in Geneva, Switzerland. As of 2024, the ISO has published over 23,000 documents covering various aspects of products, services, and systems from quality to environmental management to health and safety. Whether ISO is applicable for your company is for you to determine, however there is no doubt that your operations will run most smoothly if you clearly document the processes, but not over document or over constrain your employees. Achieving that balance is an art and a science.

Why did process management become a driving force of industry? Because many organizations attempted to operate without clearly documented processes were observed to have unpredictable results in their products or services.

Take for example the story of Zappos Call Center Chaos: In the early 2000s, Zappos was growing rapidly, but they did not have documented processes for handling customer service calls. Remember how we noted the Zappos culture for enabling employees to go above and beyond to remedy customer complaints? That culture extended to a "no scripts" policy for handling customer complaints. According to the legend, a customer called in to Zappos with a simple question about a pair of shoes. But instead of simply answering the question and ending the call, the Zappos customer service rep decided to really connect with the customer. They began chatting. The conversation went from shoes to life stories, hobbies, and even philosophical musing. Eventually, the call went on for 10 hours. Zappos management realized that going above and beyond for customers was great, but there needed to be some balance. So, while they kept their customer service ethos focused on personal connection, they did start to put some guidelines and processes in place—albeit without sacrificing their company culture of putting the customer first.

Boeing, the largest aircraft manufacturer in the world, fell victim to a lack of documented processes during the production and test of the first versions of the Boeing 707 jet, the world's first commercial jet airliner. As engineers worked to optimize the flight performance of the prototype 707s, they experimented with different wing flap designs (the hinged surfaces on the wings that help provide additional lift and can impart drag and improve stability during takeoff and landing). The flap design was constantly being modified by the engineering teams and implemented in different prototypes. For example, one plane might have version A of the design, while another prototype had version B or C of the design, and there was no standardized process for tracking which version was in use on which aircraft. Flight crews had no way of knowing which design was on the particular plane they were flight testing, or how those designs impacted performance, leading to surprises and sometimes dangerous outcomes during flight tests.

Since the beginning of the industrial revolution in the middle of the eighteenth century, businesses have attempted to find the right level of process control. A process which states "build the product however the customer orders it" is useless, because it leaves 100 percent of the operations to chance and preference of the customer and employees. On the other hand, a process which dictates every action and interaction for every employee with explicit timing and inflexible interactions will leave employees feeling devalued and frustrated, because it removes any opportunity for autonomy. The key to developing and documenting your processes is to follow a well-proven process!

Process Development Steps

- Define the Process Objectives (What is being accomplished, what is the input, and what is the output?).
- Map the process as simply as possible, using flowcharts, diagrams, or process maps (many tools are available online).
- Define one process per major activity, including all departments or roles in the company. For example, one process for "purchase parts and materials" covering the activities of everyone including designers, buyers, accounting, inventory management, and quality control.
- Evaluate the process you have drawn. Is it repeatable, specific, and measurable?
- Document the process, by writing a document which describes the process and who is responsible for which steps. The "who" could be roles (cashier, barista) or departments (sales, engineering, production, management).
- Trial-run the process by implementing it, training employees, and folding in improvements.
- Support the process with tools (software, facilities, and equipment, as we will describe later in this chapter).
- Keep the documentation up to date and provide a simple but effective method to continuously improve any process. A key concept that your organization should embrace is that of "self-correcting." If something is found to be wrong, empower employees to fix the problems in tangible ways.

There are a couple of human foibles which impact all of us to some extent. The first foible is an artifact of *Homo sapiens* learning to write and read some 5,000 years ago. Once communities became accustomed to the written word, those words somehow became sacrosanct and, in some cultures, immutable and inviolate. If something was written, it should be followed without hesitation. As processes became documented, the focus for many humans has been to become a slave to the written word, follow the instructions, and not consider what might be wrong or done better. Through this dedication to the written word, humans have lost much of their ability to look at the big picture and think holistically about complex problems. [36]

The second human foible is what I call dedication to tradition. Once something has been done a specific way, for example assembling a product, baking a cake, or running a business, that way becomes *the only way*. In many industries you will hear old-timers proclaim, "That is the way that we have always done it, because it works." The longer an organization exists, the more concrete and unassailable the business processes become, due to Institutional Complexity Creep, as we discussed in Chapter 2. Precipitating a change to the business operations becomes tantamount to changing the course of the Queen Mary: It takes time, coordination between many varied people, and substantial energy and dedication. As the founder of your new business, you are operating a small speedboat that you control, and steer wherever you desire. To be as efficient as possible, the goal is to keep your processes as simple as possible at first, then add complexity as necessary over time to address holes or issues which perhaps were overlooked in the original formulation.

Remember our discussion of your individual experiences being your superpower? Here is another opportunity to leverage your superpower. From your life experiences you have accumulated a wealth of knowledge that is unique and undeniably yours. Assuming you are starting a business where you have some passion to excel, you could overcome the two foibles listed above by applying your superpower. For your company, step back and think in the grandest terms possible about the BIG picture. Do not concern yourself with any of the millions of details but think instead of new ways that things could be done. Imagine if you were to throw all the historical methods out the window, ignore "the way we have always done it," then consider what might be possible. Perhaps the old ways can be made obsolete by leveraging a new type of software, or a new method of manufacturing? Could artificial intelligence dramatically rewrite the tried-and-true methods for your industry? How could robotics change things? If you have experience in this industry or business type, what have you observed that is wasteful or unnecessary? Things that the old-timers would cling to of course, but you could discard completely to revolutionize and create your own Elite Icon just by doing things differently?

One of my employers gave me a valuable lesson related to both of those foibles. It all came to light around 1997. This employer had a couple thousand employees assigned across a few dozen functional groups including various types of engineering, manufacturing, test, human resources, sales, accounting, health and safety, and many others. Executive management noticed that all those departments operated independently and documented their processes in diverse ways, to different levels of detail, essentially whatever each department felt was appropriate to manage processes and train new employees. The situation was comparable to a small city with dozens of independent little mom-and-pop businesses coexisting independently and without any consistency in how they operated. The company executives were unhappy about the inconsistency and decreed that all departments must document their operations with a standardized methodology. At that time, the company workload was light, and there were rumors of impending layoffs among the rank and file. Suddenly, department managers were tasking employees to each develop processes detailing processes including "the best practices" for each department as if it were a silo. In this way, each department assigned a handful of people to write the view of the process from their perspective, without collaborating with coworkers or integrating processes from other departments. As you can see, this was fertile ground for Institutional Complexity Creep.

Through this initiative, all processes were thoroughly documented and controlled. A simple activity such as "purchasing parts and material," something which required cooperation across several groups, became exhaustively documented in dozens of processes, from each department's viewpoint. However, none of the resulting process documents were a complete view or entirely correct, because each department made assumptions about other departments' activities! With company layoffs looming, employees became overzealous in writing expansive and thorough documents in order to stretch their assignment out as long as possible. Over the course of this effort, thousands of documents were created, which employees were then expected to follow to the T. Because of the mandate to include "best practices" and "lessons learned from prior problems" people might recall, the processes became overly dictatorial. Worse yet, the processes added new activities to eliminate errors and preclude accidents or issues. To make matters worse, rules and procedures were put in place which made updating or modifying any process document difficult and time-consuming. Of course, there were mistakes and inconsistencies in the first draft of the documents, but it was so difficult to make updates that people were reluctant to try. People would rather live with the problem or discreetly deviate from the broken processes.

As these processes were rolled out to approximately 2,000 employees, and eyes rolled, work slowed down, and in some rebellious corners of the company, those newly released documents were ignored. It was essentially a corporate mandated Institutional Complexity Creep! Employees grew frustrated because the documents were myopic views of the same singular activity taken from the vantage point of each department rather than a unified view of the corporate workflow. This was a clear violation of the guidance provided in step 3 of the Process Development Steps. Further evidence that the effort had missed the mark completely, this employer next set up an independent division of the company that was greenlighted to bypass or ignore any of the processes that it felt was overly onerous, to fulfill contract orders from budget-minded customers. The executives created a "fast lane" around all the complexity that had just been created! That turn of events further fueled frustration in other divisions as employees rightfully asked why they had to follow all the rules, yet people in this new "cost conscious" division were allowed to circumvent the rules. Other employees clamored to be transferred to the fast lane division.

When I started developing the process maps and documents for BCT, I leveraged my experience from that previous company. I vowed to keep the BCT processes *simple, cross-functional* (all applicable departments were included in any process), and *easy to update*. I made the simple assumption that we would hire smart people, and the processes needed only to explain the most critical parts of the workflow and the objectives. When I completed my process development effort, there were approximately 30 documents in total, focusing on the interactions between departments or roles, specifying what inputs were required, and what was produced. Over the ensuing 10 years as the company grew from 3 to 350 employees, some additional process documents were developed and released. When I left the company, about 50 total process documents were in use to cover the workflow of all the departments and all of the activities. Still a very efficient and understandable set of processes. Not perfect, but good enough to keep the company running well and enabling people to use their brains and creativity.

Thus, the golden rule of process development is to start simple, because over time the processes will only become more complex and restrictive.

The "easy to update" aspect is extremely important for reasons beyond just incorporating errors in early versions and evolving to match the reality of how people work. Your company and your workforce will grow as well, and if there is a need to pivot and change how the processes are conducted, an easy to update feature will enable your company to move nimbly, like a speedboat rather than the Queen Mary of my early employer. Giving employees latitude to shape and update the processes helps them feel empowered and enhances their job satisfaction and knowledge that they are "making a difference" (an important focus for Gen-Z and Millennials). These factors of "easy to update" and employee engagement create a **self-correcting** aspect to the company processes which will enable it to stay on the right path as people learn and grow. It's impossible to get the process definitions 100 percent correct on the first try but having a company which can correct its own errors is hugely powerful.

Philosophically, our approach was to hire intelligent employees, train them with the processes so that they understood the interactions with other groups, and allow them to use their brains to solve issues and suggest improvements. This philosophy is counter to some organizations, where overzealous executives and managers dictate processes to "error proof" the organization, disempowering the employees and eliminating their ability to innovate or act independently. In retrospect, I think that the simplicity of our processes and empowerment of employees to problem solve and innovate were not only a large part of building our inclusive culture of happy employees, but also a significant part of our business success in providing great products and services at attractively low price-points.

If your company is in an industry like manufacturing where process management is critical, you should spend some time learning about Lean Six-Sigma theory, 4S, and TQM. Alternatively, you can recruit onto your core team someone who has experience and can implement a lean, efficient set of processes. There are entire career paths (Industrial Engineering), organizations, and libraries devoted to these topics. But even if your company does not require process control, remember that even Starbucks publishes and maintains a thorough process suite to ensure the customer experience is uniform everywhere in the world, the business is profitable, and employees are well trained. Franchise businesses especially need well documented processes to become successful.

The key aspect you should consider when reviewing the processes that you develop is the *RIGHT level of bureaucracy*. If nothing is written down or mandated by processes, then chaos will ensue. If too much is written down, or what is required by processes is overly prescriptive, then the organization will be rigid and employee creativity will be stifled. You will know that you have achieved the proper level of bureaucracy when the employees are neither confused nor stifled, and the business operations are consistent and efficient. Having a flexible, self-correcting process system will allow you and your employees to adjust the level of rigor to get it just right. Have a daily walk around your company and ask people how things are going, they will let you know.

Business Software

The amount and types of business software you run in your business will be a combination of the nature of your operations, industry norms, and how you wish to differentiate yourself from the rest of the world. Business software may include functionality such as Computer-Aided Design (CAD), Timekeeping, Inventory Management, Enterprise Resource Planning (ERP), Scheduling, Point-of-Sale (POS), Customer Relationship Management (CRM), Accounting and Finance, Project Management, Collaboration and Communication Software, Supply Chain Management (SCM), and on and on. Software solutions will range from free to ultraexpensive, multimillion-dollar investments with hundreds of thousands of dollars in annual license fees. In short, you can buy, lease, or develop software for a myriad of functions and spend as little or as much as you can afford. So, where to start?

The key to developing your Business Software infrastructure is to review the Process Maps you developed in the previous section and attempt to find one piece of software that will perform all the processes and is also free. It is unlikely to be that simple, so you will have to work from that point to minimize the number of software systems and the cost of each, in balance with the cultural expectation that the software should facilitate your employees' work, not hinder it.

For some businesses, there just is not much software required beyond perhaps some timekeeping solutions, a POS system, and some accounting software. Other businesses, as we have mentioned, are software intensive. In any case, my advice to you is to look extensively for innovative software solutions that are affordable and sufficient to help your employees succeed and be happy in their tasks. This is another area to avoid being stingy. Spending a little extra on the right software could move your company from mediocre to Great. Cutting corners on software usually translates to needing to hire more people to make things happen, and people are more expensive than software. An example of effective application of business software is Amazon fulfillment centers, where software-driven robotics and AI are used for inventory management and order picking. These technologies reduce the need for human labor, maintaining high efficiency, eliminating errors, and lowering operating costs.

A tactic that we used at BCT was to "spiral develop" the software suite as the company grew. Take for example the task of parts ordering and inventory management. We started using a shared Excel spreadsheet. That worked fine when there were only a handful of employees, and it was virtually free. As the company grew, we signed up to a subscription based, simple inventory management system which would allow us to record what parts we had on hand, and place orders with suppliers and record costs, expected delivery dates, and other pertinent information. As I recall that system was about $500 per year to lease and operate, and it worked well through the point where there were about 30 employees, and we were building products for a dozen-plus customers. At that point, we researched the software industry offerings around what is called "Material Resource Planning": Software that tracks all your parts and material needs across multiple projects and organizations, tracks lead-times, helps anticipate shortages, facilitates ordering parts before you run out, as well as managing inventory and problem resolution. Software of this category can range from virtually free to millions of dollars to acquire. I searched the Internet, visited prospective companies who could provide (or custom develop) a suitable system, talked with other manufacturing companies and attended industry trade shows to see the latest developments. Eventually, I was able to identify a system which was affordable enough to fit within our budget, easy and fun for the employees to use, and had significant industry support including other companies participating in user groups. The biggest improvement was that it added significant automation, so that a small team could do the work of many people. It wasn't perfect, but it was a good combination of capabilities, affordability, and ease of use.

There are a myriad of options and opportunities to implement software solutions to boost your business efficiency, enhance employee engagement, and drive productivity. The opposite is also true, in that the wrong software can bring your organization and your employees to their knees. So be thoughtful about what you implement for software solutions. What we found worked at BCT was to select software which was easy to use and implement, automated and affordable at that time, and by our estimates would satisfy the growth of the company for at least the next 2 years. This strategy keeps expenses low and allows you to reassess and upgrade to the next better solution if and when the company outgrows the current system. Let the software do the boring mundane work, and free your employees for the creative and human-interactive operations.

Equipment

Much like software, the equipment you select will become a touchpoint for your employees and enable the efficiency of production and quality of your products. If you aren't an expert on equipment availability and the latest innovations, you should engage expertise from your employee base or find assistance online or at industry trade shows. Spending the time traveling to a trade show and exploring equipment options is an excellent way to quickly narrow down your selections and enable your company to be a fun and efficient organization. If you have employees with expertise in the equipment or operations which will be performed by the equipment, encourage them to participate in the investigation and selection.

Deciding whether to buy or lease equipment for your business is an important decision, especially when cash flow is tight. Leasing is the safest option, especially if you are not flush with cash in the bank. To help characterize your options in simplistic terms, I've provided Table 6.1.

If cash is tight, Lease It. If you are not sure you will use it, Lease It. This is especially true if you need flexibility or the equipment will require upgrading, maintenance, or replacement frequently. The typical right answer for a small company is to lease, especially if you are in Phase-0 (no revenue) or Phase-1 (limited revenue) and have the mindset to Stay Hungry.

As the company grows, a Loan to spread the cost of ownership while still building an asset base for your company becomes an attractive option. Once your company is flush and has capital reserves, just purchasing the asset and owning it may become the preferred option. The wrong choice is to spend the cash that you need to run your business day-to-day and pay your employees' wages.

The benefits of a purchase include potential depreciation write-offs and an increase in company value during a merger or acquisition.

Table 6.1 Equipment acquisition considerations

Factor	Purchase	Loan	Lease
Up-front cost	High	Low	Low
Long-term cost	Usually Lower	Higher	Usually Higher
Asset building	Good	Good	None
Cost of maintenance	Full	Full	Low or none
Ease of upgrades	May be difficult	May be difficult	Simpler
Preserving capital	Uses capital	Minimal capital outlay	Minimal capital outlay
Tax deduction	Depreciation	Depreciation	May be deductible
Business stage	Mature	Growing	Early

However, maintaining cash on hand is crucial. Therefore, leasing is often considered the safest option for major equipment acquisitions.

Facilities

With only a few exceptions, the choice between owning and leasing facilities is to always lease. The exceptions would be if the business requires ownership of real estate to function, or when a suitable lease option just doesn't exist. Owning real estate could be a smart move for businesses that require long-term stability, a physical presence in a specific location, or specialized space. A precursor to owning real estate is a predictable cash flow. However, before you commit to ownership, consider the costs, potential for appreciation, and most importantly the likelihood that your business could outgrow the space soon. If you do outgrow the space, you will then need to sell the real estate you have purchased, and perhaps have spent money to improve. If you do not have adequate cash on hand, you may not be able to afford a larger space, leaving your company in the unfortunate position of being stuck in a too small facility but unable to move someplace larger.

The Preservation of Capital rule here dictates that the smart move for every business is to begin the journey in a free space provided by an incubator or accelerator, and if those are not applicable, start in a coworking space such as WeWork or Office Evolution. An added bonus of these solutions is that they often provide services such as telephone answering and networking solutions to help your company build credibility. These options are especially useful if your company is pre-revenue (phase 0).

Once you have outgrown those options, team up with an experienced commercial realtor to help you find a great space to help your company move up to the next stage. Walk the realtor through your current facility or sit down with them and discuss your ideal solution. Factors to include in the search discussion would be:

- How much space each for offices, equipment, communal areas, and specialized spaces?
- What employee-centric spaces do you need, how much parking and other amenities?
- What factors will make your employees happy in the workplace?

- Are hard-walled offices, cubicles, or open areas preferred? How many bathrooms, break areas, lounges, and so on do you want?
- What physical improvements do you anticipate? Many times, the landlord will provide a "TI" tenant improvement budget as an incentive for tenants to occupy the space.
- How long do you anticipate needing the space before you would outgrow it?
- Is the location or appearance important to impress customers or investors?
- Would it be advantageous to be near other businesses?
- Are there any local zoning laws or regulations which apply to your type of business or would restrict your operations?

As you review these questions with your agent, be mindful that it is difficult to predict the growth of your company, especially if you are just starting out. To the maximum extent possible, you should (a) prioritize a low lease cost (minimizing cash flow), (b) select a space which satisfies the functional needs of your business, (c) make an outstanding impression on employees, customers, and investors, and (d) have flexible termination options.

What you find will be market driven. What might be possible to find in Oklahoma City might not exist in Los Angeles or might be exorbitantly expensive. What is available in Silicon Valley might not exist in other parts of the country. As we outlined in Chapter 5, some municipalities and states may offer grants to help you cover facility expenses. At BCT, we began our journey with a single office we rented from Office Evolution, then moved to a "free" incubator space, then as revenue started to come in, we worked with an experienced commercial real estate agent to find an affordable, 1,200 sq ft space that we could improve and lease for as little as 2 years, but with an option to extend. The 2 years turned out to be perfect, and we were able to move up to larger spaces for our growing team and pieces of equipment.

Once you do find a location which you think might work, ask yourself and the leadership team five questions:

- Will the employees be happy, or will they be disgruntled and quit?
- Will customers and investors be impressed (if it matters)?

- Will you be able to conduct your operations legally and efficiently?
- Is the cost affordable?
- If the company grows too fast or we don't need it anymore, do we have an option to terminate early?

Searching for, selecting, and customizing a space for your business should be exciting and fun, but it is also stressful. Putting together a team to collaborate with and share the burden will make the process smoother and more successful in the long run. It also provides an opportunity for employees to weigh in on particulars that they care about.

Depending upon your industry and ability to recruit a talented workforce, you may find it worthwhile (or outright required) to include special amenities such as indoor gardens, nap pods, on-site fitness centers, on-site daycare, creative lounges and chill zones, pet friendly spaces, soundproof quiet rooms, interactive walls or whiteboards, and on-site food and beverage options. Amazon has a puppy cuddling room at their headquarters. Yelp has a fully stocked beer keg tap room to encourage team bonding during happy hours.

The most creative workplace amenities are those that prioritize employee well-being, foster creativity, and provide opportunities for socialization and collaboration. They create an environment where employees feel valued, supported, and inspired to bring their best selves to work. When designing your office or looking for a lease space, consider what would work best for your team's needs and the culture you want to cultivate. Offering unique amenities can help recruit top talent, boost morale, improve retention, and impress customers.

Core Values Check

This chapter has focused on many aspects of getting your business up and running, as quickly and efficiently as possible. Time for a quick check-in on the key tenets of our philosophy.

First, review the proposed processes, software, equipment, and facilities for alignment with your company Myth. Suppose your Myth conveys a message of "cutting-edge technology." Do your facilities and processes support that Myth? Will customers visiting your facility and talking with your employees believe your Myth? Do your facilities, processes, and operations help build credibility for your brand?

Next, consider the culture you envisioned to create. How do the processes, software, and facilities support that culture and reinforce the key aspects of your desired culture? Will your facilities attract prospective employees who are Masters of their trade? Will the software and equipment enable the employees to work with Purpose? Will the Processes facilitate their efforts such that they can happily work Autonomously, and without feeling overly constrained?

Finally, does the amount of money you will be spending align with the phase of the company?

Great companies create an environment in which employees act like owners. They do this through clear communication, articulation of clear vision and priorities, coaching and openness to debate/discussion. I would argue that this type of environment helps people to be at their best—and helps the company to be at its best.

—Robert S. Kaplan

CHAPTER 7

Going Live! Launching Your Business

Through this point, we have discussed many aspects of creating your company, building a great Myth, how to go about recruiting a brilliant team, and enabling them to succeed in an awesome culture supported by informative but flexible processes and a dynamite facility! As noted in the introduction, your company will not grow in the order in which these chapters are presented, and often the way in which your company grows will surprise you and your cofounders. Every business startup creates a unique set of challenges, rewards, and surprises. In Chapter 6, we discussed how to go about developing the business systems, processes, facilities, and equipment to run your business—all very inward looking. In this chapter, we're going to turn the focus the other way, and look at what the customers, investors, employment candidates and the public will see when they look at your company. As illuminated in the introduction, the #1 reason for startup business failure is "poor product–market fit," and really all five of the top reasons businesses fail can be translated to "not getting the product or execution correct before running out of money." This chapter will focus on how to address that problem and determine whether your envisioned product or service is a good fit for the market, as quickly and cheaply as possible. The best way to find out is to put your company out there, assuming you can create your envisioned product or service perfectly, and if you were able to do that, would the customers be breaking down your doors to buy it? The idea is to get customer feedback to further refine what you think is a great idea for your business and allow your team to adjust course if necessary.

Time for a Website

At this point you have a solid idea for your Elite Icon opportunity, and you're refining the Myth, and starting to reach out to trusted individuals to recruit onto your team. Ideally, you do not have any large expenses yet, so you still have time to pivot if you need to as you learn how the world receives your product concept. You've thought about a facility, and systems to run your business, and what equipment you will need to be successful. Before you go too far, and before you start reaching out to customers, investors, or even bankers, you need to establish your presence on the world stage: the Internet. The reality is that when you introduce yourself or your business to anyone out there, if they are interested in what you have to say they will eventually reach for a smartphone or computer to look up you and your company and they may want to know your e-mail address. If you haven't taken the time to establish a quality presence on the Internet, your credibility is destroyed as soon as they look for you and can't find you. Or, if they find a "coming soon" or "under construction," you have just declared yourself not ready for prime time. If your website looks amateurish, they'll assume your business is just a hobby.

To build credibility for your business create a great website. Imagine what you want visitors to experience, spend some time looking for great content on the Web, and then see if it can be created. If you can publish a great website which aligns with your Myth, appeals to your target customers, and demonstrates that you are the real deal then you can build credibility. Without a website, you have no credibility, and you have lost your opportunity to make a great first impression. You may have a fantastic product idea, an innovative company concept, a good team, and a start on some funding. But the reality is that people do judge a book by its cover, and today's company "cover" is its website and social media presence. If you need some inspiration, check out the websites for Apple, Tesla, Spotify, Adobe, or SpaceX.

If funds are limited, you can make a very competent and complete website utilizing a high-quality webhosting "all-in-one" service such as Squarespace, GoDaddy, Bluehost, Dreamhost, HostGator, or a similar service. With these solutions, you can secure your domain name, create the website, host it, and market your business all from a single portal.

Some of those services will also provide a "branded" e-mail address to go with your domain name, as well as Ecommerce services if you need those for your business. To help you get started, many of them offer professional quality templates to get your beautiful site up and running quickly. Check the details of the service to confirm you are getting everything you need, including social media tools, e-mail integration, and even search engine optimization (SEO). Specific to AI research and generative AI results, you will want to make sure that your website and data have Knowledge Integration. This includes what is called "Schema Markup" (structured data) on your website to help search engines and AI systems better understand and categorize your content. This will include information like your company's name, address, phone number, and type of business. You should also create and maintain a detailed company profile on major platforms like Google, Wikipedia, LinkedIn, Stack Overflow, GitHub, and any specific to *your* industry data providers that contribute to AI responses. This is termed "Knowledge Graph Optimization," and this standard information is used by AI databases to categorize and leverage information about everything including companies like yours. Once your data are on the Internet, give it a few weeks to percolate, then start running queries through search engines and generative AI sites to see if your company is showing up as it should. If not, work with your provider to enhance the exposure for your information.

If all that website jargon just confused you, or you want to make the biggest splash, then hire a website design company, preferably near your location so that you can meet their team face-to-face and convey your company's business, product, culture, and Myth clearly. Review their industry experience and look at their portfolio. Is their previous work attractive and appealing? Ask them about AI, SEO, and CMS (content management systems) that they will use to make sure your site is maintained well and shows up high in potential customers' search results. Obviously, you want to discuss budget, development schedule, support, and ongoing maintenance costs. Getting your website up quickly, aligned with your product or services, reflecting your Myth, is critical. This website is likely how many people will form their first impressions about your company, so this is a place to spend enough to achieve the most professional, captivating website you can afford.

At BCT, we went through about four website versions over a 10-year period. We started with a site that was basic and cheap (as I recall it was something that George and I put together with some free website design software), and it looked awful. And we did not get much inbound interest from anyone, not surprisingly. Our company was being judged by our website, and the results reflected what we spent: nothing. On our second and third versions, we were able to afford a local professional website design studio to develop the content, host the site, and provide maintenance and security features. When we designed those websites, we got inspiration from competitors' websites not only in our industry but also from innovative companies in other industries. The first and second versions are shown in Figure 7.1, illustrating the evolution of our company branding. The first version was mostly text, with one static picture. The second version had scrolling pictures, interesting graphics, and a variety of colors and interactive features to keep visitors engaged. People don't want to read things on a website, they want to be entertained. The fourth version (currently in use) is even more interesting.

When you have a moment, visit a few Las Vegas casino hotel websites. Visit www.venetianlasvegas.com and think about how you react to the images, layout, and messaging. Next, visit www.oasisatgoldspike.com and compare your reaction. Both hotels are in the hospitality industry in Las Vegas, but they carefully choose a style and message to convey to their target audience. In essence, their website is conveying the company Myth. If you want a couple more, try www.circuscircus.com or www.bellagio.com. Clearly, some of those websites cost a lot more to develop and maintain than others, but you would be surprised at what you can achieve with a little creativity and vision.

If you are curious, take a moment to look over the BCT website at www.bluecanyontech.com. Scroll up and down a bit to get the flavor of the site. I think you will find that it aligns well with the Myth I discussed in Chapter 3. The website becomes interactive as you scroll around, it conveys sophistication, capability, and has some killer imagery of space, satellites, and cool hardware. The web developers leveraged the latest design capabilities to make the website as interactive and stimulating as possible. We found that the longer we could keep potential customers engaged, the more likely they were to initiate a dialog with our team and

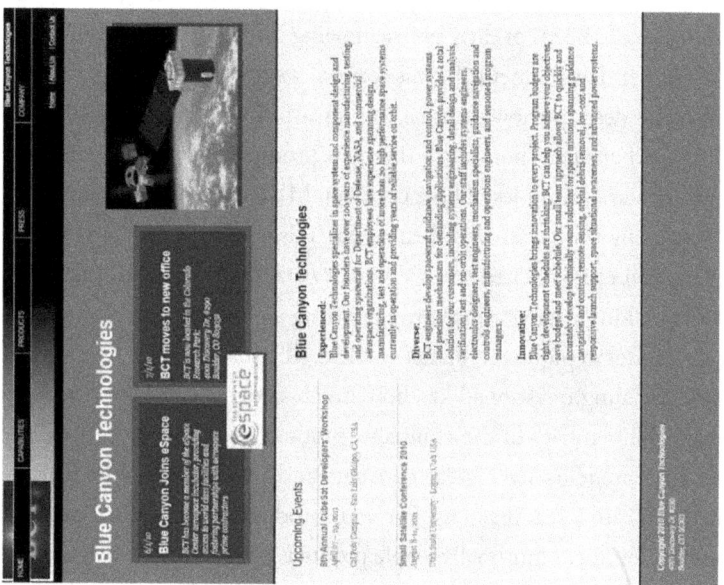

Figure 7.1 BCT's first (left) and second (right) websites

eventually convert to a sale. Once our website looked professional, the world *believed* we were legitimate. As a company, we did not change that much between the website iterations, but our *image* changed overnight from cheap and clunky, to sophisticated and technically advanced. As superficial as it may be, the world will continue to judge companies by their website, until they get to know them better, but oftentimes that first crucial sale happens because the website is rock solid.

If you are on the "Staying Hungry" path and do not have your products or services completely fleshed out and ready for shipment, hold off on aggressive social media or other marketing until everything is more mature. Having a website up and running gives your company credibility for any inbound interest, potential customers, or investors. That's enough for now, and you can switch gears to get your products and services fleshed out.

Minimum Viable Product—The MVP

Much has been written about the minimum viable product (MVP), a basic version of a product that includes only the essential features needed to meet the core needs of early users, allowing for feedback and validation before further development. In this section, we're going to expand on it a little bit and describe how to use it to jump-start your company, bring in funding, and create a shortcut to the right product. We will also examine a couple of stark examples of how useful an MVP can be when used right, and how badly things can go when an MVP is skipped.

Have you ever watched the TV show *Shark Tank*? Many of the entrepreneurs making presentations are exhibiting a prototype, first of a kind, concept model to pique the sharks' interest. The sharks are crafty, though, and ask revealing questions like "how much sales do you have?" to help ascertain the maturity of the company, product, and opportunity. Many of the entrepreneurs have great concepts and just need money to turn their dream into a real business. For your product or service is it possible for you to develop a minimally viable product, or even just a shell of your product concept, to gauge interest from the world in what you're offering? Each business and industry are unique, but I will share with you that when we attended our first industry trade show and launched our first website, BCT did not have any *complete* products. We had some crude prototypes of our product ideas with plans on what we thought we would do next, but we were carefully saving our capital until we were sure what the customer community wanted.

One of the ways we got customer feedback to identify our Elite Icon was to put up a booth at industry trade shows. We would display carefully protected prototypes enclosed in display cases where they could be seen but not held. Having face-to-face discussions with potential customers gave us excellent information to confirm what we had gotten correct, and where we had missed the boat. Having real "products" on display made our company appear more mature than it was, but we knew we could deliver the products, once we had figured out what the customers *really* wanted. The key is to spend the Minimal amount possible to create a product that is viable *enough* to not destroy your reputation yet enable you to get feedback from real-world users. Key concepts: minimal amount of schedule and money, capable enough to establish credibility, not so lacking that your reputation is wrecked. Endeavoring to describe a nonexistent product to a customer is a real challenge and can be downright awkward. The MVP gives you something tangible to reference and guide the discussion with your customer or investor.

Another common issue that the MVP overcomes is what I call "creator's goggles": Somebody comes up with a new product or service idea, and they completely fall in love with it, but can't (or refuse to) see the flaws or mismatches with what the customer truly needs or wants. The cure for creator's goggles is to develop and build enough of your product or service, get it in front of potential customers, and get their raw, honest feedback. Spend enough time and money to build an MVP in order to find out if your idea has merit, or maybe needs a bit of adjustment, or just plain sucks.

Let's review the history of Uber.[37] When Garrett Camp and Travis Kalanick created the first Uber Beta App in 2010, called UberCab, it was simple and would merely enable a person with a smartphone to "hail a cab" rather than needing to make a phone call. It was essentially a premium car service, with typical costs of $100 and up for a single ride, and only in San Francisco. The app was designed to be intuitive and allow users to see available cars nearby, request a ride and track the vehicle's arrival. Payment was processed through the app, eliminating the need for cash or a credit card reader in the vehicle. It was a simple, well-thought-out but basic idea, with the key innovation of combining GPS tracking and a real-time payment system in mobile app. Industry estimates are that gross revenue for the first year of Uber was around $300,000. Expenses for that first year are not publicly known but are estimated at $1 to $2 million. Capital raised included $200,000 in 2009 and $1.25 million in 2010, modest amounts, which I would characterize as "Staying Hungry." Through that first year, the team incorporated feedback, navigated regulatory challenges, and kept building features into the app, using San Francisco as their test market.

In 2011 and 2012, the company rebranded itself as "Uber," experimented with different pricing models including "UberX," a more affordable option for nonluxury cars, making Uber more accessible to a wider range of customers. They also introduced a service called "UberTAXI" which allowed users to book regular taxis through the app, effectively turning traditional taxis into part of the ecosystem. As the concepts gained popularity, Uber was able to attract significant investment to scale the business, including $11 million from a Benchmark Capital led Series A round in 2011. The service was able to expand into other U.S. cities and subsequently internationally. By the end of 2013, Uber had expanded into 35 cities around the world. Uber stayed hungry while they figured out the product and revenue model, then went for big funding once they knew their path.

By 2014, Uber had disrupted the transportation industry and become a household word synonymous with ridesharing. The company was able to raise billions through high-profile investors like Google Ventures and Goldman Sachs. The development team continued to evolve the business model, introducing new features in the app and addressing customer concerns about security and quality.

Somewhere along the way, UberTAXI got phased out, because it wasn't a viable product that fit into the rest of the ecosystem. Problems included resistance from the Taxi industry, lack of quality control and service inconsistency, and pricing issues trying to make the app incorporate the metered fare system of traditional taxis. The point here is that the Uber team tried something, and when it didn't work, they dropped it and moved on to better ideas. After UberTAXI was phased out, Uber continued to innovate with several other products and services, such as:

- **uberPOOL** (2014), which allowed riders to share rides and reduce costs, making the service more affordable.
- **Uber Eats** (2014), which expanded Uber's model to food delivery.
- **Uber Freight** (2017), a platform for transporting freight and goods.
- **Uber for Business** (2015), offering transportation solutions for companies.

Additionally, Uber continued to perform research and innovate in areas like autonomous vehicles, electric bikes, and flying cars, and the company kept expanding its global reach.

Now, imagine that Camp & Kalanick had not taken this development path. Suppose they had not chosen to frugally spiral upward by building a more and more viable product as the company became successful, re-investing revenue to make the service ever more capable (and discarding capabilities that fell flat on their face like UberCab and UberTAXI). Instead, suppose that Uber had come up with just a concept to provide just premium, black car services and UberTAXI, but never created a Beta App or tested the market? What if they had developed an amazing business plan, Fully Capitalized at $100 million for development, and spent all the money to roll out UberCab and UberTAXI worldwide? They would have wasted millions of dollars developing the wrong thing. Sure, they would probably have figured it all out, but would Lyft have become the dominant? As of this writing, Uber has a market capitalization of $140 billion, versus Lyft's $6.7 billion.[38]

And how did the founders fare? Travis Kalanick sold his stake in Uber for $2.8 billion in December of 2019. Garrett Camp, as of July 2024, owned approximately 3.22 percent of Uber, valued at around $4.53 billion. Now, admittedly Uber was exceptional, but this proves the point that developing the product slowly, staying hungry, figuring out the problems, THEN going big can work out just fine for everyone including the founders.

Contrast the minimal viable product approach of Uber to the strategy of Bird Global, Inc. electric scooter rentals, founded in 2017 by Travis VanderZanden, a former executive at Lyft.[39] The business model is an electric scooter sharing service which allows users to rent e-scooters via a mobile app. The company raised $15 million in 2017, shortly after the company launch, and another $400 million in 2018, then another $550 million in 2019, and more in 2020 and 2021. Somehow, the market valuation at that time rose to around $2.5 billion, making it one of the first so-called unicorns in the micromobility sector. The money raised through 2018 was spent on more scooters to expand across the United States into hundreds of cities, fund technology development, and glitzy marketing. Competitors to Bird Rides included Scoot (founded in 2012), Lime (founded in 2017), Spin (founded in 2017), and others around the world, making the e-Scooter business a vicious Red Ocean.

As early as 2019, Bird Rides was encountering resistance from city governments, regulatory challenges, and safety criticism. Local governments started imposing restrictions to block the scooters and clean up the mess of scooters littering the sidewalks of their cities. Financially, the business model didn't close: The problem was that to be attractive to the consumer demographic (younger people), the rental costs needed to be very low. However, because of the billions of dollars invested, the necessary ridership would need to be enormous to achieve a profit, even if Bird could offer rides at $3 to 4 per mile. Another problem encountered from an early stage of the company was that customers frequently experienced crashes, resulting in lawsuits against the company.

Overall, the financial performance of Bird Rides, Inc.[40] has been horrific:

- 2019: Around $100 million in losses.
- 2020: Around $190 million in losses.
- 2021: Around $100 million to $120 million in losses.
- 2022: Estimated over $300 million in losses.
- 2023: $25.5 million in losses in Q2 alone, with similar losses likely for the rest of the year.

So, what can be learned from the tale of two transportation companies? The Uber leadership team chose to develop slowly, test the market with a good enough MVP that was sufficient to test the waters and get user feedback. The user feedback was crucial in honing the product and guiding the team to the true pain point that needed to be solved: Public transportation options were very limited and, in many cases, inconvenient or downright unsafe. The Uber strategy was wise, because it was frugal and grew only as necessary to follow customer demand. As Small Biz Survival said in 2017 "Follow the Money,"[41] meaning that business leaders should see what parts of their business generate revenue, and expand upon that. Make changes to optimize the revenue in that area and eliminate things that don't generate revenue. That's what Uber did quite well. Customer demand was strong for Uber, Uber Eats, and uberPOOL because the offerings were innovative and solved a problem. UberTAXI wasn't popular (didn't generate much revenue and created customer confusion), so the leadership team phased it out. You must be brutally honest with the feedback, even if the feedback says your darling baby is ugly.

Lyft followed Uber into the Blue Ocean a couple of years later, and it turns out there's enough room for two strong successful companies, each with a unique company Myth and niche. Lyft is substantially smaller though, demonstrating the effect of the first to market advantage which Uber captured.

Remember in Chapter 2 when we introduced the Elite Icon? The four things that make up an Elite Icon are Commercially Viable, Differentiation, Value Creating New Demand, and Passion. Let's think about how Uber and Bird Rides compare with respect to these four categories, in Table 7.1. Uber clearly exhibits high marks on all four factors and is thus an Elite Icon. The issue with Bird, however, was that so many other companies were competing in the same space, and the company raised billions of dollars in capital, which made the product commercially *unviable*. If

Table 7.1 Uber versus Bird

	Uber	Bird Rides
Value creating new demand	High value, high demand	Possibly high
Passion	High	High
Differentiation	Very unique	Lots of competition
Commercially viable	Yes	No

Bird had developed a business model which would support ultralow-cost rental rides, or somehow differentiated themselves from the competition, they might have stood a chance. Instead, they've lost lots of money for many investors.

The recommendation from these stories is to develop your product with as much customer feedback as you can obtain along the way. Apply the criteria introduced in Chapter 2 to project whether you can actually be profitable, including the invested capital. The lesson from Chapter 5 on Getting funded is that the more outside capital you accept, the more you lose control and become committed to whatever concept you sold to your investors. Do not assume that your great idea is perfect, even if you are able to convince a large group of investors to give you millions of dollars (or billions like Bird). Regardless of how you secure capital, use it wisely and be willing to experiment, learn, iterate, and spiral develop your way into a true Elite Icon.

Failing Fast and Other Best Practices

Nobody is quite sure who coined the term "Fail Fast," but it was popularized by Eric Ries, the author of *The Lean Startup* (2011), an excellent read. It is like the MVP, except that Fail Fast can extend to *how* you do business, permeating your entire organization. Eric espoused the concept of testing ideas quickly, learning from failures, and adapting rapidly to feedback from users, developers, and laypersons. Moving quickly through this cycle of iteration helps minimize waste, keeps the development team engaged and focused, and gets your product to market faster than the competitors, ideally. If an idea isn't working, it's OK to abandon it and pursue concepts which are more promising. Developing a fun and innovative workplace which utilizes different ways of creating products or services can be the whole reason that a company is successful in the long run. Try new things and learn what works and what doesn't work.

Unfortunately, in many arenas, failure carries a heavy negative connotation. But in developing a product, a service, or a business, failure is how you learn and discover what will work, and thereby become successful. If your team can view the failures as a way to learn, make improvements, iterate, and improve quickly, they will save money and time. The key to this is to get through that process before you commit to a solid plan. Premature commitment can occur when you get a big bomb of cash, such as via Venture Capital. It can also happen if you fail to create a prototype of your product and service and never solicit customer feedback.

At BCT, we embraced the MVP for our products and Fail Fast for our production methods. It was a companywide mentality, and we also empowered our engineers to use rapid prototyping to test out concepts, using affordable 3D printers. Sometimes, we would spray-paint those 3D parts and take them to trade shows as if they were actual products. Most of the time, customers wouldn't even ask, they assumed the pretty hardware inside the enclosed glass case was real, not 3D printed. Being able to look at the hardware encouraged a dialog between our team and the prospective customers. We also invested extensively in automated test equipment, simulation software, and encouraged everyone to take part in assembling and testing new products, all of which helped foster the culture we wanted to curate. Specifically, we wanted everyone to feel safe and empowered to try new things, explore new ideas, incorporate what worked, and dismiss what didn't work.

In some cases, failing fast meant that we found out that what we thought would be a great product or way of doing business was a real dud. We found that out quickly before spending a significant amount of money or time and then moved the team on to other ideas. Using these approaches, we left any potential competition in our dust.

Another company famous for the Fail Fast approach is SpaceX. From the beginning, founder Elon Musk and the team adopted a mindset of rapid prototyping, where they designed and built rockets quickly, tested them, and learned from the results. The early rockets (Falcon 1) went through multiple failures before achieving success. The company's willingness to launch and test rockets, often under conditions of financial strain, allowed them to gather real-world data and make improvements. This approach would have been too costly for traditional aerospace companies but was central to SpaceX's model. Falcon 1 had three failed launches before achieving success on the fourth attempt in 2008. Each failure provided valuable information that helped SpaceX refined its designs. There are stories that if the fourth launch had not been successful, the company would have been out of money and had to shut down operations and file bankruptcy.[42]

Besides failing fast, you can develop other approaches applicable to your company which will assist your growth and improve your odds of success. One method which assisted us at BCT was "Automation Everywhere," with the idea that anything which was mundane should be automatic. We didn't like the idea of paying smart people to perform routine, mundane tasks. Product testing (which was repeated on every piece of hardware we built and shipped) was automated so that a human could set up the test, push a button on a computer, and come back later for a completed test report. Some manufacturing and assembly steps could be automated with equipment we purchased from various suppliers or in some cases built in house. The culture that we embraced, and I advocate for you to do the same, was that employees are smart, and should be taking care of things that require brainpower. Mundane, repetitive tasks should be automated and handled by machines. Adopting this mentality and communicating it throughout the company tells every employee that you think they are valuable.

The key to enabling your company to be lean and efficient, as we're describing in this chapter, is to think about everything that happens as part of a big organism, everything works together. Don't just dwell on the details, rather look at the big picture, and keep in mind that your employees are your most expensive and your most powerful resources. Do not squander your most important resource on mundane busy work. Engage them in finding ways to make the company become more innovative and efficient. Finally, how might AI change your industry, your business, the operations of a single department in your company, or even eliminate tasks that humans are paid to perform currently?

Pitching to Customers and Investors

When it comes to high pressure situations, nothing quite beats the experience of pitching your business concept to prospective customers and investors. At first, it will feel like you're an actor playing a part in a surreal Hollywood B movie. That's perfectly normal. With repetition and an open mind and accepting feedback from your audience including non-verbal cues, you will improve quickly. Practice first with a friendly group of reviewers rather than waiting for the big opportunity to see if your material and pitch are great. Here are some recommendations to improve your presentation quality:

- Decide on the *Message* you're trying to deliver and stick to it. You should have a clear goal in mind for what you intend to accomplish with the presentation.
- Be able to briefly dive deep if there are questions but rely on the presentation as an anchor to guide and control the discussion and keep to the Message you selected in #1.
- Do not make your presentation overly detailed, but do make it *visually appealing*, informative and reflect the Message you're delivering. In presentations, if your audience gets lost or confused, you've ruined your opportunity to impress and convince. Instead, they are trying to figure out what's going on.
- Arrive early in time to set up and make acquaintances before presenting (perhaps build some allies in the audience?) Be *enthusiastic*, but comfortable in yourself (meaning, don't pretend to be someone you're not). Dress comfortably but appropriate for the setting and in keeping with your industry norms.
- Open strong, to *capture everyone's attention*. Everyone has short attention spans in this era. Consider starting with a startling statistic or an interesting image, or attention -grabbing video.
- *Tell a story.* People love to hear stories. It could be personal, about a brand, or previous experience or even a story about consumers, to support the Message you established in Step #1. It could be personal, about a brand, or previous experience or even a story about consumers, to support the Message you established in Step #1. Stories connect with people much more than statistics, figures, quotes or even academic results (all of which are important to support the Message). Steve Jobs was famous for framing Apple's newest innovations in stories of revolutions, "changing the whole computer industry," and "changing the music industry." These were stories of change that brought the product, the consumer, and the exciting times of change together and made the audience embark on a journey. You could tell your audience how you got where you are, and what makes

you believe in your business. Keep it short, but interesting so that you can make an emotional connection with your audience which they'll remember long after your fancy diagrams or bullet points in PowerPoint.

- *Interact with the audience* to build trust, solicit their feedback and connect with them. The last thing you want is the audience getting bored or inattentive. Make eye contact, smile comfortably (not creepy), and look to different parts of the audience routinely.

- If you get a question you can't answer, *admit it*. Do *not* attempt to guess or lie. Just admit you don't know, but you can get back to them with a follow-up (and make sure you do so). Also, this question may lead to your opportunity to seize the moment.

- Seize the Moment: At some point in your presentation, someone in the audience is going to ask you a question which may feel in the moment as if it were the question you'd prefer they not ask, such as, "What problems have you had?" or "Why aren't your sales stronger?" You need to respond to this question with the reason that you are talking to the audience in the first place. If possible, explain how they can help you with the problem, sales issue, and so on. Essentially, you are trying to convert the audience into members of your team to work with you. Explaining how both parties will benefit is a key to making this conversion.

- Appoint someone from your team to *take notes* (for two reasons): First, you need to make sure you respond to all requests for additional information. Secondly, you need someone who can observe the audience's emotions and reactions to your presentation. The information you gather by *observing reactions* can help you refine your future presentations or guide you to make strategic follow-ups to seal the deal.

At BCT, we spent a lot of effort polishing presentations and developing standard material that supported numerous meetings, new business efforts, and eventually acquisition presentations. One rule which was effective when we were starting out was the Guy Kawasaki 10–20–30 rule, which states that for a general presentation, you should present 10 slides, in 20 minutes, using 30 pt font. Whenever possible, use pictures instead

Figure 7.2 A BCT presentation from 2014 showcasing our growing company of 12 people

of words, like the example in Figure 7.2. People often prefer pictures over text due to short attention spans and a lack of time or interest in reading.

The 10–20–30 rule means 10 slides to allow presenters an ample amount of space to summarize the information and whet the audience's appetite for additional information. More than 10 slides, the audience may lose focus and doze off. A period of 20 minutes is how long you should present, with ideally 40 minutes of Q&A follow-up from an interested audience. A 30 pt font means that everyone can read the presentation, even from the back of the room.

Your presentations can become less overview and more specific as the company grows and you hone the message. You can decrease the font size and increase the number of slides to more effectively address important topics in greater detail.

In 2015, when BCT was starting to book more and more customers with an expanding portfolio of satellite hardware products, we were invited to Toulouse, France, to present to Airbus Defence and Space, a major player in the European satellite industry with some 34,000 employees that had delivered over 70 satellite systems. We were over the moon to be invited for this opportunity, and spent a lot of time deciding what information we would present, and who would travel on this expensive trip.

Because this was a big opportunity, we decided that we should send four people on the trip: Steve as the chief technical officer to present the mechanically awesome technical details of our exquisite products; Dan as the technology wizard and chief storyteller; Gary as the brilliant electrical engineer; and myself as the facilities, production, and test expert. By sending high-ranking people from the organization, we were telling our prospective customers that we were serious about the opportunity. In the days leading up to the trip, we each worked individually to assemble and polish each of our presentations. During the long flight over from Denver to London, we were comparing notes on our presentations and discovered that Dan was still working on his presentation, but he promised to finish it as soon as he got to the hotel. There were some weather problems which delayed our flights, and we ended up stuck sitting in Heathrow Airport for most of the day, then flew late that night to Toulouse, France, and landed in the middle of the night. We were inexperienced travelers, and it took a while to secure transportation, communicate with the taxi driver in our Ameri-French to direct him to our hotel, and eventually get to our rooms and crash for a few hours' sleep.

The next morning, we all met in the lobby, dressed in our newly purchased suits with our laptops in hand ready to go to meet our prospective big new customer. We called for a taxi and loaded into the small sedan: one person up front, three in the back, with Dan sitting on the "hump" in the middle of the back seat. As soon as we started off, Dan pulled out his laptop and started working on his presentation! With the weather delay and late night, he hadn't had any time to complete it yet, so there he was with his laptop balanced on his lap (of course!) and asking one of us to hold a mousepad so that he could use his mouse while he worked on the presentation.

Toulouse was founded by the Romans and was the capital of the Visigothic Kingdom in the fifth century, long before cars were invented. To say that the roads twist and turn in downtown Toulouse is a huge understatement. As the taxi driver sped down narrow bumpy alleys and around tight corners, Dan kept losing control of his laptop or mouse and started swearing at the taxi driver in frustration. I'm hopeful the driver didn't understand English. It was a 30-minute drive to the Airbus facility, which turned out to be just enough time for Dan to reasonably complete his presentation. When we all presented our material to the Airbus team, the information was well received, and Dan's ability to tell great stories and weave a compelling technical presentation really blew the customers away. He has an uncanny ability which combines technical wizardry with an ability to make the technology approachable via simple relatable stories. Relief flooded through our team when Dan put the customers under his spell, and we should have known that Dan would come through, as he always did. Not surprisingly, Dan has found his career after BCT in Hollywood as a movie producer.

Another tactic which served us well as our company grew was for the founders to curate a library of standard presentation templates, which anyone in the company could access. We integrated important messages into the templates which substantiated our Myth and subtly reinforced key messages we wanted the customers, investors, and employees to receive. Having canned information made sure the information delivered to customers was always consistent, so our message was reinforced in the marketplace. It also saved everyone time, and that means saved money too, of course.

It is best to prepare and review your material well ahead of time to make sure you are properly crafting and delivering your Message. Dan's ability to tell engaging stories, work on the fly (and in the taxi!) and under pressure is unique. If you can find somebody like him to join your team, consider yourself blessed!

Ways to Add Value and How to Protect It

As you start to hone in on your product and your way of doing business, you are developing the special things that will set your company apart, in other words, the "secret sauce." There are a variety of methods to simultaneously protect these innovations and enhance the value of your company, including patents, trademarks, copyrights, and trade secrets. Let's review these options and how they might be applicable to your company situation.[43]

Trade Secrets are the catch-all of invention, process, chemical formulas, plan or idea protection. There is no public disclosure requirement, and thus no external costs associated with creating and using a trade secret. The trade secret is oftentimes used as interim protection until a patent is approved. From a pure protection standpoint, a trade secret may be the most powerful, but there is essentially no way to protect a trade secret from walking out the door or being developed independently by a competitor. It is your secret, but that does not mean it will be unique forever. Different states have adopted different standards of protection for trade secrets, so you should investigate your own situation. Intentional theft of trade secrets is a federal crime as well as in most states and can be punished as such, as described in the Economic Espionage Act of 1996.[44] If, on the other hand, the trade secret is "found out" through independent means by another company, there's nothing you can do about it. In the right situation, a Trade Secret can add tremendous value to your company. Restricting access to the secret, marking documents, and requiring employees to sign nondisclosure agreements can help protect your secret sauce.

Patents are exclusive rights approved and granted by the government to an inventor or an assignee for a fixed period (usually 20 years) in exchange for the disclosure of an invention. The costs of patents are usually between $5,000 and $10,000 but can be higher depending on the type of patent or complexity of the invention.

The obvious benefit of a patent is that it enables the inventor or assignee to be the sole practitioner of the functionality, assuming it is useful or beneficial, so you can manufacture amazing widgets, for example. The power of the patent comes from the rule that the government has authorized the patent holder the right to create and maintain a monopoly for the life of the patent. This creates an artificial market limitation, which gives the patent owner the right to raise prices higher than the market would normally accept. Thus, a patent can help you defend your Elite Icon from potential intruders. As we will discuss in the final chapter of this book, related to selling your business, patents can provide a definitive value adder when negotiating the transaction price with an acquirer.

The downside of a patent is that the government requires that the inventor disclose the exact nature of the patent, including how it works, what problems are addressed, and how the design is novel. The U.S. Patent system was established in 1790, when accessing published papers was quite a bit more difficult than today, when anyone with access to https://patents.google.com/ can see the explicit details of your patent if they have the right search criteria. By publishing your patent, you are providing explicit detail to competitors, both current and future. Anyone can learn from your design and potentially create their own patent which improves upon your design. Fortunately, patents can be defended in a court of law, and if a competent authority determines willful infringement, you will be entitled to damages from the competitor.

The Patent quandary arises because you want to protect your advantage, but you don't want to divulge your innermost secrets. The strategy utilized most often is to protect the most precious "crown jewels" via trade secret, and patent some equipment, process, or ancillary design element which is necessary but not precious to your invention. In this manner, you provide a couple of layers of protection, without exposing your Top Secret details. This is the strategy utilized by Coca-Cola, they protect the formulation of the drink via Trade Secret (internal eyes only), and then maintain patents on equipment, packaging innovations, and production techniques.

Trademarks provide inexpensive protection for brands, slogans, logos, and similar items. A trademark has unlimited life protection as long as the owner maintains the registration, uses the trademark and defends the rights. The power of the trademark is the ability to brand and create demand for a product, which in turn can be used to drive the price above what consumers would expect to pay for an unbranded product. This type of pricing leverage is powerful but can also be expensive to promulgate. Occasionally, the market will overadopt a trademark to the point where the power is lost completely, for example in the cases of Jet Ski (registered to Kawasaki), Kleenex (Kimberly-Clark), Post-it (3M), and Styrofoam (DuPont). The original trademark names have become so ubiquitous that any power originally held has been overcome by the fact that everyone uses the trademark term to describe the universe of products. Very few people sneeze and look for "facial tissue" versus "a Kleenex" or go on vacation at the beach and ask to rent a "stand-up personal watercraft" instead of a "Jet Ski."

When used well and promoted creatively, a good Trademark can enhance your Myth and your Elite Icon, build esprit-de-corps among your employees, and add value to an eventual exit. Some unfortunate cases have occurred where companies attempt to imitate, or downright violate another company's trademark. Such events can cause damage to all parties, and cost time and significant money to resolve.

Copyrights are inexpensive and like patents in that they represent exclusive rights granted by the government for a creation but focus on works of authorship rather than designs. Copyright protection extends to 70 years beyond the life of the author and provides protection for the author for actual damages and any additional profits enjoyed by the infringer, as well as statutory damages. Here's the kicker, though: Copyrights protect how an idea is expressed, not the idea itself, so there is not a lot of protection and the value is only attributable to the work itself. There really are not many opportunities to protect business information with Copyrights in most industries.

Security and Protection

As your company grows, attracts customers and overcomes obstacles, it will become more successful and visible to the public and to the bad guys. With success will come attention and not all of it will be desirable. Some industries are more prone than others to industrial espionage, but any commercially successful organization will eventually become the target of predators of one sort or another. Building in protection to your policies, procedures, facilities and equipment is easiest done early, rather than waiting to attempt to "bolt it on" later.

The U.S. Patent and Trademark Office estimates that U.S. businesses lose $250 billion each year in trade secret and proprietary information theft. The loss can occur via a wide range of mechanisms both intentional and accidental, such that it doesn't even require an active infiltrator to seriously hurt your business. Consider for a moment that a single 64 GB USB flash drive can store the equivalent of 4 million printed pages of information, enough to fill an 18-wheeler semitruck.[45]

The first step of protecting your company is to identify what information, processes, designs, or activities are key to your Elite Icon advantage?

What would you least like your competition to know or be able to do? That is your "secret sauce" and should be protected through all feasible mechanisms, including physical security, cybersecurity, and personnel security.

Best practices in physical security include controlling access to your facilities, equipment, and operations. To help in these endeavors, consider employee ID badges, security systems, locked or restricted areas, and logs of visitors. In addition, have a published employee and visitor conduct protocol which stipulates what is allowed in terms of photography, videos, or copying information of any kind. Keep track of documents and implement requirements for disposal. You can even consider how to handle the topic of trade secrets in your employee termination plan.

Cyber security is a constantly evolving technology which can help you protect your information when performed correctly or expose you to additional threats if performed poorly. The importance of this aspect of your protection cannot be underestimated, both during day-to-day operations and for the long-term future of the company. Of all the things that will be scrutinized if you ever sell the company, go public, or get acquired, cybersecurity and accounting are likely to be big focus areas. Why? Accounting because it is the calculation of actual revenue, costs, and profitability, as well as preventing fraud and embezzlement. Problematic accounting calls into question the true financial value of the company. Cybersecurity will be a focus because the value of your company may rest in the trade secrets, patents, know-how, or other secret sauce which is documented on your computers and networks. If cybersecurity has been compromised, then your competition or a foreign company may have obtained the information. At this point, the secret has been compromised and may now be just "sauce." Whether it ended up in China, or your eager competitor's hands, the value has been severely reduced if it is no longer a secret. Both the FBI and Homeland Security have resources to help businesses in the event of cybercrimes, if you should be so unlucky as to fall victim to an attack. The FBI has an Office of Private Sector to help protect the nation's economy and national security.[46] The acquisition of BCT took about a year, and probably 75 percent of the scrutiny during due diligence centered around accounting and cybersecurity. If those had not met muster, the deal would have collapsed.

In this chapter, we've discussed how to create an outward-facing presence for your company, via the website primarily and augmented by social media to the extent it makes sense in your industry. We've discussed getting a minimally viable product in front of customers, and how to go about putting together marketing materials in the form of presentations for customers and investors. Finally, we've discussed some tactics to start protecting your secret sauce and crown jewels. The major goal of these efforts is to get your company exposed to the potential customer base to determine whether your product or service idea has a strong product–market fit, as well as getting as much feedback to modify your plans to maximize your chances of success in the long term. And since you are going to start exposing your idea to the public, you need to start thinking about how to protect your ideas from being stolen. In the next chapter, we will introduce the joys of accounting, taxes, and cash flow management, all key to making your company financially robust.

An organization's ability to learn, and translate that learning into action rapidly, is the ultimate competitive advantage.

—Jack Welch
Chairman and CEO, General Electric (1981–2001)

CHAPTER 8

Don't Go Broke: Bookkeeping, Accounting and Cash Flow

Cash starvation is the most pervasive and permanent death for a small business.

—Anonymous

Startup businesses have a voracious appetite for money! It's like a teenage boy participating in "2 a day" football practices. No matter how much you feed it, it will still need more. Whether it is buying equipment, on-boarding new employees, paying rent, or funding marketing and website development, there are a thousand different things that the business needs to survive, and they all require money. Fortunately, there are some expenses that are necessary now, and some that can wait for later.

Creating and having a plan to keep your expenses on track is a critical component of getting the business up and running. If you run out of cash, and cannot make payroll, your employees will start to abandon you and take their talent and your investment in them out the door. If you cannot pay your suppliers, they will lose confidence in you and refuse future orders, or start demanding payment up front. If you miss a loan payment or two, the Bank may call your loan and request that you pay it off in full. Running out of money even for a few months can be fatal to a growing business. These and other unpleasant experiences await the business owner who loses track of the company's financial status.

In this chapter, I will outline a strategy for you to enable you to manage the cash, know the financial status, be ready for tax filings, and have a robust financial management system in place to help the company grow.

In addition, if your goal is to go public, or enter into a merger or acquisition, your financial management must be robust.

Taxes, Taxes, Taxes!

Get ready. Your business will have to pay Income Taxes, Payroll Taxes, Sales and Use Taxes, Self-Employment Taxes and possibly Excise Taxes, Property Taxes, Value-Added Tax, and Customs Duties and Tariffs if you import or export. That's a lot to keep track of, and you will want to confirm your business accountant is tracking as much of it as possible. There is a lot of information to coordinate, it must be done accurately and on time, and you need to focus on other issues. Thus, the need for a competent accountant. First, we will review payroll, then come back to bookkeeping and accounting.

Payroll will become a large part of your expenses in getting your company up and running. If you've never experienced the process, the tax obligations can be confusing. Here's a quick primer to help understand and estimate payroll taxes as a percentage of salary. The specific percentage that goes toward payroll taxes depends on both employee and employer contributions. Here's a breakdown of the main payroll taxes and how they apply[47]:

1. Social Security Tax (FICA: Federal Insurance Contributions Act)
   - Employee Contribution: 6.2 percent of salary (on income up to the annual wage base limit).
   - Employer Contribution: 6.2 percent of salary (matching the employee contribution).
   - Total Social Security tax: 12.4 percent (employee + employer combined)
2. Medicare Tax (also FICA)
   - Employee Contribution: 1.45 percent of salary (no income limit).
   - Employer Contribution: 1.45 percent of salary (matching the employee contribution).
   - Total Medicare tax: 2.9 percent (employee + employer combined)

3. Additional Medicare Tax (for higher earners)
   - Employee Contribution: An additional 0.9 percent on income over $200,000 for single filers ($250,000 for married couples filing jointly).
   - This additional Medicare tax applies only to employees, not employers.
4. Federal Unemployment Tax (FUTA: Federal Unemployment Tax Act)
   - Employer Contribution: 6.0 percent on the first $7,000 of each employee's wages (though employers usually get a credit of 5.4 percent, making the effective rate 0.6 percent).
   - Employees do not contribute to FUTA.
5. State Unemployment Tax (SUTA: State Unemployment Tax Act)
   - Employer Contribution: This rate varies significantly by state, ranging from 0.5 to 6.0 percent (or higher) on a certain portion of wages, often up to $7,000 to $40,000 per employee |per year.
   - Some states also impose a small employee contribution, though most do not.

To estimate the total payroll tax cost for an employee, we can combine the contributions for the employee and employer. Here's an example of what this might look like for an employee earning $50,000 annually:

Social Security:
- Employee: 6.2 percent of $50,000 = $3,100
- Employer: 6.2 percent of $50,000 = $3,100
- Total for Social Security: 12.4 percent of $50,000 = $6,200

Medicare:
- Employee: 1.45 percent of $50,000 = $725
- Employer: 1.45 percent of $50,000 = $725
- Total Medicare: 2.9 percent of $50,000 = $1,450

FUTA:
- Employer only: 0.6 percent on the first $7,000 = $42
- (Note: This is for the employer's portion only; employees do not pay FUTA taxes.)

SUTA:
- Varies by state; let's assume a rate of 3.0 percent on the first $7,000 = $210 (again, this is only for the employer).

Total Payroll Taxes
- Employee's share of payroll taxes (Social Security + Medicare): 7.65 percent of salary
- Employer's share of payroll taxes (Social Security + Medicare + FUTA + SUTA): 7.6 percent (assuming typical state SUTA rate)

So, the Employee's payroll tax burden is 7.65 percent of salary (for Social Security + Medicare, plus any additional Medicare tax if applicable). While the Employer's payroll tax burden ranges from 7.6 to 10 percent of salary, depending on the state's unemployment tax rate.

There's a lot to keep track of when it comes to taxes. Fortunately, there are experienced, reputable and affordable payroll services which can take on this burden on your behalf, so you don't have to become an expert or worry about making mistakes. They will handle the paperwork, transact through the banks, handle direct deposits, and file forms.

Bookkeeping, Accounting and Financial Management

First, let's get a few roles ironed out, because many people confuse the roles and responsibilities. A *bookkeeper* is a person who keeps track of the records of financial transactions, usually recording them in a journal or online bookkeeping program. The bookkeeper may also be entrusted with the payroll procedure. An *accountant* is a more experienced, senior level person who analyzes the information entered by the bookkeeper and puts together reports to assess the health of the company, as well as submitting relevant tax forms. A *CPA* is an accountant who specializes in tax law, processes and filings. A *CFO* is the chief financial officer for a business, and typically participates in strategic planning sideby side with the CEO and the board of directors.

As soon as your company starts to make financial transactions such as purchasing equipment, making payroll, or accepting payment from customers—you need a bookkeeper. Do not try to be your own book-keeper unless you have a background in accounting. It is tempting to buy a subscription online program and do it yourself, but you will be neglecting your duties as a founder if you do so. You will end up spending your time trying to learn bookkeeping and accounting processes instead of being the Mythmaker, Culture-Czar, and leader of the company. There are plenty of bookkeeping and accounting services available that can pro-vide you with the amount of support you need at a reasonable price, so you will only have to pay for what you need.

Let the bookkeeping service help you manage the finances of the com-pany. Entrusting a reputable firm or hiring a qualified bookkeeper and accountant (once you have enough work to justify it) will benefit your company in a myriad of ways:

- Tax and Legal compliance
- Payment of taxes and filings such as VAT, Social Security, Payroll Tax, and Medicare
- Financial analysis of the company's performance, supporting strategic decisions
- Reporting to investors
- Budgeting support
- Records organization in preparation for tax filings, audits, or mergers and acquisitions
- You will sleep better at night (I know this from personal experience)

In addition to those tangible benefits, you will be able to keep an eye on the bigger picture, and you will learn things that fill in your knowl-edge gaps you may have in the financial realm. Many unexpected insights come from reviewing and discussing the financial reports of your business with a professional who is viewing the books from a different perspective.

Accounting Methods for Your Business

Accountants learn all types of different "methods" of performing the accounting for a business, and they essentially revolve around *when* things are recognized as "hitting the books." For example, in a simple small business where expenses occur and your business receives payment more or less immediately or concurrent with the expense of creating whatever was sold, the accountants will tend toward the *Cash* accounting method. This means that revenue is recognized when cash is received, not when the sale is made, and expenses are recorded when they are paid, not when they are incurred. This method is the simplest because things happen quickly, when they occur, and the accounting system clearly illustrates the position of the company and closely matches the bank account balances. The cash method is simple and does not usually confuse the leadership team.

However, as your company grows, and especially if there are significant delays between when the customer orders something and when you deliver it and when you get paid, then the *Accrual* accounting method is preferred. If you receive payments over time, have inventory to manage, or need detailed insights for investors or regulators, then definitely *Accrual* is your method. Under this method, revenue will be recognized when it is earned, for example when you ship the product (not when you receive payments). Similarly, expenses will be recorded when they are incurred, not when they are paid. The beauty of the accrual method is that it matches the expenses and the income, so there is a clear connection between income and the costs of producing your product or services. Here's the catch, though: Because of the timing disconnect between receiving money and earning revenue, and the timing disconnect between incurring an expense and paying that expense, there can be significant month-to-month differences between the accounting system numbers and your bank balances. Your bank is recording things as they occur. Your accounting system is recording things when your business makes a commitment to buy something or fulfills a promise to ship something. While the accrual method is more appropriate for bigger businesses, it becomes confusing for the leadership team. Fortunately, we will introduce a tool later in this chapter to help you stay on top of the financial health of your business.

We've just touched the tip of the iceberg on accounting. In addition to the cash method and accrual method, there are hybrid methods and modi-fied methods which are outside the realm of our need to know at this point.

As your company grows, the accounting needs will grow proportion-ally. You must find a bookkeeping service that is reputable, affordable, and has enough depth to support your needs while you grow. As the company gets larger and the finances become more complex, you can consider adding a part-time or full-time accountant. When the company gets considerably larger (>$10 million in revenue) or you are starting to consider going public, a merger, or an acquisition then it is time to hire a CFO either part or full-time.

Inaccurate or incomplete bookkeeping can hurt your business in a variety of ways including missed opportunities to invoice customers, in-correct payments, missed filings resulting in fines or fees, and worst of all fraud or embezzlement. Suffice it to say that a competent and trustworthy bookkeeping and accounting service can ensure you pay the proper amount of money at the right time and avoid missed opportunities to make more money.

Cash Management—The Life of a Growing Business

As mentioned above, managing the growth of the business is perhaps your most challenging task as the founder. Grow too fast and you run out of money and go out of business. Grow too slowly and you miss out on the Blue Ocean market opportunity.

*Note: Bookkeepers and accountants may want to skip this section, because it does not pertain to **actual** accounting. But the founder (who presumably does not have an accounting background), needs a tool that can help plan and manage the upcoming months and years. What is about to be discussed should not be confused or comingled with the bookkeeping or accounting processes. Note also that if the company is using the Accrual method, the business exec-utive or someone in operations is going to have to maintain a view of the cash position of the company reflecting projected bank balances over the coming months and years.*

The best way to grow successfully is to create and follow a plan (sub-ject to change at any time, of course!) such that you don't run out of cash if the business grows very fast, and you don't go bankrupt if the business doesn't grow fast enough, or you spend too quickly trying to grow. As daunting as it may seem to walk this tightrope, it can be easy and fun for you and the leadership team, as an exercise in visualizing the possible future of your business. The key is to have a 3- to 6-month look-ahead window of how much money you will have in your bank accounts so that you aren't surprised and don't run short of money. A fundamental part of the plan will be a cash flow model which I recommend you manage personally as the founder or have someone on the leadership team own it. The core categories you should include in a spreadsheet, tabulated monthly, are:

a. Equity: cash on hand in bank accounts, share capital, other investments.
b. Income: sales or products or services, interest income, grants or contract payments.
c. Expenses: cost of goods sold, rent, utilities, marketing, and so on.
d. Liabilities: bank loan payments, tax payments, accounts payable, and salaries.

Start by creating a spreadsheet with the four categories I've outlined, then start plugging in your company's specific cash status in the appropriate category. As an example, let's look at the Cash Management Model for *A Great Company*.

- In January 2025, A Great Company has $100k in savings, and $200k in checking for a total of $300k of equity. Things haven't gotten started yet, so there's no income yet. But there are expenses for rent, and utilities totaling $1,300. In addition, you anticipate $11,000 in payroll and payroll taxes each month. Thus, at the end of January, the company will have $287,700 left in checking and savings, and if nothing changes you will still have $149,900 at the end of the year, as shown in Figure 8.1. You and the other founders can sleep at night!
- Now refer to Figure 8.2. In February, you win a contract with the "A" customer, worth $50,000 and that customer sends a check in

		Jan-25	Feb-25	Mar-25	Apr-25	May-25	Jun-25	Jul-25	Aug-25	Sep-25	Oct-25	Nov-25	Dec-25
						A Great Company Cash Management Model							
Starting Equity	total:	$ 300,000	$ 287,700	$ 275,400	$ 263,100	$ 250,800	$ 238,500	$ 223,700	$ 211,400	$ 199,100	$ 186,800	$ 174,500	$ 162,200
	Savings	$ 100,000	$ 100,000	$ 100,000	$ 100,000	$ 100,000	$ 100,000	$ 100,000	$ 100,000	$ 100,000	$ 100,000	$ 100,000	$ 100,000
	Checking	$ 200,000	$ 187,700	$ 175,400	$ 163,100	$ 150,800	$ 138,500	$ 123,700	$ 111,400	$ 99,100	$ 86,800	$ 74,500	$ 62,200
Income	total:	$ -	$ -	$ -	$ -	$ -	$ -	$ -	$ -	$ -	$ -	$ -	$ -
Expenses	total:	$ 1,300	$ 1,300	$ 1,300	$ 1,300	$ 1,300	$ 3,800	$ 1,300	$ 1,300	$ 1,300	$ 1,300	$ 1,300	$ 1,300
	Rent	$ 1,000	$ 1,000	$ 1,000	$ 1,000	$ 1,000	$ 1,000	$ 1,000	$ 1,000	$ 1,000	$ 1,000	$ 1,000	$ 1,000
	Internet	$ 150	$ 150	$ 150	$ 150	$ 150	$ 150	$ 150	$ 150	$ 150	$ 150	$ 150	$ 150
	Electricity & Gas	$ 150	$ 150	$ 150	$ 150	$ 150	$ 150	$ 150	$ 150	$ 150	$ 150	$ 150	$ 150
	Insurance						$ 2,500						
Liabilities	total:	$ 11,000	$ 11,000	$ 11,000	$ 11,000	$ 11,000	$ 11,000	$ 11,000	$ 11,000	$ 11,000	$ 11,000	$ 11,000	$ 11,000
	Payroll	$ 10,000	$ 10,000	$ 10,000	$ 10,000	$ 10,000	$ 10,000	$ 10,000	$ 10,000	$ 10,000	$ 10,000	$ 10,000	$ 10,000
	Payroll Tax	$ 1,000	$ 1,000	$ 1,000	$ 1,000	$ 1,000	$ 1,000	$ 1,000	$ 1,000	$ 1,000	$ 1,000	$ 1,000	$ 1,000
	Loan Payments												
	Supplier Bills												
Month end	Cash On Hand	$ 287,700	$ 275,400	$ 263,100	$ 250,800	$ 238,500	$ 223,700	$ 211,400	$ 199,100	$ 186,800	$ 174,500	$ 162,200	$ 149,900

Current Month

Figure 8.1 January 2025 Cash Management Model

A Great Company Cash Management Model												
	Jan-25	Feb-25	Mar-25	Apr-25	May-25	Jun-25	Jul-25	Aug-25	Sep-25	Oct-25	Nov-25	Dec-25
Starting Equity *total:*	$ 300,000	$ 287,151	$ 324,152	$ 311,303	$ 298,454	$ 285,606	$ 270,257	$ 257,408	$ 244,559	$ 231,710	$ 218,861	$ 206,012
Savings	$ 100,000	$ 100,000	$ 100,000	$ 100,000	$ 100,000	$ 100,000	$ 100,000	$ 100,000	$ 100,000	$ 100,000	$ 100,000	$ 100,000
Checking	$ 200,000	$ 187,151	$ 224,152	$ 211,303	$ 198,454	$ 185,606	$ 170,257	$ 157,408	$ 144,559	$ 131,710	$ 118,861	$ 106,012
Income *total:*	$ -	$ 50,000	$ -	$ -	$ -	$ -	$ -	$ -	$ -	$ -	$ -	$ -
Customer A		$ 50,000										
Expenses *total:*	$ 1,300	$ 1,300	$ 1,300	$ 1,300	$ 1,300	$ 3,800	$ 1,300	$ 1,300	$ 1,300	$ 1,300	$ 1,300	$ 1,300
Rent	$ 1,000	$ 1,000	$ 1,000	$ 1,000	$ 1,000	$ 1,000	$ 1,000	$ 1,000	$ 1,000	$ 1,000	$ 1,000	$ 1,000
Internet	$ 150	$ 150	$ 150	$ 150	$ 150	$ 150	$ 150	$ 150	$ 150	$ 150	$ 150	$ 150
Electricity & Gas	$ 150	$ 150	$ 150	$ 150	$ 150	$ 150	$ 150	$ 150	$ 150	$ 150	$ 150	$ 150
Insurance						$ 2,500						
Liabilities *total:*	$ 11,549	$ 11,699	$ 11,549	$ 11,549	$ 11,549	$ 11,549	$ 11,549	$ 11,549	$ 11,549	$ 11,549	$ 11,549	$ 11,549
Payroll	$ 10,499	$ 10,499	$ 10,499	$ 10,499	$ 10,499	$ 10,499	$ 10,499	$ 10,499	$ 10,499	$ 10,499	$ 10,499	$ 10,499
Payroll Tax	$ 1,050	$ 1,050	$ 1,050	$ 1,050	$ 1,050	$ 1,050	$ 1,050	$ 1,050	$ 1,050	$ 1,050	$ 1,050	$ 1,050
Loan Payments												
Supplier Bills		$ 150										
Month end|Cash On Hand	$ 287,151	$ 324,152	$ 311,303	$ 298,454	$ 285,606	$ 270,257	$ 257,408	$ 244,559	$ 231,710	$ 218,861	$ 206,012	$ 193,163

Current Month

Figure 8.2 February 2025 Cash Management Model

that amount. Payroll varies a bit each month due to overtime and other variations, so you enter the actual amounts each month. Other expenses and liabilities were the same as January, with the addition of a supplier invoice that needs to be paid for $150.

At the end of the month, you've still got $324,152 in the bank account and you anticipate $193,163 on hand at the end of the year. So far, so good!

- But now you need to hire more employees to work on the "A" Contract, you estimate those expenses starting in May. In addition, you decide to build 10 of product "B," and must order $5,000 in parts in order to build them. It will take about 2 months to build 10 B's, and you anticipate selling them in May for $25,000. You're getting busy, so you plan on hiring eight more employees. We're keeping the numbers simple by paying each employee $5,000 per month.

- More great news! You've been notified by the State that you won that grant you applied for, but they won't be able to fund it until August. You enter the $30,000 in August, and you plan to use that money to fund a $25,000 marketing blitz in September, with a follow-up in December of approximately $5,000, so you enter the anticipated expenses for those months. You also have an insurance premium due in June, and supplier bills are anticipated in April, June, and September, so you enter those amounts accordingly.

- Let's move to Figure 8.3 now and assume that it is currently March. You've been loading in actual expenses for things like payroll, and you've got estimates for everything you can think of loaded for future months. How do things look?

- There's a problem starting in September. Even though you've won some contracts and anticipate selling 10 of the B product, and you've won a State grant, that revenue will come in later in the year, and you can't meet your expenses in the near term. You will be bouncing checks if you don't do something about it. Since you've been making a forecast, you have about 6 months to develop a solution.

- What can you do? Since the checking account is getting low in July, you can plan on moving half of your savings to checking

A Great Company Cash Management Model

		Jan-25	Feb-25	Mar-25	Apr-25	May-25	Jun-25	Jul-25	Aug-25	Sep-25	Oct-25	Nov-25	Dec-25
Starting Equity	total:	$ 300,000	$ 287,151	$ 324,152	$ 262,852	$ 206,102	$ 174,802	$ 115,302	$ 59,002	$ 32,702	$ (49,498)	$ (105,798)	$ (162,098)
	Savings	$ 100,000	$ 100,000	$ 100,000	$ 100,000	$ 100,000	$ 100,000	$ 100,000	$ 100,000	$ 100,000	$ 100,000	$ 100,000	$ 100,000
	Checking	$ 200,000	$ 187,151	$ 224,152	$ 162,852	$ 106,102	$ 74,802	$ 15,302	$ (40,998)	$ (67,298)	$ (149,498)	$ (205,798)	$ (262,098)
Income	total:	$ -	$ 50,000	$ -	$ -	$ 25,000	$ -	$ -	$ 30,000	$ -	$ -	$ -	$ -
	Customer A		50,000										
	Product B					$ 25,000							
	State Grant								$ 30,000				
Expenses	total:	$ 1,300	$ 1,300	$ 6,300	$ 1,300	$ 1,300	$ 3,800	$ 1,300	$ 1,300	$ 26,300	$ 1,300	$ 1,300	$ 6,300
	Rent	1,000	1,000	$ 1,000	$ 1,000	$ 1,000	$ 1,000	$ 1,000	$ 1,000	$ 1,000	$ 1,000	$ 1,000	$ 1,000
	Internet	$ 150	$ 150	$ 150	$ 150	$ 150	$ 150	$ 150	$ 150	$ 150	$ 150	$ 150	$ 150
	Electricity & Gas	$ 150	$ 150	$ 150	$ 150	$ 150	$ 150	$ 150	$ 150	$ 150	$ 150	$ 150	$ 150
	Marketing Blitz									$ 25,000			
	Parts for B			$ 5,000									$ 5,000
	Insurance						$ 2,500						
Liabilities	total:	$ 11,549	$ 11,699	$ 55,000	$ 55,450	$ 55,000	$ 55,700	$ 55,000	$ 55,000	$ 55,900	$ 55,000	$ 55,000	$ 55,000
	Payroll	10,499	10,499	50,000	50,000	50,000	50,000	50,000	50,000	50,000	50,000	50,000	50,000
	Payroll Tax	1,050	1,050	5,000	5,000	5,000	5,000	5,000	5,000	5,000	5,000	5,000	5,000
	Loan Payments												
	Supplier Bills	150	150		450		700			900			
Month end	Cash On Hand	$ 287,151	$ 324,152	$ 262,852	$ 206,102	$ 174,802	$ 115,302	$ 59,002	$ 32,702	$ (49,498)	$ (105,798)	$ (162,098)	$ (223,398)

Current Month

Figure 8.3 March 2025 Cash Management Model

A Great Company Cash Management Model

		Jan-25	Feb-25	Mar-25	Apr-25	May-25	Jun-25	Jul-25	Aug-25	Sep-25	Oct-25	Nov-25	Dec-25
Starting Equity	total:	$ 300,000	$ 287,151	$ 324,152	$ 262,852	$ 206,102	$ 174,802	$ 115,302	$ 59,002	$ 32,702	$ (49,498)	$ (105,798)	$ (162,098)
	Savings	$ 100,000	$ 100,000	$ 100,000	$ 100,000	$ 100,000	$ 50,000	$ 50,000	$ 50,000	$ 50,000	$ 50,000	$ 50,000	$ 50,000
	Checking	$ 200,000	$ 187,151	$ 224,152	$ 162,852	$ 106,102	$ 124,802	$ 65,302	$ 9,002	$ (17,298)	$ (99,498)	$ (155,798)	$ (212,098)
Income	total:	$ -	$ 50,000	$ -	$ -	$ 25,000	$ -	$ -	$ 30,000	$ -	$ -	$ -	$ -
	Customer A		$ 50,000										
	Product B					$ 25,000							
	State Grant								$ 30,000				
Expenses	total:	$ 1,300	$ 1,300	$ 6,300	$ 1,300	$ 1,300	$ 3,800	$ 1,300	$ 1,300	$ 26,300	$ 1,300	$ 1,300	$ 6,300
	Rent	$ 1,000	$ 1,000	$ 1,000	$ 1,000	$ 1,000	$ 1,000	$ 1,000	$ 1,000	$ 1,000	$ 1,000	$ 1,000	$ 1,000
	Internet	$ 150	$ 150	$ 150	$ 150	$ 150	$ 150	$ 150	$ 150	$ 150	$ 150	$ 150	$ 150
	Electricity & Gas	$ 150	$ 150	$ 150	$ 150	$ 150	$ 150	$ 150	$ 150	$ 150	$ 150	$ 150	$ 150
	Marketing Blitz									$ 25,000			
	Parts for B												$ 5,000
	Insurance			$ 5,000			$ 2,500						
Liabilities	total:	$ 11,549	$ 11,699	$ 55,000	$ 55,450	$ 55,000	$ 55,700	$ 55,000	$ 55,000	$ 55,900	$ 55,000	$ 55,000	$ 55,000
	Payroll	$ 10,499	$ 10,499	$ 50,000	$ 50,000	$ 50,000	$ 50,000	$ 50,000	$ 50,000	$ 50,000	$ 50,000	$ 50,000	$ 50,000
	Payroll Tax	$ 1,050	$ 1,050	$ 5,000	$ 5,000	$ 5,000	$ 5,000	$ 5,000	$ 5,000	$ 5,000	$ 5,000	$ 5,000	$ 5,000
	Loan Payments												
	Supplier Bills		$ 150		$ 450		$ 700			$ 900			
Month end	Cash On Hand	$ 287,151	$ 324,152	$ 262,852	$ 206,102	$ 174,802	$ 115,302	$ 59,002	$ 32,702	$ (49,498)	$ (105,798)	$ (162,098)	$ (223,398)

Current Month

Figure 8.4 March 2025 Cash Management Model (move $50,000 from savings in June)

in June. That will keep you from bouncing checks, but it hasn't helped with the year-end problem. Savings (and lines of credit) buy you time, but to grow your business you must have increasing sales (income).

- Figure 8.4 shows the plan to move some savings in June and you now have until about September before things get bad again. If things stay on track, however, you will still be overdrawn by $223,398 at the end of the year. You've bought yourself a couple of months to generate more income.

- What else could you do to get more time? Fortunately, you established a line of credit with the bank, and you could leverage the entire $150,000 from the line and transfer that money to checking in August. But then you will have to start making loan payments of $2,000 per month starting in August, so you should reflect that in each month's liabilities as shown in Figure 8.5.

- This demonstrates that a LoC, just like savings, is just buying you time. You need to generate more income, at least $100,000 but more would really help. Proactively, you assign your top sales agent (Sales Wizard) to go visit with Customer A and ask them how things are going, and if they could use more help from your company, and if they're interested in your B product?

- Your Sales Wizard comes back from visiting Customer A and says they are extremely pleased with your company's performance on the "A" contract. They plan to expand the scope of your contract in October by $75,000 as well as order 100 of your "B" products in November! You reflect those amounts in Figure 8.6.

- In addition, you see that you will probably be able to pay off the Line of Credit in December, so you include that transaction as well. Things will be tight, but it is a plan. And you have 8 months to develop new customers, make sales, and expand your business.

- What other plans could you consider? You could consider using the remaining $50,000 from savings. That could buy you a month. But that doesn't solve the problem.

- You could send the Sales Wizard out to sell more "B" products. How many could he sell, and when?

A Great Company Cash Management Model	Jan-25	Feb-25	Mar-25	Apr-25	May-25	Jun-25	Jul-25	Aug-25	Sep-25	Oct-25	Nov-25	Dec-25
Starting Equity total:	$ 300,000	$ 287,151	$ 324,152	$ 262,852	$ 206,102	$ 174,802	$ 115,302	$ 359,002	$ 332,702	$ 248,502	$ 190,202	$ 131,902
Savings	$ 100,000	$ 100,000	$ 100,000	$ 100,000	$ 100,000	$ 50,000	$ 50,000	$ 50,000	$ 50,000	$ 50,000	$ 50,000	$ 50,000
Checking	$ 200,000	$ 187,151	$ 224,152	$ 162,852	$ 106,102	$ 124,802	$ 65,302	$ 159,002	$ 282,702	$ 198,502	$ 140,202	$ 81,902
LoC Draw								$ 150,000				
Income total:	$ -	$ 50,000	$ -	$ -	$ 25,000	$ -	$ -	$ 30,000	$ -	$ -	$ -	$ -
Customer A		$ 50,000										
Product B					$ 25,000							
State Grant								$ 30,000				
Expenses total:	$ 1,300	$ 1,300	$ 6,300	$ 1,300	$ 1,300	$ 3,800	$ 1,300	$ 1,300	$ 26,300	$ 1,300	$ 1,300	$ 6,300
Rent	$ 1,000	$ 1,000	$ 1,000	$ 1,000	$ 1,000	$ 1,000	$ 1,000	$ 1,000	$ 1,000	$ 1,000	$ 1,000	$ 1,000
Internet	$ 150	$ 150	$ 150	$ 150	$ 150	$ 150	$ 150	$ 150	$ 150	$ 150	$ 150	$ 150
Electricity & Gas	$ 150	$ 150	$ 150	$ 150	$ 150	$ 150	$ 150	$ 150	$ 150	$ 150	$ 150	$ 150
Marketing Blitz									$ 25,000			
Parts for B			$ 5,000									$ 5,000
Insurance						$ 2,500						
Liabilities total:	$ 11,549	$ 11,699	$ 55,000	$ 55,450	$ 55,000	$ 55,700	$ 55,000	$ 55,000	$ 57,900	$ 57,000	$ 57,000	$ 57,000
Payroll	$ 10,499	$ 10,499	$ 50,000	$ 50,000	$ 50,000	$ 50,000	$ 50,000	$ 50,000	$ 50,000	$ 50,000	$ 50,000	$ 50,000
Payroll Tax	$ 1,050	$ 1,050	$ 5,000	$ 5,000	$ 5,000	$ 5,000	$ 5,000	$ 5,000	$ 5,000	$ 5,000	$ 5,000	$ 5,000
Loan Payments									$ 2,000	$ 2,000	$ 2,000	$ 2,000
Supplier Bills		$ 150		$ 450		$ 700			$ 900			
Month end Cash On Hand	$ 287,151	$ 324,152	$ 262,852	$ 206,102	$ 174,802	$ 115,302	$ 59,002	$ 332,702	$ 248,502	$ 190,202	$ 131,902	$ 68,602

Current Month

Figure 8.5 March 2025 Cash Management Model (Leverage LoC in August)

A Great Company Cash Management Model

		Jan-25	Feb-25	Mar-25	Apr-25	May-25	Jun-25	Jul-25	Aug-25	Sep-25	Oct-25	Nov-25	Dec-25
Starting Equity	total:	$ 300,000	$ 287,151	$ 324,152	$ 259,442	$ 199,282	$ 164,572	$ 101,662	$ 191,952	$ 162,242	$ 149,632	$ 87,922	$ 126,212
	Savings	$ 100,000	$ 100,000	$ 100,000	$ 100,000	$ 100,000	$ 50,000	$ 50,000	$ 50,000	$ 50,000	$ 50,000	$ 50,000	$ 50,000
	Checking	$ 200,000	$ 187,151	$ 224,152	$ 159,442	$ 99,282	$ 114,572	$ 51,662	$ 141,952	$ 112,242	$ 99,632	$ 37,922	$ 76,212
	LoC Draw								$ 150,000				$(150,000)
Income	total:	$ -	$ 50,000	$ -	$ -	$ 25,000	$ -	$ -	$ 30,000	$ 75,000	$ -	$ 250,000	$ -
	Customer A		$ 50,000			$ 25,000							
	Product B									$ 75,000		$ 250,000	
	State Grant								$ 30,000				
Expenses	total:	$ 1,300	$ 1,300	$ 6,300	$ 1,300	$ 1,300	$ 3,800	$ 1,300	$ 1,300	$ 26,300	$ 1,300	$ 1,300	$ 6,300
	Rent	$ 1,000	$ 1,000	$ 1,000	$ 1,000	$ 1,000	$ 1,000	$ 1,000	$ 1,000	$ 1,000	$ 1,000	$ 1,000	$ 1,000
	Internet	$ 150	$ 150	$ 150	$ 150	$ 150	$ 150	$ 150	$ 150	$ 150	$ 150	$ 150	$ 150
	Electricity & Gas	$ 150	$ 150	$ 150	$ 150	$ 150	$ 150	$ 150	$ 150	$ 150	$ 150	$ 150	$ 150
	Marketing Blitz			$ 5,000									$ 5,000
	Parts for B									$ 25,000			
	Insurance						$ 2,500						
Liabilities	total:	$ 11,549	$ 11,699	$ 58,410	$ 58,860	$ 58,410	$ 59,110	$ 58,410	$ 58,410	$ 61,310	$ 60,410	$ 60,410	$ 58,410
	Payroll	$ 10,499	$ 10,499	$ 53,100	$ 53,100	$ 53,100	$ 53,100	$ 53,100	$ 53,100	$ 53,100	$ 53,100	$ 53,100	$ 53,100
	Payroll Tax	$ 1,050	$ 1,050	$ 5,310	$ 5,310	$ 5,310	$ 5,310	$ 5,310	$ 5,310	$ 5,310	$ 5,310	$ 5,310	$ 5,310
	Loan Payments									$ 2,000	$ 2,000	$ 2,000	
	Supplier Bills		$ 150		$ 450		$ 700			$ 900			
Month end	Cash On Hand	$ 287,151	$ 324,152	$ 259,442	$ 199,282	$ 164,572	$ 101,662	$ 41,952	$ 162,242	$ 149,632	$ 87,922	$ 276,212	$ 61,502

Current Month

Figure 8.6 *April 2025 Cash Management Model (Customer A contract, Sales of B Product)*

- Could you work with Customer "A" to expand the scope of their contract even more? Developing other customers would be a good idea, too.
- Should you go to some trade shows to exhibit your fine products and try to boost sales? Be sure to estimate the expenses of those shows in the proper month.
- You're spending $25,000 on the September marketing blitz. When will that effort generate sales and how much?

At BCT, our CEO George was constantly updating the Cash Management Model, often multiple times per day as the company grew, new expenses were identified, new contracts won or lost, and sales were booked. It was never a perfect model, and it was always simplistic and as easy to operate as possible. But the power of such a model cannot be understated because it gives you the business leader a 6- to 12-month look-ahead of the financial status for the company. Without such a tool, you are essentially flying blind. With adequate warning, you have time to take actions to avoid running out of cash.

The model helped us answer questions like

- "Can we afford to expand to a larger facility? And when?"
- "If we spend $x to develop a new product by next March, and can sell 100 of them per month starting in July for $y, and the production cost is $z each, how much money will we make? Is it a good idea?"
- "If we purchase an automated machine that reduces assembly costs by 25 percent for the 100 products we produce each year, how much can we spend such that the machine is paid for by year 2?"
- "Will we have enough cash each month to make payroll? Will we have enough cash to make loan or line of credit payments on time?"
- Should we demand partial payment from the customer up front? Many industries are iron clad with the expectation that payment will be made by the customer once services are rendered or product is delivered. However, if you are in any sort of situation where you are customizing or tailoring your services or products for

your customer, it is in your best interest and perfectly acceptable to stipulate that you must be paid a significant percentage of the product cost up front.

The uses for a Cash Management Model are pretty much unlimited, bounded only by your imagination. As the company grows and starts to become successful, someone will come up with a "Great" idea. Putting the cost and benefits of the proposed idea into the model, along with associated costs for labor, materials, and anticipated monetary benefits allows you as the leader of the company to quickly determine how "great" it really might be. Can you afford it? When will it provide a benefit to offset the cost? Without an objective, realistic way to model the costs and income of the activities of your company, you are subject to emotional responses or the loudest voice carrying the day.

You can build your model however you like, and what fits your style. The example we reviewed here is very simple to illustrate the concept. Add details to your model to capture cash flows in and out and predict long-term (multiyear) financial status to enable you and your leadership team to make strategic decisions, avoid running out of cash, and maximize your Elite Icon opportunities.

Never take your eyes off the cash flow because it's the lifeblood of business.

—Sir Richard Branson

CHAPTER 9

Managing Growth and Problems

At this point, you will have your company up and running, your website is live, you are developing a portfolio of customers, and perhaps you've even started to book some revenue. Congratulations!

How do you like the culture at this point? Remember, the culture is the result of the people you hire combined with how you behave and the policies you put in place. Culture is like a garden where you plant seeds, spread fertilizer and water routinely, and let the sun go to work. You can't control it, but you can plan and cultivate. And it's easier to ruin than to fix. Assuming you've done a good job on recruiting a positive group of people, you can now encourage them to build out the cultural concepts by asking for their participation. Just to refresh a few concepts from the Culture chapter: If you want to bring some fun into the workplace, you could consider providing a ping-pong or foosball table, or an arcade game for your break room. At BCT, we had ping-pong, which seemed to appeal to a lot of people, as well as an ancient Asteroids video game, which appealed to other parts of the team. If you want to inspire a nice morning ritual, you could bring gourmet coffees and teas, for example, or breakfast sandwiches on occasion. Get imaginative! These little touches bring a touch of personality into the workplace as well as helping people relax around new acquaintances and coworkers.

As a founder of the company, you should not be spending a significant amount of your time, day after day, micromanaging your employees. If you find yourself in that role, you should first look to yourself to determine whether the problem is with your employees or perhaps related to your difficulty letting go. If the employees aren't clear on how to perform their roles, then you should revisit Chapter 6 to determine if perhaps you haven't documented the processes that you expect your team to execute.

Engage them in assisting you to enhance the process maps and documents and iterate and correct them as often as necessary to get them right.

My experience as a founder at BCT was that one of the challenges of building a team and getting them all "on the same vector," as Elon Musk would say, is to find out what they're working on. As the company starts growing, once you have more than 5 or 10 employees, it is easy for some of your employees to start to drift without purpose, being too shy or embarrassed to ask for assistance. Maybe they're a "worrier"? A great morning ritual which we established at BCT (and it is widely used in many industries) is the Morning Stand-Up Meeting (MSM). Designate a reasonable time for the MSM to start. A time that is within your "core" hours that you designate in your employee handbook, and early enough that people don't idle away too much time if they arrive early.

At BCT, we were very production and test focused, so the MSM was coordinated by whomever was leading the production and test effort at that stage of the company. Everyone would meet in front of a large whiteboard (floor to ceiling, about 30 ft across), which was magnetic and had individual magnets to identify all the pieces of hardware in various stages of production and test. A magnet for each part would enter the whiteboard on the right side. As the actual hardware made progress through the assembly and test functions, the corresponding magnet would move incrementally to the left, until it reached the left side and was ready for shipment. People in the company were assigned to specific functions, so they would focus on their "section" of the whiteboard, what magnets were in their zone, and what was coming their way. It was a great visual aid to help coordinate people's work. More importantly, it forced people to start *talking* about issues, concerns, or opportunities. During the high-growth phase of BCT, every employee attended those morning stand-up meetings, including members of the sales team, the founders, and even the person handling our marketing. Everyone was learning from everyone else, and that morning meeting was also a critical opportunity for the founders to tweak the culture, reinforce that it was a safe environment, and get help for anyone who was struggling. While a big whiteboard may not be appropriate for your company, some other activity might make sense, with the goal of coordinating everyone's activities and providing opportunities for newer employees to grow and learn.

Here's an example of how the whiteboard can help you. If an employee has been struggling to learn his role, they will show it with either a negative attitude or say that they are not sure they will complete a task on time. Such instances become a perfect opportunity for the founders to take notes and offer to help that person or assign someone else to mentor or assist this employee. In this manner, you reinforce key cultural points, that you are a team that helps each other out in times of struggle, and it is a safe environment.

One of my earlier employers had a similar morning ritual but slightly more individualized and free form. At that employer, the leader would start the meeting with any interesting news regarding sales, or company growth, or other high-level information which employees like to hear about. The leader would then state the team's objective for the day and for the week, with some encouraging words about the goals being important and we should all work together to make those objectives. After that, each person, in turn, got a chance to speak, identify any concerns they had over their responsibility, and give a statement about their personal goals for the day and who they needed assistance from in order to achieve those goals. This format made each employee come to the meeting already preloaded with some plans for the day, rather than arriving empty-headed and waiting for directions from a manager. The MSM can instill a culture of teamwork and self-direction that eliminates the need for managers or founders to do much more than correct the occasional person who was confused about their objectives.

Both abovementioned formats were effective because they aligned with the type of work being performed and the culture the leadership wanted to instill. Your industry, product, or service may lend itself to other types of coordination meetings. Whatever you pick, be sure to set and abide by time limits, because people really don't like to stand around all morning listening to unnecessary chatter. Communicate an agenda and format to the team, eliminate unnecessary distractions, and utilize visual aids whenever possible to help clarify the discussion and keep people on track. Finally, make sure everyone participates as much as possible.

The large whiteboard at BCT that I mentioned earlier, and other visual aids around the company on walls, doorways, and other prominent places can help your employees learn more quickly about the company, as

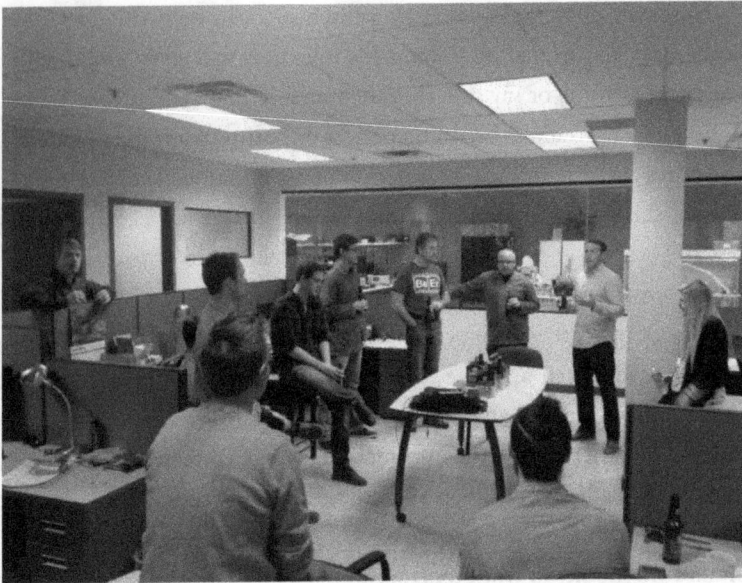

Figure 9.1 Circa 2014: BCT's CEO George (second from the right) giving a "Beer Friday" Update and letting us know that Inc. Magazine ranked us #322 fastest-growing companies in the United States

well as serve as discussion points for visiting job candidates, customers, or prospective investors. Anything you can display which is relevant, informative, and visually appealing will do the trick.

Should you feel so inclined, you can start a tradition like "Beer Fridays" where the founders bring in a few six packs on Friday afternoons and everyone can relax a bit and ask questions of the founders. Employees have taken a career gamble by joining a startup, and they're going to want to know what is going on with the company, good or bad. It's another opportunity to build a stronger team and a closer understanding of each other, as you can see in Figure 9.1.

The Art of Being a Founder

Through the course of every day and every interaction, founders are in the spotlight and under a magnifying glass. Employees will watch founders to gather clues about how the company is performing, customers will assume that founders' conduct represents the entire company's, and investors will try to determine if founders are trustworthy. The other thing that other founders have pointed out to me is that an organization will start to adopt the personality and demeanor of the founder, as if it was just a big game of grown-up follow-the-leader.

William James (1842–1910), the father of American psychology, said "Act as if what you do makes a difference. It does." James was spot on. When you carry yourself and act with integrity and purpose, you will inspire others to reach farther and try harder in everything they do for the company. Imagine yourself in the shoes of your employees and customers and demonstrate the ideals of your culture. Any deviation will gather proportions over time; as the company becomes larger and more successful, you are primed for success only if there are not any skeletons in your closet, much like a hopeful presidential candidate.

As a founder, you will also discover that your time is in high demand and depending upon the size of the organization and your delegation abilities, you may receive any number of surprise, "pop up" issues to deal with each day.

When I was interviewing other founders and CEOs in the course of writing this book, I stumbled across a few founders who had obviously let the success of the company go to their heads. They were arrogant and spoke as if they alone had achieved the success of their 100+ person company. The arrogant founder trap is unfortunately commonplace, and it can wreak havoc on a company culture very quickly. Remember that your employees are your team; you need to lead them and know that they will be there to support the company when needed. The better mindset for the founder is to humbly recognize that success is the result of teamwork, dedication, and sacrifices.

The Problem of a Struggling Company (Three P's)

Every company will eventually experience either low sales or inability to meet customer expectations. It will feel as if the company has somehow missed the target, making founders feel lost and confused as to how to identify and remedy issues. Most of these situations can be traced and remedied by reviewing the three P's: Product, People, and Place.

Product: Does your product or service meet the objectives laid out for an *Elite Icon*?

- Does your product provide *unique value* to the customer?
- Are you operating in an *uncontested market space*?
- Is the product or service *commercially viable*? Meaning, will people pay your price?

People: Have you provided your team with the *MAP*?

- Mastery: Does your team need additional training to master their roles?
- Autonomy: Can they work independently without constant oversight?
- Purpose: Do they understand how their role supports the company objectives?

Place: Is your company sufficient to support the business objectives? Verify with *COMFERT*:

- *Customer Service:* Are you meeting the needs of your customers in a timely fashion?
- *Operations:* Are your company processes and software enabling you to deliver?
- *Marketing:* Is the value proposition effectively communicated to the target audience?
- *Facilities:* Are your buildings the right size, configuration and in a good location?
- *Equipment:* Do your employees have access to the best equipment?
- *Resources:* Do you have the parts and materials available on time to deliver the product?
- *Team:* Do you have a good team and is the culture healthy?

Review of the three P's will identify one or more issues which need to be remedied for the company to achieve healthy sales and desired growth.

Examples of prominent companies that struggled and how the three P's identified their problems include WeWork, which signed expensive leases for *Facilities* worldwide before they had sufficient demand (too many *Competitors*, not an Elite Icon), leading to chapter 11 bankruptcy in 2023; Pets.com, which spent heavily on marketing, but neglected profitability (effective *Marketing*, but the *Operations* were expensive and inefficient) leading to bankruptcy just 9 months after their IPO in 2000; and Peloton which was unable to meet customer demand during the COVID-19 pandemic due to shortages of parts from their supply chain (inadequate *Resources*).

Growing Too Fast

Growing too fast may seem like not a problem, but it has been a struggle for many otherwise successful organizations. It happened to Chipotle Mexican Grill in the early 2010s, when their supply chain was unable to keep pace with food quality and safety, resulting in several foodborne illness outbreaks. Tesla struggled with explosive growth and demand for the Model 3 when they were unable to manufacture the cars fast enough due to manufacturing bottlenecks and quality issues. We struggled with rapid growth at BCT, because we could not hire fast enough to meet the demand of our growing customer orders. To address excessive growth, turn to *COMFERT-P* (the same *COMFERT*, with an added factor for *Pricing*):

- *Customer Service:* Communicate the problem and that you are addressing the issues.
- *Operations:* Can you expand or upgrade processes and software?
- *Marketing:* Is the value proposition effectively communicated to the target audience?
- *Facilities:* Do you need more or larger and better buildings?
- *Equipment:* Will better or more automated equipment improve quantity and quality?
- *Resources:* Do you have the parts and materials available on time to meet growth?
- *Team:* Can you expand the team quickly enough, and train them fast enough to improve quantity and quality? Should you restructure?

The final piece of addressing explosive growth is to address *Pricing*: Have you overachieved with your Elite Icon such that you are giving the customer too much value at too low of a price? Should you be charging more? Many business owners are afraid of increasing prices for fear of driving customers away. If your organization cannot keep up, you need to do something immediately before the problem gets worse. If addressing COMFERT isn't sufficient to address the rapid growth, increasing pricing will provide two benefits to the company:

1. Increasing pricing will slow the growth and allow your team to catch up, staff up, improve training or make changes;
2. Increasing prices will provide additional revenue to hire staff or resolve whatever is lacking in COMFERT. Once the growth is manageable, you can revisit the pricing if necessary to recapture market share or fuel the growth.

Adjusting pricing is akin to a throttle that you can use to accelerate or slow down the growth of your company.

As you can see, the problem of not being able to achieve sales (growing too slowly) or not being able to meet customer demand (growing too quickly) are just two sides of the same coin with respect to your company. Either of these problems simply indicate a problem with the three P's (or four P's if you include pricing), and once you have addressed the issues the performance of the company should improve.

When Something Bad Happens

Eventually, there will be a crisis or problem at your company, perhaps with uncertain degrees of impact. You can't respond to every bit of bad news with a full court press. You need to develop a system to determine the extent of an issue and develop a response. One strategy we successfully employed at BCT included immediate triage of these types of issues to determine if it was a critical, must-be-handled-now issue, or could wait a bit until a measured response could be developed. We called this the "glass ball, rubber ball" system. Critical issues must be handled immediately (or the glass ball will shatter when it hits the floor), whereas a rubber ball will bounce, giving you time to catch it later or on a future day. Pay immediate attention to the glass balls, let the rubber balls bounce, and worry about them later.

Another successful technique when trying to build out a good support system was to ask the individual who brings you the issue what they think might be the best first step. This is helpful if you have a capable but underconfident employee that you're trying to encourage to grow, and it also starts to engender a self-correcting culture and workforce that can make progress when you aren't immediately available. You aren't committing to their idea. If you want to soft-pedal it, you can also ask some clarifying questions to help them develop the plan, which will in turn help you learn more, as well as aid them in developing their skills. Once you're confident in their handling of those types of issues, you can encourage them to operate more autonomously but keep you informed, if you prefer.

Overcommunicate

As the founder of a young and growing business, you are at the epicenter of communication to your investors, your customers, and your employees. At no point in my 35-year career in business have I ever heard a customer or investor complain that they are getting too much information from a company executive. In fact, the opposite is true: If a company leader does not provide regular and informative communication, people will begin to assume that there are problems, or that the leader is intentionally withholding information.

When it comes to Investors, the communication protocol should include regular (quarterly at least) updates on the health and status of the company, as well as a dialog of any ongoing issues and plans for resolution. The introduction of new opportunities, solutions, or news of impact should always be included.

Employee communication should be regular and as transparent as reasonable. My recommendation is at least monthly to provide updates on company growth, business opportunities, and financial performance in a general manner. For example, it is perfectly acceptable to inform the employees that revenue has grown $XX\%$ over the past year, without specifically citing dollar amounts. Always remember that a company is a fertile rumor mill, providing ample opportunity for gossip both positive and negative. If you do not provide regular and informative updates to your employees regarding corporate status, you can be sure that incorrect information, usually dramatic, incorrect, and negative, will begin to circulate. Regular monthly company meetings can also be a great way to celebrate successes, welcome newly hired employees, and continue to foster your cultural dynamics. If you are an uncomfortable public speaker, use these opportunities to improve your skills and practice delivering information before you must present to investors or merger and acquisition teams.

Be sure to celebrate successes and milestones with visible company events, like a summer BBQ picnic and photo shoot, like the one which we took when we expanded into a much needed bigger, new facility (Figure 9.2).

Customer communication is equally important, with an added risk that customers who feel ignored are likely to take their business elsewhere. If you are in an industry that operates with sales representatives or program managers, then you should set requirements for your employees assigned to each customer dictating the cadence and content of customer

Figure 9.2 Circa 2018 company picture. We were making bigger satellites, too!

communication. Regular and semitransparent communication with the customers will build trust and mutual respect which may serve as collateral in the bank if problems arise.

Perfect customer communication may be the most difficult to consistently achieve. As the company grows, employee schedules become increasingly chaotic. Establishing and maintaining customer relations will become more problematic. Take for example an early customer we had at BCT who operated a very small business of their own on the other side of the country from our location. As our company grew and became quite busy, we neglected to prioritize this customer's products. To make matters worse, we did not assign anyone the task of keeping this customer updated and informed. As months passed and our team was virtually silent, this customer grew more and more suspicious that our silence indicated something nefarious or that we were covering up problems. They chose to file a lawsuit against BCT, which immediately got our attention. It took over a year of dedicated work and regular communication to resolve the issues, deliver the customer's satellite, and avoid further legal proceedings. But in the meantime, that customer received constant communication, and his products got attention at the highest levels of the organization. In hindsight, it was a blunder by our management team. If we had kept this customer informed, that would have sustained a good working relationship between our two organizations. More importantly, it would have prompted our team to pay more attention to this customer's product status and contract requirements. Instead, we both spent a bunch of money on lawyers, lost money in other ways due to the distraction of being sued and created a lot of tension and sleepless nights. Lesson learned: If you leave your customer in the dark, they may become unpredictable and create really big problems.

Risk-Informed Decision Making

When you are making major decisions for the company, it is natural to focus on the positive and desirable outcomes, while either overlooking or downplaying the potential risks which might occur. That is a natural response for an optimistic founder, and it helps to develop some methods to evaluate plans objectively. It helps to have an objective framework so

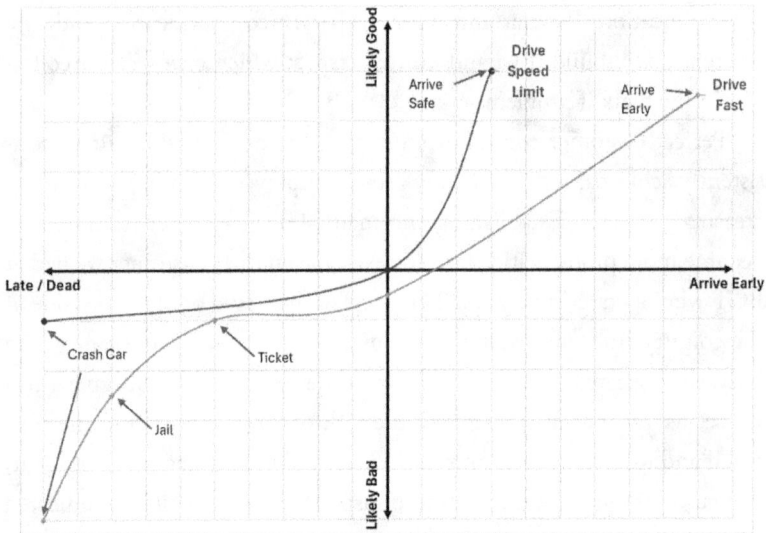

Figure 9.3 Example of risk–reward graph evaluating driving speed to make a car trip

that you and your team can explore the drawbacks as well as the potential benefits. This objective tool is called the Risk–Reward Graph and the concept is that the *x*-axis represents your desired outcome as well as the opposite, undesirable state. The *y*-axis represents the degree of good or bad possible results which might occur. For example, in Figure 9.3, I have the hypothetical case of taking a road trip, and either driving very fast, or driving the speed limit, with the desired goal of arriving early.

The upper right datapoint reflects our desired outcome to arrive early if we drive fast. The lower left quadrant has some undesirable outcomes which might occur, including getting a speeding ticket, going to jail, or getting in a crash. Connecting these points with a line gives us a feel for the risk–reward of our plan of driving fast. Alternatively, we could drive the speed limit, which has a higher likelihood of arriving safe, but not as early, as depicted by the upper, right middle datapoint. Note that it is still possible to be in a car crash, but not as likely, as depicted by the point at the far left with small likelihood. Connecting the datapoints shows that this course of action has an overall better chance of a good result but does not maximize our goal of arriving early. But, as a driver, we can select a plan and follow it with objectivity, making an informed choice after

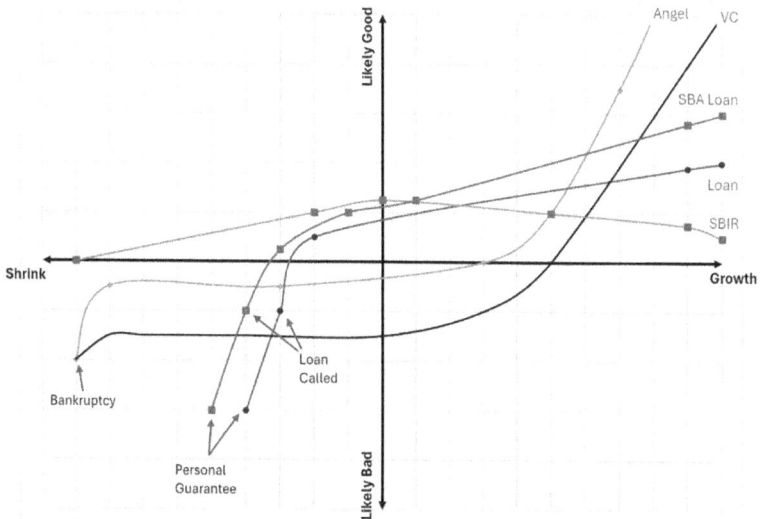

Figure 9.4 **Risk–reward chart depicting various outcomes of capital raising efforts if successful or unsuccessful**

considering the consequences of bad outcomes in addition to what most optimists will focus on: the thing we want to happen.

As a business example in Figure 9.4, we have the desire to grow our company through the use of a variety of methods to raise capital discussed earlier in Chapter 5. The desired company growth is shown to the right, with the opposite (shrinking, and ultimately bankruptcy) shown to the left. The y-axis then represents how significant the impact of various types of capital raising might be.

For instance, an SBIR grant has pretty much the same impact on the company's growth whether the company expands or not. It's always a positive, but minimal effect to secure an SBIR grant. Similarly, a conventional bank loan can help a company grow, even if the company struggles a bit. But if the company can't make the loan payments or violates the covenants, the bank can call the loan, and in the worst case require the company owners to make good on the personal guarantee to pay off the loan (highest negative impact). An SBA loan, on the other hand, has more favorable terms and maybe a lower interest rate, making it more beneficial than a conventional loan (once you get through the paperwork). VC and Angel funding can have a very strong impact for the company once it grows enough to offset the equity dilution. The dilution is present whether the company is growing or not, and the typical terms of VC funding shifts the benefit/impact lower (less desirable) than Angel funding in the chart. This is just one example of how a risk–reward chart can be used to help you objectively evaluate different solutions. The beauty of the risk–reward chart is that it allows you to characterize scenarios depicting both the desired positive as well as undesired negative outcomes and contrast different options which your team might be evaluating to help you select a solution to match your risk tolerance.

Bad News Never Ages Well

Unlike fine wine, bad news does not get better with time. While building your business, it is inevitable that something bad will happen at some point. When the unexpected and undesirable happens, you absolutely must get in front of it, understand the nature of the problem, and begin to formulate a plan. The plan doesn't necessarily have to be one of recovery, it can simply be a plan of understanding at first. As a founder, your behavior during a crisis and your response to bad news will influence your organizational culture. Crises significantly shape and reinforce, or potentially undermine, the culture through the actions and words of the leadership as they manage challenging situations.

Step one is to understand the extent and impact of the problem. Who is impacted by the issue, and to what extent? Are there other, consequential problems that will be generated because of the primary problem? Gather your team, bring in outside expertise if necessary, and make sure you have done everything you can to halt the damage and begin understanding the issues.

If you have cultivated a culture of learning, and Fail Fast as we described in Chapter 7, then you already have many of the mechanisms necessary to turn a failure into future successes. Employees need to feel safe to experiment, fail, and innovate. If you respond to failure with calmness and acceptance and provide support, your team will respond positively and lift everyone to become better. Never ever scapegoat or penalize an employee publicly or immediately upon failure. Even a single misstep in this arena will result in substantial damage to your culture and morale. If, after contemplation and review of the pertinent facts, you determine that a reprimand or termination is necessary, perform the necessary actions methodically, privately, and with relevant documentation.

Who, Five Whys, and What

When something bad occurs, your key responsibilities as a leader and founder of the company are to do three things as quickly as possible (meaning within a couple of days at most):

1. Who: You must understand which stakeholders are impacted (customers, employees, investors, or the public). "The Who."
2. 5 Whys: Work with your team to develop a plan to fully understand why the problem occurred, including the five Whys methodology presented below. "The Why."
3. What (are you going to do about it): Communicate to all stakeholders the problem, the impacts, and your plan to understand the issue fully and why it happened. Do not feel compelled to immediately communicate a recovery plan—because that could take significant time. "The What (are you going to do about it)" needs to eventually be explained.

Is it really important to communicate the bad news promptly? Put yourself in your customer, investor, or employee's shoes. If the leader of the organization withheld this important information, there must have been a compelling reason, right? What possible reasons make sense?

- The leader was attempting to cover up the problem.
- The leader didn't think it was a serious issue.
- There are other problems that I haven't been informed about.
- The company does not care about me, or my product/investment/ career.
- Or, they're just plain incompetent and can't be trusted.

Unfortunately, there are not any good reasons to withhold information. Any of the above explanations are damning and will impart lasting damage within your organization and with the relationships with that customer. Companies that built the club of withholding information and having to suffer the resulting fallout include Enron (2001 financial scandal), Boeing (737 Max), and Wells Fargo (fake accounts).

Communicating as early as practical, even if only with the admission that there is a problem and your team is working on it, will build trust and confidence with your stakeholders. Once you have alerted the necessary people you can return your focus to problem investigation and developing recovery plans.

As you dig into the problem, go beyond surface-level issues to identify the reason behind the failure. A good mental cue is to keep asking "why" things happened, five times. Toyota Industries statistically demonstrated that asking the question "why" five levels deep will achieve a full understanding of the root cause of any failure.

For example, let's review the Ford Pinto design from the 1970s. Pinto was a compact car produced by Ford as a small, low-cost, economical, entry-level car in response to the 1973 oil crisis. Unfortunately, once the car was in production and many were on the roads, the car became notorious for deadly fuel tank explosions in the event of rear-end collisions. Even in low speed collisions, the fuel tank could rupture, causing fires resulting in deaths and serious injuries. Ford was aware of the issue but failed to correct it before releasing the car to market. The failure to address the safety risk is considered a major manufacturing and ethical failure which resulted in significant legal and financial repercussions for Ford.

Example of "Five Whys" analysis of the Ford Pinto manufacturing failure:

1. Why did the Ford Pinto have a dangerous fuel tank design?
   a. The Pinto's fuel tank was in a position where it could rupture easily in a rear-end collision, leading to explosions and fires.
2. Why was the fuel tank in such a vulnerable position?
   a. The design placed the fuel tank behind the rear axle, which made it more prone to damage during a rear-end collision.
3. Why was the fuel tank placed behind the rear axle, despite the risk?
   a. Ford made the decision to place the fuel tank in that position to reduce the car's cost and improve fuel efficiency. It was a design

choice driven by the desire to make the car more competitive in the market.

4. Why did Ford prioritize cost-cutting over safety in the Pinto's design?

   a. Ford's management was under significant pressure to produce the Pinto quickly and at a low price to compete in the growing small-car market. Cost and speed of production were prioritized over thorough safety testing and design adjustments. Additionally, Ford performed a cost–benefit analysis that concluded the cost of fixing the fuel tank design was higher than the potential costs of legal claims and accidents.

5. Why did Ford use a cost–benefit analysis that undervalued human life and safety?

   a. Ford's management, particularly in the early 1970s, viewed the Pinto's design failure as a financial issue rather than an ethical or safety issue. The cost–benefit analysis conducted by Ford estimated that the cost of making changes to the design (about $11 per car) would exceed the cost of potential lawsuits, which was seen as a lower financial risk compared to the benefits of getting the car to market quickly and cheaply.

So, the problem was not actually a manufacturing failure but rather a failure of management policies and priorities. It would have been very simple for Ford management to direct the engineering and production teams to redesign and rebuild the defective cars. But management's choice to save $11 per car resulted in the deaths of 27 people with another 24 people burned but not killed.

Back to our principle that *Bad News Never Ages Well.* Imagine the discussions in Ford Motor Company when the prototype testing of the first Pintos revealed the design flaw. Was the news of the fatal flaw immediately communicated to upper management? According to testimony, yes it was. Did management develop a plan to control the situation and proactively develop a recovery plan? It doesn't appear so.

When you are dealing with your own problems, once the root cause of the problem has been identified, you need to implement tangible *written-down* changes to your company to preclude reoccurrences. The written changes can occur electronically, but they must be written in order to become effective. Word of mouth just won't create a lasting, reliable change. Whether the change is to a process, a policy, the approval or disapproval of a supplier or partner, or the termination of problematic employees, make the change, then monitor the results. These are the reasons that you want a business that embraces self-correcting mechanisms, as we discussed in Chapter 6. Self-correcting means you don't have to always be the one to fix every problem. Problems will occur, mistakes will be made, and hopefully nobody will be hurt. Having a company mindset and systems which can quickly respond and implement improvements will allow your bad news day to become a "lesson learned, won't happen again, on to better things" day.

I would like to believe that the Ford Motor Company executives in 1973 did not openly prefer that people would die and that was better than spending an additional $11 per car. I believe there was a failure of communication and appreciation of the extent of the danger.

Remember the story about Theranos from Chapter 3? I hope that Ms. Holmes did not drop out of Stanford with the specific intent of misleading investors, doctors, and patients in order to get rich. I'd like to believe that as a founder, she had a passion to help people and believed that her discovery would revolutionize health care for the betterment of mankind. I believe that as the bad news started to surface, she failed to stop, consider altering plans, and communicate it clearly to all her stakeholders. Instead, she chose to withhold the bad news, and press on in hopes of better results, eventually needing an impossible miracle, until it was too late.

The antidotes to the illnesses which afflicted Ford and Theranos are integrity and transparency. Recognize there is a problem and address the issues. Treat your employees, customers and investors with the respect they deserve as partners with a vested interest in the outcome. Once the problems are resolved you can continue building a Great Company.

Management is about persuading people to do things they do not want to do, while leadership is about inspiring people to do things they never thought they could.

—Steve Jobs

CHAPTER 10

Bringing It All Back Together

Through the various sections in this book, we have discussed methods to raise capital, how to identify market opportunities which enable the highest probability of success, and how to go about setting up your company to make it operate smoothly. We've reviewed business successes and failures, and what aspects made them each evolve into what the world now recognizes as the brand and the Myth. More than any of those factors, it has become clear that the people are what made each company successful or not. People from the first founder through each employee contributed to what the company became.

You as the founder of your business have the latitude to build and prioritize whatever capital you do raise however you choose (provided you abide by any covenants or conditions stipulated in the agreements!). Hopefully, throughout this book, we've made some good arguments for being frugal about expenses that don't matter yet spend generously on the critical items that will make your company grow, including attracting and retaining the best team.

Suppose you have partnered up with two other entrepreneurs and you've identified an Elite Icon opportunity that you all believe could be captured based upon your industry knowledge, experience, and education. Each of the founders has agreed to invest $100,000 of their own money from savings, friends and family, and you were lucky enough to impress a wealthy Angel investor with your pitch, and she decided to give you $700,000 to get your company started, in exchange for 10 percent of the equity. What an amazing offer! You have the liberty to spend the money on facilities, salaries, benefits packages, marketing, furniture, proof-of-concept products, or whatever makes sense to you. However, your Angel has let you know that this is the only money she will be able to invest with you, and she would like to see at least a 5× return on her investment within 5 years. Obviously, $1 million won't run a viable company for 5 years, so you're going to have to develop a plan to bootstrap from this seed money into a successful business. Using the strategies we have outlined, how would you go about developing such a plan?

The key to this challenge is to *begin at the end*. What does your company need to look like to be self-sustaining in that Elite Icon opportunity in the next 3 to 5 years? Does it need 5 employees? 25? 100? Does it need nicer facilities? More equipment? Put together some rough calculations including estimates of product sales, salary & benefits, production costs, and other expenses including rent, utilities, equipment, insurance, taxes and marketing. Don't agonize about making a perfect prediction but do attempt to include a number for every category of expenses. Your estimate will likely be high in some areas, low in others, but if you have something reasonable for each of the major items, you've got something to work with.

I've always said there isn't a problem that can't be solved with a spreadsheet, and estimates of this kind are easy to put together and adjust for different scenarios. You can create a time-phased plan of when you hire people, their salaries and benefits, and all the other monthly expenses. This process will help you get an estimate of the total cost to build out a self-sufficient company under different conditions.

As you put together your plans for how many people to hire when and how much to pay them, consider what we discussed in Chapter 4: Highly qualified, experienced, and productive employees will outperform less qualified, inexperienced, and unproductive employees. Provided you can attract them, the higher pay and cost of benefits are eliminated by the extra productivity, indeed often you get more productive for less money from an experienced, go getter. In addition, those highly experienced and motivated employees are more likely to become creative and develop innovative solutions which further add value to the business to build a successful future position in the market.

The next step of the plan should focus on the near-term activities which can leverage that $1 million you have sitting in the checking account now, into more revenue on the path to being able to fund the fully self-sufficient company. Can you win an SBIR contract or two, or secure any State or Federal grants, raise capital through crowd funding or one of the other strategies we covered in Chapter 5?

Through this type of exercise, you can develop some strawman plans which embody both the actions and the costs of getting your business to the point where it is making revenue and can eventually become cash flow positive. In 1748, Benjamin Franklin wrote "Time is Money" in his essay "Advice to a Young Tradesman," a letter aimed at helping young people navigate the world of business and personal finance. He wrote:

> *Remember that time is money. He that can earn ten shillings a day by his labour, and goes abroad, or sits idle one half of that day, though he spends but sixpence during his diversion or idleness, it ought not to be reckoned the only expence; [sic] he hath really spent or thrown away five shillings besides*[48]

Let's put Ben's decree to the test. For this evaluation, we're going to consider two hypothetical companies, "Spacely Sprockets," founded by Cosmo Spacely and "Cogswell Cogs," founded by Cecil Cogs. Both of these founders are experienced in the industry of space widgets and are developing similar product ideas which will leverage the latest advances in artificial intelligence, self-driving cars, and 3D printing manufacturing. They have each secured $1 million in startup capital to pursue a new market opportunity and coincidentally start their fledgling businesses on the same day.

Cecil Cogs is an experienced businessman, and he sets up his business, leases an average facility, and begins hiring his team. He does his research, recruits a qualified team to develop the product as well as an accountant and various support staff. He budgets for other major expenses such as utilities, standard benefits, taxes, equipment, insurance, material to build their new product prototypes, and marketing expenses. He estimates that it will take his team 10 months to develop their product and get it onto the market.

Cosmo Spacely has just read this book, so he has a slightly different strategy in mind. He will look for an exceptional facility in order to attract the top talent, he will offer better than industry average pay and company ownership, and he will provide better benefits, even though all of these things are going to cost him more each month. Cosmo doesn't want an average company; he wants a Great Company! His strategy is to hire the best, let them flourish, and count on his team to be innovative and efficient. The team hired by Spacely develops their design 20 percent faster than an "average" team. Finally, Spacely budgets an additional 20 percent more for marketing in order to put together an impressive campaign. All these additional costs add up to 8 percent higher costs per month as shown in Table 10.1. Spacely is spending more per month, but since his team is more efficient, they are able to complete the project 20 percent earlier, in just a little over 8 months compared to Cogswell's team at 10 months.

By completing the development sooner with its high-powered team, the Spacely company actually saves over $100,000 (a 10 percent savings) versus Cogswell's team. Since Spacely's team completes their work faster, they can file for a patent and trademark first, securing intellectual property rights. Best of all, Spacely is first to market, capturing the consumers

Table 10.1 Comparison of Cogswell and Spacely budgets

	Cogswell	Spacely	
Estimates (thousand $)	Typical	Exceptional	
Monthly Rent	$ 12,000	$ 14,400	Nicer facility
Util	$ 6,000	$ 6,000	
Mgmt/Support Salary	$ 30,000	$ 30,000	
Dev Team Salary	$ 30,000	$ 36,000	Hire the best
Benefits	$ 9,000	$ 9,900	Better benefits
Taxes	$ 5,400	$ 5,940	Taxes scale with salary
Equipment	$ 5,000	$ 5,000	
Insurance	$ 1,500	$ 1,500	
Marketing	$ 1,000	$ 1,200	Better marketing
Material	$ 20,000	$ 20,000	
Monthly Total	$ 119,900	$ 129,940	8%
Time to market:	10	8.3	months
Development Cost:	$ 1,199,000	$ 1,082,833	k dollars
		9.7%	savings

interest in this innovative new device which is disrupting the industry. Consumers start buying Spacely's product before Cogswell's product is even finished being designed.

Another advantage that Spacely can capitalize upon is that once his development team completes their work in month 8, he can assign them on a new project and get a 2-month head start on Cogswell's team. Spacely could also take advantage of this time to have his team apply for some Grants or SBIRs, getting a jump on securing some smart capital to help fuel the business growth. It's highly likely that Spacely's team had some discoveries during the development of the first product, and they could either pursue those ideas, propose them as SBIR concepts, or seek customer input to flesh out their concepts. The banking account balances for both companies are shown in Figure 10.1 illustrating the financial performance over the first 18 months. As you can see, Cogswell ran out of money in August and had to take out a loan for $200,000 to keep his company running. Fortunately, he can pay off the loan in April of the following year, once he starts generating revenue.

The final part of this story between Cogswell and Spacely occurs at month 18 (in May) when a holding company approaches each of the company owners to discuss acquiring the company through a stock

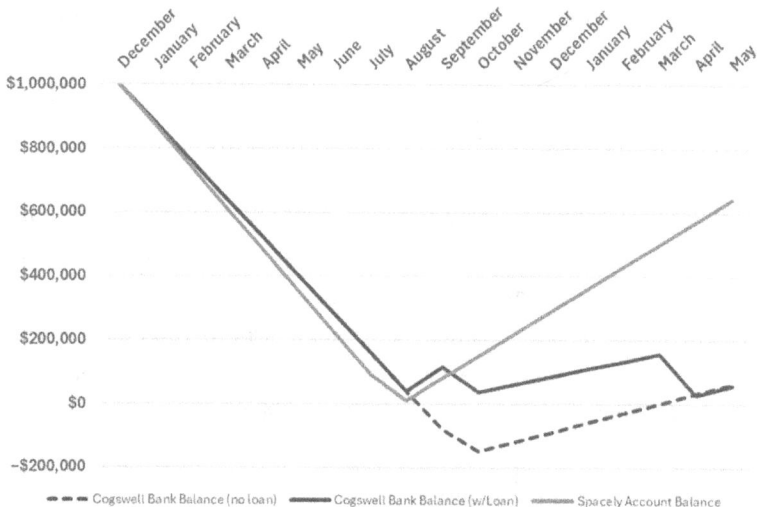

Figure 10.1 *Spacely and Cogswell Company performance—first 18 months*

buyout. The valuation offered by the holding company is 20× the earnings over the prior 12 months. For Cogswell, the previous 12 months were a loss, so the calculation is meaningless, and the holding company isn't sure how to estimate a valuation, other than to trust Cecil's prediction that the company is now going to be operating profitably in the future. For Spacely, the previous 12 months showed modest earnings of $290,000, and the holding company offers 20× which is $5.8 million. Cosmo Spacely and his founding partners consider the offer but decide to hold onto their growing business because they know they've built something special, they're having a great time, the employees are happy, and the future is bright.

With gratitude to Hanna-Barbera Productions, creators of *The Jetsons*, Spacely Sprockets and Cogswell Cogs, we have been able to confirm that Benjamin Franklin was correct, *Time is Money*.

When competing in business, the sooner that your team completes a project, and can start collecting revenue, the more revenue you can generate. Especially if you are first to market! This isn't a complicated concept, but it is somehow lost on many business owners who elect to cut corners or delay pursuing an opportunity. While being first is helpful, you must also have good timing, and a world-class team that can execute and maximize your chances for success. Just look at the difference between Uber with a market capitalization of $140 billion, versus Lyft's $6.7 billion, as of December 2024. Another way to view this dynamic is that as of March 2024, Uber accounted for 76 percent of the U.S. Rideshare market, compared to Lyft's 24 percent.[49]

Let's discuss the rate of growth of your company for a bit. As I outlined in the Introduction, consider three phases of growth for your company: *phase 0*, when the company is just you and your cofounders with zero revenue, developing plans; *phase 1*, when you start to hire critical employees who are fundamentally necessary to bring in revenue and grow the company to achieve those plans; *phase 2*, where the company becomes more self-sufficient, and you can expand the employee pool to support the growth.

In phase 0, when it is just you and your founders, if possible, you should avoid paying anyone a salary. Moonlight if possible and hoard your capital as much as you can, while you identify your Elite Icon and test the waters with a prototype of your product or service. Let the market inform you whether your idea is desirable, or whether changes are necessary. Your goal in phase 0 is to become *credible*, including legal business formation; a professional looking website, e-mail, and physical addresses; and a team which instills confidence in prospective customers, investors, or employees.

The people you hire in phase 1, as I outlined in Chapter 4, should be multitalented exceptional contributors who will fulfill the promise of creating something special. Phase 1 is where you hire the Great team and help them create the core of the company which will maximize your chances of success. Keep the team small and nimble during phase 1, and don't be surprised if you must wear a lot of hats to fill in the gaps where you haven't had time or capital to devote to end-to-end operations yet. Your goal in phase 1 is to have a company Myth, a product or service you are pursuing, and a source of revenue or capital, and some marketing underway.

Phase 2 is when you start to round out the company, the staff, the facilities, and the overall operations to become a long-term self-sustaining organization. You will flesh out many of the holes in the operations, processes, and team during phase 2. This is the time to start delegating some of the less critical parts of your responsibilities to other people within the company. Your goal in phase 2 is to achieve financial stability and operational consistency so that your company is viewed as a trusted supplier of the product or services. You know you've achieved phase 2 if you can go on vacation for 2 weeks and not have to call into the office even once to make sure everything is OK.

Next, let's examine an example of a company named "3C Institute for Social Development," established in 2001 by Dr. Melissa DeRosier, a clinical psychologist focused on connecting research with practice in education. Dr. DeRosier earned her doctorate from UNC-Chapel Hill in 1992 and completed a 2-year fellowship at Duke University Medical Center. While working on a 5-year federal grant focused on bullying and violence prevention in the Wake County Public School System, she noticed that many schools were relying on non–evidence-based programs to address social and emotional learning. This observation (her superpower) inspired her to establish 3C Institute to create web and games-based solutions for improving social and emotional skills for children and families.[50] She wanted to stay in North Carolina, so she turned to SBIR opportunities to bring smart money to her doorstep. Dr. DeRosier wrote her first SBIR grant proposal from the attic office in her home, and was delighted to win the grant, which allowed her to move into a 600 sq ft office space and hire two employees but wasn't enough to allow her to take a salary that first year. She had failed in some prior business startups, and was rewarded for her persistence with not only the federal SBIR grant from the National Institute of Health, but also was able to apply for and receive a matching grant from the State of North Carolina to help her build the business and perform marketing for 3C Institute. Fortunately, the success continued. 3C Institute pursued and secured SBIR phase 2 as well as additional phase 1 awards, totaling $250,000 in 2002, $200,000 in 2003, and $1.6 million in 2004 (a good growth pattern using smart money). Since its inception, the company has grown to employ 75 staff members and has received $25 million in SBIR funding from organizations like the U.S. Department of Education, the National Institutes of Health, and the Centers for Disease Control and Prevention.

Along their journey, 3C Institute evaluated Angel Investors and Venture Capital opportunities, but could not find a synergistic match between the profit motives of investors and the social priorities of improving the health and well-being of children and families.

In 2014, 3C Institute launched a corporate spin-off, Personalized Learning Games, to commercialize its social-emotional learning games and expand their reach.[51] However, after the 2016 election, some of the previously awarded grants were defunded, including a $1 million program for bullying prevention. Dr. DeRosier recognized the need to pivot, and began transitioning to a services business model, and away from reliance on SBIR and other grants. Today, the company is 80 percent supported by Services and Software sales, and only 20 percent from Grants. Enough grant money to continue research to build the future for the company. 3C Institute is an excellent example of how the SBIR system was designed: Assist a business startup to develop core products and services and serve as a pipeline to fuel innovative research until the company can commercialize their products and become a standalone success.

Another example of a company that grew with assistance from the SBIR program is BioSensics, Newton, MA, which was founded in 2007 by three scientists from Harvard University. The company pursued and received over $2 million of funding from the U.S. Department of Health and Human Services as well as Department of Defense in support of health monitoring for elderly and people with cognitive issues. Since that time, BioSensics has emerged as a global leader in the development of wearable-based medical devices and digital health technologies for clinical trials, patient monitoring and health assessment.[52] The company has also incorporated novel techniques such as Tai-Chi, innovative carpet materials, and other concepts to provide a holistic approach to addressing the dangers of falling and other health issues. BioSensics was awarded the Tibbetts Award in 2020 by the U.S. Small Business Administration, recognizing it as one of the most innovative and impactful small businesses in the country. The company has utilized the U.S. Patent system to protect their technology and grown to employ more than 20 people with diverse backgrounds and skill sets.

Transitioning away from SBIRs, BioSensics has developed and commercialized several wearable-based medical devices and digital health technologies to create a viable and commercial revenue stream. Their products provide objective assessments of gait and fall risk and support aging at home. The products have been integrated into various clinical trials and health care settings, contributing to advancements in patient monitoring and health assessment.[53]

The Myth of BioSensics could be described as a journey that began with a vision by three Harvard scientists with a mission to transform health care by leveraging wearable technology to provide objective, accessible, and precise health insights. The founders identified a Blue Ocean in the medical field: the need for real-time, reliable data to improve patient outcomes and enable preventative care. They envisioned a world where advanced technology could seamlessly integrate into everyday life, enhancing health monitoring and reducing health care costs for individuals and institutions alike. The company's Myth is reinforced by its significant impact: BioSensics' technologies are utilized by thousands of individuals and have been incorporated into numerous clinical trials, thereby advancing medical research and enhancing patient care.

When it comes to your own company, always keep an open mind and be ready to pivot in response to customer and employee feedback. Your Myth, products, services, and Culture will always be a work in progress. If those things aren't evolving, you are probably being overtaken in the marketplace by competitors. Be creative and leverage as many *simultaneous* funding avenues as you can to create a robust and redundant income stream while you're getting the company off the ground.

The biggest priorities for you as a founder are (1) developing sources for capital to get the company started, (2) building a wonderful team, and (3) finding customers who believe in your products and services. Success in those endeavors will all hinge upon your company Myth and the passion which you and your founders bring to work with you each day as you navigate the labyrinth of building your business in your market. The goal for you as the founder is to stretch the money you do receive as long as necessary to prove out your products and services, and bring in enough cash to keep everyone employed long enough to figure out how to become successful. You can do that by bringing in lots of money, spending frugally, and being creative in your marketing. I recommend all three.

What you envision as your company and your product when you start out on this adventure will likely not be the final product or service which supports the business. It may turn out that your vision is accurate, and the initial ideas you start out to pursue yield a vibrant company. More often, however, company founders realize along the way that the customers and marketplace need slightly different or evolving solutions. Expect to learn along the way and follow the clues that the world will give to you.

Everyone needs to have a purpose in order to give their life meaning. A reason to get out of bed in the morning and be useful for family, society, and humankind or the planet. Most of us must work to pay our bills. So, if you are going to work, why not do something that you are passionate about? Alongside fun and interesting people who share your passions. People you enjoy working with and building a great Myth, and turning that into a relevant, durable business? There really is not anything more fulfilling than working with a team that you help lead, building a Great Company, doing something special that nobody has done before. It is an exciting way to spend your days and leave a legacy.

I hope that you have enjoyed reading this book as much as I enjoyed compiling the stories, lessons learned, and guidelines. Thank you for your time, and best of luck building a Great Company! I would love to hear from you if you have interesting experiences on your journey.

—Matt Beckner

Epilogue: Exit Stage Left

The philosophies and methodologies presented throughout the chapters of this book were targeted toward building an organization where the founders retain control, provide a positive work environment for the employees, but stay flexible in defining the path of growth. As you undoubtedly experienced along your journey of growing your company, there is no single, predictable path from startup to exit. There were numerous surprises both good and bad along the path, some of them exhilarating, some disappointing. Not everyone will decide to sell their business. Many founders continue to enjoy the amazing workplace and people. Running a Great Company where employees are happy and customers are satisfied is an unequivocal success!

However, what you may experience at some point in the company's growth is what Scott Tibbets refers to as "the Founders Ceiling,"[54] essentially the size of the company that you personally as a founder or your combined leadership team is equipped to manage. The skill set and priorities for the leader of the company will evolve as the company grows. I found that I was most comfortable in my role as a founder for the company when it was between 25 and 100 people. Smaller than that, and I felt that we didn't have enough horsepower to operate reliably—people were having to wear too many hats. Once the company got over 100 people, the types of challenges and opportunities were far enough outside my comfort zone that I became less and less effective as a leader. George and Steve had higher ceilings. Our combined management team at BCT did fairly well up to about 300 people in the company, but as we grew beyond that it became clear that we had met or crashed through the ceiling and it was time to hand over the leadership to a different team for the good of the company and the employees. Everyone's ceiling is different, and some founders never reach theirs.

The recommendations in Chapter 5 regarding capitalization leaned most strongly into nondilutive funding mechanisms such as Grants, Friends and Family funding, Crowd funding, and Bank Loans so that the founders could retain control of the company. Leveraging modest means of capital raising also kept the leadership team laser-focused on responding to customer feedback in order to maximize revenue and the success of your startup. In addition, retaining ownership in those nondilutive strategies will give you the most options and control if it is time for an exit.

On the other hand, if along the way it was necessary to accelerate growth through a large, dilutive cash infusion, not to worry. Whether you accepted dilution via Angel Investment or Venture Capital, you should have created a much bigger pie in the process, and even though you will get a smaller slice, your overall economic benefit should be proportionally larger. Obviously, the more dilution, the less control you retain.

As the company grows and if the time comes to contemplate an Exit, you have many options available to you. The remainder of this chapter is devoted to summarizing the exit methods that align best with your goals, then planning and executing the exit.

Exit Considerations

Before we dive into specific exit structures, however, let's consider key factors related to your business, your goals, tax consequences, and impacts on employees and customers.

Business Valuation: How to determine the value of any given business is an art and a science unto itself. "Experts" will typically cite *earnings multiples by sector or industry*. Or, instead of earnings, the multiple may be based off of revenue, but that in my opinion is a fallacy because nobody is excited to buy a business with high revenue but even higher operating expenses! The assumption may be that high revenues eventually translate into profitability, but that isn't always the case.

So, "earnings" will most likely be defined as EBITDA = Earnings Before Interest, Taxes, Depreciation, and Amortization. One of the challenges of EBITDA is that it is not an officially recognized metric under GAAP (Generally Accepted Accounting Principles, the rules your CPA follows), so it isn't readily available from your accounting department. You may have to do some gymnastics to get your accountant to calculate and track it. All the pieces are available from your accounting system, just not the calculation itself. A benefit to you and your company is that

EBITDA will often paint a more attractive picture of your company than other metrics. For this reason, savvy buyers will attempt to discredit the EBITDA multiplier method.

If you can leverage the EBITDA multiplier with your prospective buyers, then you can lean on "industry norms" for EBITDA multiples to calculate your business' value. Again, the challenge here is to agree upon the appropriate multiple. Various "experts" will get their data from different sources and achieve different multipliers. For example, in a review of "EBITDA Multiples by Industry" that I conducted at the end of 2024, I found surprisingly varied opinions on multiples, as shown in Table E.1.

The problem with the EBITDA multiplier methodology is obviously that sellers prefer big multipliers and buyers prefer small ones. For your own sanity, before you decide to go to market, consider both extremes for your situation and decide if you and your equity partners would be satisfied with either end of the spectrum.

Table E.1 Industry EBITDA multiples from various sources (December 2024)

Industry	Equidam[55]	Eval[56]	Eqvista[57]
Advanced Medical Equipment and Tech.	21.66	20.76	28.9
Advertising and Marketing	11.94	13.29	14.31
Aerospace and Defense	17.91	23.91	33.08
Investment Banks	17.98	10.61	17.03
Biotechnology	15.32	N/A	23.77
Business Support Services	9.43	18.33	N/A
Entertainment Production	15.78	26.65	24.39
Fishing and Farming Equipment	9.75	15.31	11.81
Food Retail and Distribution	9.35	12.90	22.64
Homebuilding	8.03	12.68	29.54
IT Services	14.68	14.54	25.18
Leisure and Recreation	11.79	26.65	38.36
Oil and Gas Drilling/Services	6.44	12.82	6.42
Paper Products	10.15	8.54	26.75
Real Estate Services	16.5	23.37	25.81
Software	28.48	34.47	35.49
Wireless Telecom Services	7.37	6.54	8.85

EBITDA multiple valuation methods are applicable in situations like acquisitions and mergers, but at best can only provide general guidance for other types of transactions.

What we found at BCT was that the "industry normalized EBITDA multiplier" was merely a number around which to start a discussion between the acquirer and the company being acquired. With any organization that we met with, the question would be posed as to how much we expected to sell the company, and leveraging this method provided a defendable starting point to respond. Founders do have a fiduciary duty to achieve a good valuation for the shareholders, regardless of whether the company is private or public. Founders should also concern themselves with continuity of operations, ability to continue satisfying customer obligations, employee retention, corporate culture, and overall continuity of the company legacy. Consider weaving these factors into your negotiations with any prospective buyer. We developed a scorecard at BCT where we ranked each potential acquiring company on all of those factors.

The new owners of BCT have been able to continue the Myth, retain most of the employees, and continue to increase the annual revenue to over $135 million and employ 450 people.[58] The reviews on Glassdoor indicate that the culture has eroded somewhat. Culture is one of the most difficult things to maintain after the founders exit. Reviews include "Great people, good environment, fun programs," "Leading edge technologies with great culture," and "Good benefits and pay." The negative reviews most notably cite: "Inexistent/unexperienced management."[59] So, maybe we shouldn't have left the company after all?

Getting back on track of determining valuation: In addition to the EBITDA multiplier, there are a variety of methods to simultaneously enhance the value of your company and protect your market advantage, as we discussed in Chapter 7. These factors should be prominent during any discussions about selling the company, and you should highlight the trade secrets, patents, trademarks, copyrights, industrial design rights, exclusive contracts, and strategic partnerships you have been able to establish.

While the value of the company is important, there are several factors to consider during such negotiations:

Personal Goals: Consider what you want from the exit. Is it maximum financial return, a smooth transition, or a specific legacy for the business? Some owners want to continue to remain with the business in a leadership capacity to stay active and ensure that their legacy is protected, and their employees are well taken care of. Other owners want a clean break so they can head to the marina, buy their ocean yacht, and never look back. For each of the major shareholders at BCT, there was a different answer. And once the exit is complete, plans may change as well. When we discuss the different types of exits, you will notice that there are preferred exit methods appropriate for different personal goals. If your goal is to pass the company on to a family member, some of the methods are simply not applicable.

Timing: Market conditions, business performance, and personal life stages can all affect the best time to exit. While market conditions can be difficult to predict, you will likely have a better insight into those factors than the general public and may be better informed than the people looking to acquire your business. Timing will involve a bit of luck, because most people find that an exit is determined mostly by personal desires and business performance. Whether that occurs during bullish or bearish market conditions is really outside your control.

Employee and Customer Impact: Consider how your exit will affect employees, customers, and other stakeholders. One of our key objectives throughout this book is to maintain a business that you, your employees, and your customers respect and enjoy.

If the company got off track somewhere along the way, and has become a burden, suffers from a negative culture, or has simply gotten out of control, then the time may be right to part ways and let some fresh perspective steer the ship into better waters. In this scenario, your exit could enable a series of changes for the betterment of the organization and employees. That doesn't necessarily mean that you were the root of the problems. It is equally likely that the company has outgrown your skill sets and although you've done an amazing job to that point, the time has come to part ways and transition the company to a different suite of capabilities to continue to grow and thrive. The founders at BCT felt we had overseen the growth of our company to the best of our abilities, but now it was time for the organization to leave us so that it could continue to flourish under more experienced leadership.

If things have gone well, and you have indeed achieved a remarkable workplace where employees are happy, customers are satisfied, and stakeholders believe in the company from top to bottom, then you have an obligation to consider all of those perspectives in your pursuit of an exit.

Tax Implications: Some exit strategies have more favorable tax treatment than others (e.g., selling to family members or through an ESOP). In my opinion, tax considerations should be used as a tiebreaker between competing opportunities that otherwise satisfy your personal and financial goals and the impact on your employees and customers.

Whichever method you pursue, you should embrace the process and enjoy it as much as possible. Being the founder of a company which proves valuable enough to attract attention from third party buyers is a monumental achievement, one which few people get to experience. Celebrate this amazing success! Have fun as much as you can, regardless of the exit method, and most importantly *Don't Forget to Run the Business*. Many founders get caught up in the time demands and excitement of the exit process. They neglect the health and performance of the company resulting in a loss of value and in many cases a failure to complete the exit. Also, be ready for "deal fatigue": As the negotiations go on, then pass into due diligence, there will come times when you are exhausted and ready to just accept any deal. Don't give up, there are some acquisition strategists who will try to wear you down, so stay strong.

Select Your Great Exit

1. **Acquisition: Sale to an Outside Party**
   - **Description**: Selling the business to an outside party, such as a larger company within your industry, a competitor, a private equity firm, or an investor, is the most common exit strategy. It can be achieved through an asset sale (selling assets like equipment, buildings, inventory, and intellectual property) or a stock/share sale (selling ownership shares of the company).
     - **Pros**: Potential for a large payout, especially if the business is well established and profitable. In addition, it is often the best way to achieve an immediate exit from the business. If you already have a buyer lined up, this can be a great way to quickly

make your exit. Establishing a valuation that is acceptable to all parties may be a challenge. You may be able to execute a partial sale, to liquidate some of your equity but not all, and remain involved in the business operations.

- **Cons**: Depending upon the market conditions, it can be a lengthy and complex process, involving negotiations and due diligence. From a total financial picture, it will probably involve paying capital gains tax on the sale. Whether any or all the current owners stay with the company is up to what can be negotiated with the acquirer. During due diligence, every aspect of your business will be evaluated, every document subject to review, and any lingering skeletons can derail the process or significantly impact the negotiated price. Appoint a person in authority to manage the due diligence for your team in order to avoid confusion or errors.

- **Recommendation**: If you do not have a specific buyer already lined up but are planning to "go to market," the best way to ensure you get a good settlement for you, your employees and your stakeholders is to hire an investment banker knowledgeable in your industry. Not only can an investment banker control the process to make sure your interests are protected, but they can also find multiple interested buyers to drive the price higher as well as make sure that the transaction is legally conducted in accordance with regulatory requirements. A good investment banker can also provide a realistic valuation for your company based upon the actual performance and strategic value of your company, as well as defend that valuation from assault by the acquiring entity.

2. **Merger**
   - **Description**: In a merger, your business combines with another company, creating a new entity or one company taking over the other. This can often involve sharing ownership or a buyout.
     - **Pros**: Mergers of small companies can result in a more significant entity with greater market power and resources. There is also the possibility of a financial exit for one or more equity owners with continued involvement in the merged company for other owners.

- **Cons:** Requires finding the right merger partner. The process can be complex, and simply put, there will almost always be a culture clash. Typically, the larger entity will dominate the culture integration, as well as the Myth. In some cases, this might be a benefit to the smaller company.
- **Recommendation:** Look for a partner with strengths that complement your company's weaknesses. Visualize what the future combined entity could achieve, the resulting Culture and Myth.

3. **Management Buyout**
   - **Description:** In a management buyout (MBO), the existing management team or key employees buy out some or all the owner's shares or assets. This is a good option if the owner wants to ensure that the business continues to run with familiar leadership. If you wish to liquidate a portion of your ownership but retain some ownership and stay involved in the day-to-day operations, the MBO can be structured accordingly.
     - **Pros:** Obviously, this method enables an easier transition, as the management team already understands the business. It is assumed that the existing management team is comfortable with the incoming team, or else it wouldn't be an option. If it is desirable, some or all the owners can maintain a level of control or involvement. In some cases, an MBO makes sense to execute in phases or gradually over time rather than an immediate transition of throwing the new team into the deep end of the pool and hoping they figure out how to swim.
     - **Cons:** Requires the management team to have the necessary financial resources, which may involve securing external financing. Depending on your situation, the gradual exit may not be desirable. The MBO is typically also the most difficult to execute a total break between the old team and the new team (again, maybe that's a pro for your situation).

4. **Employee Stock Ownership Plan (ESOP)**
   - **Description:** This is one of the best ways to convert your hard work and years of dedication into an equitable result, as well as providing flexibility for you and other members of the leadership team to maintain control, if that is your desire. In this method,

the ESOP allows the business owner to sell the company to the employees as shares. You will need support from an experienced business attorney and CPA knowledgeable in the process. The simplest description is that a trust is set up under the guidance of a "third party administrator" to purchase the company shares, and employees gradually acquire ownership over time.

- **Pros**: The ESOP allows your employees to share in the ownership and potential success of the business. Because it will be a gradual transition, there is the least likelihood of disruption to the business operations, the culture, or the Myth. For the owners, there will be a significant tax advantage in comparison to an Acquisition, since the gains will be spread over time.

- **Cons**: The ESOP requires careful planning and execution to be performed legally. There will be associated costs for lawyers, accountants, and filings. In order for the ESOP to form an effective exit method for the principal owners, it works best to start the ESOP years before any owner wishes to cash out. Getting the details of the ESOP plan correct is critical to ensure it meets the requirements of the Internal Revenue Code.

- **Recommendation**: Consult with a reputable adviser or ESOP consultant to establish a valuation before you embark on this course of action. The consultant should be able to help you locate and work with an experienced commercial bank to facilitate the process as well as provide financing if you want to execute the exit faster than the employees are willing to purchase the stock. In this manner, the commercial bank will own a significant number of shares in the trust which will be purchased over time by the employees.

5. **Family Succession**
   - **Description**: This strategy involves transferring the ownership and leadership of the business to family members. It works well for businesses that are family-owned and have multiple generations involved or interested in taking over. This is a form of Management Buyout but may be less formal and appropriate for smaller businesses.

- **Pros**: It can provide continuity and maintain your culture, the Myth, and your family legacy. Every situation is unique, but generally a family succession will enable a smoother transition than selling to outside parties.
- **Cons**: The process can lead to family conflicts, especially if there are disagreements over leadership or financial matters. Not all family members may have the skills or desire to run the business. Finally, you should anticipate that there will be some disgruntled employees and potentially issues for your family to overcome after the succession.

6. **Initial Public Offering (IPO) (also discussed in Chapter 5)**
   - **Description**: An IPO is when a private company goes public by offering its shares on a stock exchange for the first time. This can provide significant capital and liquidity for the owners. Of all the exit strategies we discuss, this one is the most complex and requires the most up-front planning. You will need investment bankers, legal advisers, outside accounting firms, and auditors in order to execute the IPO, complete the filings with the SEC, and launch the IPO. If there is any chance that you will pursue an IPO, you should begin with that in mind early in the setting up of the company's accounting system, processes, and internal controls. All these aspects will come under intense scrutiny during the IPO process, which will take up to a year or longer.
     - **Pros**: There is a potential for a large payday if the company is successful and the IPO goes well. If the company is strapped for cash, or needs to grow, an IPO may be able to open up new capital markets in addition to the influx of cash from the launch. An IPO is an excellent way to increase market visibility within the industry and with consumers. Going public provides the opportunity to achieve a level of legitimacy that can't be replicated by a privately held company, provided everything is in order and there aren't any skeletons in the closets. The impacts on Culture and Myth can be minimized but cannot be eliminated.

- **Cons**: An IPO is the most expensive and labor-intensive exit process. Your ownership in the company will be diluted, so you need to become comfortable with the expected results. As a large equity owner, you will also be subject to a lock-up period, which is typically 90 to 180 days after the IPO. Longer lock-ups are possible in certain circumstances. To even qualify for an IPO, you will need on the order of a full year of independently audited financial statements including Balance Sheet, Income, Cash Flows, and records of any changes in equity ownership. Once public, financial data, executive compensation, legal matters, and other sensitive information must be disclosed to the public.

- **Recommendation**: For the business owners, an IPO represents both a huge opportunity and a major responsibility. It is extremely rare that a successful founder (who typically understands their industry very well from the bottom up, and is talented at leading smaller teams) can transition to becoming an executive of a large publicly traded company. The focus shifts to new roles such as regulatory compliance, governance, shareholder value, and industry strategy. Obviously, the process needs to start with a credible Investment Bank ranging from large global banks such as Goldman Sachs and J.P. Morgan to smaller firms such as Evercore, Stifel, and Baird.

7. **Liquidation or Closing the Business**
   - **Description**: If the business is not profitable or the owner is ready to exit, they may decide to liquidate the company's assets and shut it down. This could involve selling off physical assets, paying off debts, and closing the doors.
     - **Pros**: Relatively straightforward and immediate way to exit, no need for negotiations with buyers or investors, and you don't have to worry about the impacts on Myth or Culture.
     - **Cons**: In general, the business will not be worth much after liabilities are settled. This is a classic case of the parts not being equal to the conglomeration.

8. **Franchising**
   - **Description**: If the business is well established and has a proven model, franchising can be an exit strategy. In franchising, the business owner licenses the business model and brand to other entrepreneurs. Businesses which are well suited to franchising are typically low-cost, high-volume, consumer-focused businesses such as fast-food restaurants, fitness centers, service providers such as cleaning, repair or pet services, and retail businesses.
     - **Pros**: Potential for continued income through franchise fees and royalties. You can dictate how the Culture and Myth of your company must be preserved, provided you can capture those aspects in the written regulations of the franchising agreement. You can still retain ownership of the brand while expanding the business.
     - **Cons**: Requires a strong, replicable business model and significant up-front investment in training, marketing, and support systems. You will have to manage the franchise network, which can be complex or rewarding, depending upon your disposition.
     - **Recommendation**: If you suspect that franchising might be in your best interest, focus closely on documenting all of your processes and procedures clearly.

Regardless of the type of exit, be prepared for significant demands on your time and energy. You are still the founder of a great company, and unless you've found yourself a good clone, you will be expected to keep the company afloat and on a positive trajectory through the exit. Some entrepreneurs spend 2 to 3 years coordinating the exit, and arrive at the finish line exhausted and in poor health.

Do not hesitate to call in reinforcements, hire expertise, and augment your leadership team as necessary to complete the exit. We hired an experienced CFO at BCT with the specific goal of getting the company ready for an acquisition, then helping the management team throughout the process. We also retained the services of investment bankers, auditors, and additional legal support. All those entities cost money but add significant value to the market price you will be able to negotiate for your business. Most important of all, adding those support services allows the management team to keep running the business, maintain a great culture, and achieve the best results for the employees, customers, and new owners.

Starting, growing, and operating a business is an endeavor unlike anything else in the world. It can be one of the most rewarding, demanding, and occasionally terrifying endeavors you could contemplate. If you make smart decisions, follow your heart, act with integrity, and hire a good team, you will be successful. Life is short; why not make it interesting and spend your time doing things you enjoy?

Notes and References

1. CB Insights. 2021. "The Top 12 Reasons Startups Fail." www.cbinsights. com/research/report/startup-failure-reasons-top/.
2. Pitchbook. (n.d.). "Blue Canyon Technologies Company Profile: Acquisition & Investors." Accessed November 30, 2024. https://pitchbook. com/profiles/company/128686-78.
3. Punjwani, Mehdi, and Lauren Holznienkemper. 2024. "What Percentage of Startups Fail?" *Forbes*, October 23. www.forbes.com/advisor/business/ software/startups-failure-rate/.
4. Rawlinson, Nik. 2017. "History of Apple: The Story of Steve Jobs and the Company He Founded"." *Macworld*, April 25. www.macworld.com/ article/671584/history-of-apple-the-story-of-steve-jobs-and-the-company- he-founded.html.
5. GEICO. n.d. "Geico History." Accessed December 8, 2024. www.geico. com/about/corporate/history/.
6. Uber Newsroom. 2018. "The History of Uber." 2 May. www.uber.com/ newsroom/history/.
7. Wikimedia Foundation. n.d. "Uber." Accessed November 13, 2024. https:// en.wikipedia.org/wiki/Uber.
8. Kim, W. Chan, and Renée Mauborgne. 2016. *Blue Ocean Strategy: How to Create Uncontested Market Space and Make the Competition Irrelevant.* Harvard Bus Review Press.
9. History.com. 2009. "Ford's Assembly Line Starts Rolling." A&E Television Networks. www.history.com/this-day-in-history/fords-assembly-line-starts- rolling.
10. Ford Corporate. n.d. "The Moving Assembly Line and the Five-Dollar Workday." Accessed January 2, 2025. https://corporate.ford.com/articles/ history/moving-assembly-line.html.
11. Wikimedia Foundation. n.d. "Jerry Pournelle." Accessed December 30, 2024. https://en.wikipedia.org/wiki/Jerry_Pournelle#Iron_Law_of_Bureaucracy.
12. Sydell, L. 2006. "Google Unveils Censored Search Engine in China." *NPR*, January 25. https://www.npr.org/2006/01/25/5172204/google-unveils- censored-search-engine-in-china.
13. Pierson, Brendan. 2022. "The Rise and Fall of Theranos Founder Elizabeth Holmes." *Reuters*, January 4. www.reuters.com/world/us/ rise-fall-theranos-founder-elizabeth-holmes-2022-01-04/.

14. Inc.com. (n.d.). "These 18 Words from Elon Musk Will Totally Transform How You Think About Leadership." https://www.inc.com/jessica-stillman/these-18-words-from-elon-musk-will-totally-transform-how-you-think-about-leadership.html.

15. Make Fun Of Life! (n.d.). "Teamwork Lessons from the Geese" by Robert McNeish.http://www.makefunoflife.net/everyday-inspiration/teamwork-lessons-from-the-geese-by-robert-mcneish

16. Indeed.Com, n.d. "10 Workplace Personalities (and How to Work with Each)." | Accessed December 1, 2024. www.indeed.com/career-advice/career-development/workplace-personality.

17. Robinson, Bryan. 2023. "70% of Workers Lie on Resumes, New Study Shows." *Forbes*, November 5. https://www.forbes.com/sites/bryanrobinson/2023/11/05/70-of-workers-lie-on-resumes-new-study-shows.

18. Wigert, Ben. 2022. "The Top 6 Things Employees Want in Their next Job." *Gallup*, February 21. www.gallup.com/workplace/389807/top-things-employees-next-job.aspx.

19. Harari, Yuval Noah. 2015. *Sapiens: A Brief History of Humankind*. Harper Collins.

20. Pink, Daniel H. 2011. *Drive: The Surprising Truth About What Motivates Us*. Riverhead Books.

21. iHire. 2024. "Top 10 Reasons Why People Quit Their Jobs in 2024." November 25. www.ihire.com/resourcecenter/employer/pages/reasons-why-people-quit-their-jobs-in-2024.

22. Wikimedia Foundation. n.d. "Derek J. de Solla Price." Accessed November 14, 2024. https://en.wikipedia.org/wiki/Derek_J._de_Solla_Price.

23. Kohan, Shelley E. 2022. "Patagonia's Bold Move Shakes up the Ideas of Capitalism and Consumerism." *Forbes*, November 8. www.forbes.com/sites/shelleykohan/2022/09/15/patagonias-bold-move-shakes-up-the-ideas-of--capitalism-and-consumerism/?utm_source=chatgpt.com.

24. "SBIR/STTR. n.d. America's Seed Fund—Powered by the Small Business Administration." Accessed December 6, 2024. www.sbir.gov/.

25. Tibbitts, S. 2024. *From the Garage to Mars: Memoir of a Space Entrepreneur*. Henschel Haus Publishing.

26. U.S. Small Business Administration. n.d. "7(a) & 504 Lender Report." Accessed December 12, 2024. https://careports.sba.gov/views/7a504LenderReport/LenderReport?%3Aembed=yes&%3Atoolbar=no&utm_source=riverbender&utm_medium=article_link.

27. "The American Angel." *HBS*, Accessed December 11, 2024. www.hbs.edu/ris/Publication%20Files/American%20Angel_50333d06-b332-4221-9919-2c35057ca468.pdf.

28. Harlem Capital. n.d. "What Are VCs Really Looking For in an Investment???" *HCP*, Accessed February 6, 2021. https://harlem.capital/what-are-vcs-really-looking-for-in-an-investment/.

29. "Saas Growth Report: Bootstrapped vs VC-Backed." *ChartMogul*. Accessed January 2, 2025. https://chartmogul.com/reports/saas-growth-vc-bootstrapped/.

30. Stock Analysis. n.d. "IPO Statistics." Accessed December 1, 2024. https://stockanalysis.com/ipos/statistics/.

31. Stock Analysis. n.d. "Biggest Car Company Stocks." Accessed December 6, 2024. https://stockanalysis.com/list/car-company-stocks/.

32. The Investopedia Team. n.d. "What Are the Listing Requirements for the NASDAQ?" Accessed December 1, 2024. www.investopedia.com/ask/answers/nasdaq-listing-requirements/#toc-required-financial-standards.

33. U.S. Securities and Exchange Commission. n.d. "Going Public." Accessed December 1, 2024. www.sec.gov/resources-small-businesses/going-public.

34. PricewaterhouseCoopers. n.d. "Considering an IPO? First Understand the Costs." Accessed December 1, 2024. www.pwc.com/us/en/services/consulting/deals/library/cost-of-an-ipo.html.

35. Smith, Ray A. n.d. "The Number of Americans Wanting to Switch Jobs Hits a 10 Year High. *Wall Street Journal*. Accessed January 4, 2025. www.wsj.com/lifestyle/careers/job-satisfaction-low-gallup-data-detachment-17bc183c.

36. Harari. 2015. *Sapiens*.

37. Blystone, Dan. n.d. "The History of Uber." *Investopedia*. Accessed December 6, 2024. www.investopedia.com/articles/personal-finance/111015/story-uber.asp.

38. FinanceCharts. n.d. "Lyft vs Uber Technologies." Accessed December 6, 2024. www.financecharts.com/compare/LYFT,UBER.

39. Dugan, Kevin T. 2021. "How Bird, the High-Flying Scooter Company, Went Broke." *Intelligencer*, December 21, 2023. https://nymag.com/intelligencer/2023/12/how-bird-the-high-flying-scooter-company-went-broke.html.

40. Curry, Rachel. 2022. "Bird Rides IPO: What to Know About a 2021 Public Offering." *Public*, May 9. https://public.com/learn/bird-rides-ipo-what-to-know?wpsrc=Organic%2BSearch&wpsn=duckduckgo.com.

41. Muske, Glenn. 2017. "Follow the Money." *Small Biz Survival*, April 19. https://smallbizsurvival.com/2017/04/follow-the-money.html.

42. Wikimedia Foundation, n.d. "SpaceX." Accessed January 5, 2025. https://en.wikipedia.org/wiki/SpaceX.

43. *Business Valuation Resources.* 2018. "What Are the Advantages and Disadvantages of Patents, Copyrights, Trademarks, and Trade Secrets?" www.bvresources.com/blogs/intellectual-property-news/2018/03/12/what-are-the-advantages-and-disadvantages-of-patents-copyrights-trademarks-and-trade-secrets#:~:text=First%2C patents are expensive to,the application includes foreign jurisdictions.

44. Farkas, Brian. n.d. "Trade Secret Basics FAQ." *Nolo.* Accessed December 1, 2024. www.nolo.com/legal-encyclopedia/trade-secret-basics-faq.html#protecting-trade-secrets.

45. "7 Steps to Protecting Your Trade Secrets." Accessed November 30, 2024. www.uspto.gov/sites/default/files/documents/CRS-LA-OBrien-trade-secrets.pdf.

46. Public Intelligence. 2020. "Office of Private Sector." publicintelligence.net/organization/office-of-private-sector/.

47. Goldsmith, Jonathan. 2024. "Payroll Taxes in the US: An Employer's Guide." *Blog*, November 29. https://remote.com/blog/payroll-taxes-united-states.

48. Wikimedia Foundation. (2024, October 14). *Time is money (aphorism).* Wikipedia. https://en.wikipedia.org/wiki/Time_is_money_(aphorism)

49. Kaczmarski, Michal. 2024. " Uber vs. Lyft: Who's Tops in the Battle of U.S. Rideshare Companies." *Bloomberg Second Measure*, April 15. https://secondmeasure.com/datapoints/rideshare-industry-overview/.

50. Wikimedia Foundation. 2021. "3C Institute." https://en.wikipedia.org/wiki/3C_Institute.

51. Ibid.

52. BioSensics. (n.d.). "Home Page." https://biosensics.com/.

53. SAE Media Group. 2023. "NIH Awards $3M to BioSensics to Develop First-in-Kind Wearable Sensor." *Medical Design Briefs*, September 26. https://www.medicaldesignbriefs.com/component/content/article/49156-nih-awarded-3m-to-biosensics-to-develop-first-in-kind-wearable-sensor.

54. Tibbitts. 2024. *From the Garage to Mars.*

55. Gray, Dan. 2025. "EBITDA Multiples by Industry in 2025." *Equidam.* www.equidam.com/ebitda-multiples-trbc-industries/.

56. eVal. 2021. "Valuation Multiples by Industry." www.eval.tech/valuation-multiples-by-industry.

57. Sarath. 2024. "EBITDA Multiples across Industries (2024)." *Eqvista*, November 19. https://eqvista.com/ebitda-multiples-by-industry/.

58. Growjo. n.d. "Blue Canyon Technologies Revenue and Competitors." https://growjo.com/company/Blue_Canyon_Technologies.

59. Glassdoor. n.d. "Blue Canyon Technologies Reviews." https://www.glassdoor.com/Reviews/Blue-Canyon-Technologies-Reviews-E1794638.htm.

Author Bio

Matthew Beckner is a father, engineer, and entrepreneur, best known as the cofounder of Blue Canyon Technologies (BCT), an innovative aerospace startup that achieved remarkable success under his leadership. A graduate of the University of Colorado, Beckner started his early career at Ball Aerospace, which was shaped by a deep expertise in spacecraft design, product manufacturing, testing, and operations—skills that he would later leverage to help build one of the most influential small satellite companies in the industry.

In 2008, Beckner cofounded Blue Canyon Technologies, alongside a small group of passionate engineers, with the goal of making space more accessible through the development of affordable and innovative satellite systems.

Blue Canyon Technologies grew organically from its humble beginnings into a 350-person company, gaining worldwide recognition for its innovative products, including high-performance small spacecraft and satellite systems.

The company won the AIAA Small Satellite Mission of the Year in four consecutive years 2016 to 2019. The company was recognized on the Inc. 5000 list in 2021 as one of the fastest-growing privately held companies in the United States and was awarded the "Best of 2020" award by SpaceNews.

Raytheon Technologies completed its acquisition of Blue Canyon Technologies in 2020, marking a major milestone in the company's growth, reinforcing the value of BCT's technology and further expanding its reach in the aerospace sector.

Index